DATE DUE

GLOBAL LEADERS FOR THE
TWENTY-FIRST CENTURY

SUNY series in
Management-Communication

Robert C. Morris and Susanne R. Morris
editors

GLOBAL LEADERS

for the

TWENTY-FIRST

CENTURY

Michael J. Marquardt
Nancy O. Berger

STATE UNIVERSITY OF NEW YORK PRESS

Published by

STATE UNIVERSITY OF
NEW YORK PRESS, ALBANY

© 2000 State University of New York

For information, address
State University of New York Press
90 State Street, Suite 700
Albany, NY 12207

Production and book design, Laurie Searl
Marketing, Patrick Durocher

Library of Congress Cataloging-in-Publication Data

Marquardt, Michael J.
    Global leaders for the twenty-first century / Michael J. Marquardt, Nancy O. Berger.
        p. cm. — (SUNY series in management-communication)
    Includes bibliographical references and index.
    ISBN 0-7914-4661-1 (alk. paper) — ISBN 0-7914-4662-X (pbk. : alk. paper)
    1. Industrial management. 2. Leadership. 3. Executive ability. 4. International trade.
    5. Industrial management—Case studies. 6. International business enterprises—
    Management—Case studies. I. Berger, Nancy O., 1951–   . II. Title. III. Title: Global
    leaders for the 21st century. IV. series.

HD31.M2987 2000
658—dc21   99-088562

10 9 8 7 6 5 4 3 2 1

Contents

Tables

Preface

The twentieth century had its share of great leaders, from Alfred Sloan of General Motors to Jack Welch of General Electric, who were called by Noel Tichey "the first and the last great leaders of the twenty-first century" (Tichey and Cohen, 1997). They led effectively, but in a century much slower in pace and less intensive in competition than the one that leaders of the twentieth century will face.

For organizations, the next century (and millennium) will bring much greater complexity and tougher challenges that we can only begin to imagine. We know that we can anticipate increasingly fierce competition, environmental catastrophes, and political, religious, and social strife, but also exciting technological breakthroughs and new discoveries about the world around us—all will contribute to a need for a special kind of leader.

History has shown that the leaders of the old way are often the last to embark onto new paths. Whether for Newtonian physicists, Swiss watchmakers, or mainframe computer companies, success in an old paradigm all too often became inertia in the new. As Lew Platt, former CEO of Hewlett Packard succinctly states, "Yesterday's recipe for success clearly will not be tomorrow's recipe for success."

So what might leadership in the next millennium look like? In June 1997 the United Nations University initiated its new International Leadership Academy. The Prime Minister of Jordan, Dr. Abdul Salim Jamali, set the tone for the Academy with this definition of leadership:

> Leadership is by its nature both a science and an art: A science because it consists of identifiable skills which can be developed and acquired. An art because it as an "état d'esprit" given to articulating visions, taking risks, and pursuing goals undeterred by obstacles. Effective leadership is neither the bureaucratic exercise of routine administrative prerogatives, not the wielding of power for its own sake. It is the visionary and wise exercise of power, and achievement of common goals, in the service of others. (Cleveland, 1997)

Future leaders need beware. They simply cannot manage future complexities by using the concepts that seemed to serve them so well in the industrial era that is fast becoming history.

Leaders Chosen for This Book

We have chosen 12 leaders who are globally recognized for how they are preparing their organizations or countries for the twenty-first century. They possess amazing business sense, but also strong character and integrity that make people proud to be their colleagues. They are people of vision, service, innovation, global mindset, technology, systems thinking, spirituality, and learning.

They were chosen not only for their unique leadership attributes, which are carrying their institutions into the twenty-first century, but also because they represent the fact that great leadership is found everywhere. They come from every region—three are from Asia, one from Africa, three from Europe, one from South America, and four from the United States. They represent corporate, public, and political institutions, men and women, young (30s) and old (60s), and a wide variety of industries.

Overview

In chapter 1 we examine what the world of work will look like in the twenty-first century based upon the impact of globalization, technology, restructuring of the world of work, customer power, emergence of the knowledge era, changing roles of workers, biotechnology, and ever more rapid change and chaos. Chapter 2 presents the eight attributes most needed by men and women to lead in that new world, namely: vision, innovativeness, systems thinking, global mindset, servant relationship, spirituality, understanding of the power of technology, and being a continuous learner.

In chapters 3–14, we introduce the 12 leaders who best exemplify these attributes: John Chambers of Cisco Systems (chapter 3), Ricardo Semler of Semco (chapter 4), Kofi Annan of the United Nations (chapter 5), John Browne of British Petroleum (chapter 6), Carol Bartz of AutoDesk (chapter 7), Felipe Alfonso of the Asian Institute of Management (chapter 8), Ken Chenault of American Express (chapter 9), Mary McAleese, President of Ireland (chapter 10), Cheong Choong Kong of Singapore Airlines (chapter 11), William Carris of Carris Community of Companies (chapter 12), Nobuyuki Idei of Sony (chapter 13), and Jorma Ollila of Nokia (chapter 14).

In the fifteenth and final chapter, we explore the special problems and challenges faced by leaders in the twenty-first century, investigate how organizations such as GE and Intel are preparing future leaders for their organizations, and describe how action learning has become the tool of choice in developing twenty-first century leaders.

Need for Great Leaders in the Twenty-First Century

Leadership becomes ever more necessary as we enter the chaos and competition of the twenty-first century. People are needed who have vision and the confident ability of systems thinking, who can inspire and serve with strong ethics, and who understand the power of technology and the complexity of globalization. We have much to learn from those great leaders at the end of the twentieth century who are blazing the path toward the new millennium. We hope this book will serve as a useful guide for all of us as we enter this new age.

CHAPTER ONE

A New Century Requires
New Types of Leaders

New times demand new kinds of leaders. The global world of the twenty-first century will require new, worldclass leaders: leaders with a unique combination of attributes and personal characteristics. In a technological workplace that may be more virtual than physical, where information bytes and cyberspace need to be managed more than people, leaders will have to be able to function amid high chaos and continuous change. Organizations surely will not be "organized." Corporations will be collaborating and competing at the same time.

Leadership styles and skills that may have worked in stable, predictable environments will be inadequate in an era of radical uncertainty, at a time when organizations "can't even define the problem, much less engineer a solution." The pattern for success in the old paradigm might in fact be a recipe for failure in the new paradigm of the twenty-first century.

To be a leader of emerging organizations in these turbulent times will require one to have capabilities and skills far different from the skills of those who were deemed successful in the twentieth century. The new leaders for the new global environment will have the ability to continuously change themselves without changing their values and virtues. To be an effective leader in the twenty-first century one will need to possess eight key attributes: (1) an ability to develop and convey a shared vision; (2) a service/servant orientation; (3) commitment to risk-taking and continuous innovation; (4) a global mindset; (5) comfort and confidence with technology; (6) competence in systems thinking; (7) recognition of the importance of ethics and spirituality in the workplace; and (8) a model for lifelong learning.

These attributes have become essential because of eight fundamental shifts that have occurred in the work world and in our society as we complete the twentieth century. In this chapter, we will examine emerging transformations of the workplace. In chapter 2, we will identify and describe the leadership capacities needed to respond to these paradigm shifts.

Eight Major Transformations in the World of Work

The eight forces (see Table 1.1) that will dominate the business world of the twenty-first century are: (a) globalization, (b) technology, (c) radical restructuring and reengineering of the world of work, (d) increased customer power and demands, (e) emergence of knowledge and learning as an organization's most valuable assets, (f) changing roles and expectations of workers, (g) biotechnology, and (h) ever more rapid change and chaos. Let's briefly explore the powerful impact of each of these forces.

Table 1.1

Major Transformations of the Twentieth Century Workplace

1. Globalization and the global economy

2. Computer technology

3. Radical transformation of world of work

4. Increased power and demands of the customer

5. Emergence of knowledge and learning as a company's and country's greatest assets

6. New roles and expectations of workers

7. Biotechnology

8. Speed of change—moving from a Newtonian world to a quantum world of chaos

1. Globalization and the Global Economy

We have entered the Global Age. We are a more global people, we share many global values and practices, we are more and more working for global organizations. Globalization has caused a converging of economic and social forces, of interests and commitments, of values and tastes, of challenges and opportunities. We can easily communicate with people 10,000 miles away because we share a global language (English) and a global medium for communications (computers and the Internet).

The signs of the global marketplace are all around us:

— U.S. corporations have invested $1 trillion abroad and employ over 100 million overseas workers; over 100,000 U.S. firms are engaged in global ventures valued at over $2 trillion. Over one-third of U.S. economic growth has been due to exports, providing jobs for over 11 million Americans.

— 10% of U.S. manufacturing is foreign owned and employs four million Americans; Mitsubishi USA is America's fourth largest exporter and Toyota has displaced Chrysler as the third largest in U.S. auto sales. Foreign investment in the United States has now surpassed the $3 trillion mark.

— McDonald's operates more than 12,500 restaurants in 70 countries and is adding 600 new restaurants per year.

— Many Gulf countries have more foreign-born workers than native population. More than 70% of the employees of Canon work outside Japan.

— Financial markets are open twenty-four hours a day around the world.

— Over half of the PhDs in engineering, mathematics, and economics awarded by American universities in 1997 went to non-U.S. citizens.

— Global standards and regulations for trade and commerce, finance, products, and services have emerged.

— More and more companies—InterContinental, Xerox, Motorola, Honda, Samsung, Pentax—are manufacturing and selling chiefly outside their country of origin. We hardly know whether a company is French, Japanese, Swedish, or American.

— Coca-Cola earns more money in Japan than in the United States

— Over 70% of profits for the $20 billion U.S. music industry is from outside the United States. Most big-budget movies depend on global viewers for big profits.

Four main forces have quickly brought us to this global age—technology, travel, trade, and television. These four T's have laid the groundwork for a more collective experience for people everywhere. More and more of us share common tastes in foods (hamburgers, pizza, tacos), fashion (denim jeans), and fun (Disney, rock music, television). Nearly 2 billion passengers fly the world's airways each year. People are watching the same movies, reading the same magazines, and dancing the same dances from Boston to Bangkok to Buenos Aires.

Ever more of us speak a common language. English is now spoken by more than 1 billion people in over 100 countries where it is either the first or second language. English has become the global language of media, computers, and business, and like all languages, it carries cultural and social values with it.

The global economy has in turn forced the creation of global organizations, companies that operate as if the entire world were a single entity. They are fully integrated so that their activities link, leverage, and compete on a worldwide scale. Global firms emphasize global operations over national or multinational operations. They use global sourcing of human resources, capital, technology, facilities, resources, and raw materials. They deem cultural sensitivity to employees, customers, and patterns to be critical to the success of the organization. An organization is globalized when the organization has developed a global corporate culture, strategy, and structure, as well as global operations and global people (Marquardt, 1999).

The single global marketplace/workplace has been created by 10 factors, or global drivers:

— Global technology and telecommunications (enhanced by fiberoptics, satellites, and computer technology).

— Competitiveness of global corporations.

— Converging of global lifestyles and values, accelerated by global language.

— Emergence of global market drivers.

— Lowering of costs of doing business globally.

— Globalization of financial markets, resources and services.

— Emergence of the knowledge economy and era.

— Privatization and globalization of government services.

— Emergence of open and unrestricted free trade.

Although certain industries globalized earlier than others (especially telecommunications, electronics and computers, finance and banking, transportation, automotive, pharmaceutical, petroleum, and biotechnology), every industry now has global players, and success now depends upon the organization's ability to compete globally for every industry and sector throughout the world. Even the largest companies in the biggest markets will not be able to survive based on their domestic markets alone. More and more companies, whether small or large, young or old, recognize that their choice is between becoming global or becoming extinct.

Thinking and operating globally will be ever more critical to organizational survival and growth in the twenty-first century. Thus twenty-first century leaders will need to understand the global marketplace and develop a global mindset.

2. Computer Technology

Welcome to the new technological workplace with tele-training, info-structures, and ubiquitous computers! Alvin Toffler writes how the advanced global economy and workplace cannot run for 30 seconds without the technology of computers. Yet today's best computers and CAD/CAM systems will be "stoneage" primitive within a few years (Toffler, 1990). The workplace will demand and require ever more technological advancements and innovations.

Already we have technologies such as optoelectronics, DVDs (digital videodiscs), information highways, LANs (local area networks) and WANs (wide area networks), groupware, virtual reality, and electronic classrooms. The power of workplace computer technology has progressed from mainframe to desktop to briefcase portable to the user's hand. More and more of a company's operations require computer-generated automation and customization.

These technologies have become necessary to manage the "data deluge" so that we can learn faster in rapidly changing, turbocharged organizations. Working in a global economy in which "being informed, being in touch, and being there first" can make all the difference between success and second-best, technology provides a big advantage indeed!

Technology will increasingly require that managers manage knowledge rather than people. Technology will alter how and why workers learn. Employees will need to train themselves. And workplace learning will no longer be in a fixed time and location with a group of people for just-in-case purposes; instead, it will be implemented on a just-what's-needed, just-in-time, and just-where-needed basis. The technological forces that have already restructured work will force those who are responsible for employee development to "create ever more flexible and responsive learning and performance solutions" (Bassi, Chenny, and van Buren, 1997).

To better prepare us for how technology will transform work, workers, and the workplace, it is important for us to grasp some of the emerging ideas and applications of technologies. This understanding can help us redirect that technology and thereby accelerate learning and better manage knowledge in the workplace.

We are living in a world where virtual reality and interactive multimedia technologies are becoming commonplace. Personalized intelligent agents will soon be available as built-in, on-line experts looking over one's shoulders. Artificial intelligence technologies (expert/knowledge-based systems, user interfaces that understand speech and natural language, and sensory perception) will be commonly available. Intelligent tutoring systems will allow learner-based, self-paced instruction. Personalized digitized assistants, telecommunications and network advances, desktop videoconferencing, and groupware (also known as collaborative software or group systems technology) will be widely prevalent in the next five years.

And the speed and impact of technology continues to accelerate! Trying to figure out the capabilities and future directions of this rapidly changing technology is impossible. Let's look at just a few of the already existing powers of technology:

— Superconducting transmission lines can transmit data up to 100 times faster than today's fiber-optical networks. One line can carry 1 trillion bits of information per second, enough to send the complete contents of the Library of Congress in two minutes.

— Neural networks are changing how computers "think": today's computers process preprogrammed commands sequentially; a neural network uses associative "reasoning" to store information in patterned connections, allowing it to process complex questions through its own logic.

— Expert systems, a subset of artificial intelligence, are beginning to solve problems in much the same way as human experts.

— Telephones are being made small enough to wear as earrings.

— Highly-reliable connectivity is becoming available that works regardless of time or place and is easy and affordable around the world.

— Cellular phones can now respond to e-mail.

One of the most amazing and transforming technological additions to our lives is the Internet. The use of the Internet is one of the fastest-growing phenomena the business world has ever seen—building from a base of fewer than 1,000 connected computers in the early 1980s, to over 100 million host computers today.

Intranets (in-company Internets) are rapidly catching up. The implementation of Intranets is growing three times faster than that of electronic commercial applications, with over 70% of major corporations currently having or planning Intranet applications. As the evolution of Intranet sites continues, more and more features will emerge. For example, real-time training that combines a live mediator, on-line information and several remote attendees is already possible. By the end of 1997, nearly 90% of all businesses had recognized that it was critical to develop comprehensive strategies for using both Intranets and the Internet.

The new high-tech learning machines have been called the most powerful learning tool since the invention of the book. With virtual reality, the mind is cut off from outside distractions and one's attention becomes focused on the powerful sensory stimulation (light-sound matrix) that bombards the imagination. It becomes possible for ideas and mental images to float in and out of a person's consciousness.

Technology is becoming more and more a part of all products and the total GNP, including aerospace, advanced industrial systems, and automotive. Already, nearly 20% of an automobile's value is the electronics within it. The computer service and computer software market has grown to over $420 billion, an increase of 50% in the last four years! Information technology is expected to form the basis of many of the most important products, services, and processes of the future.

In addition, an array of technological developments have recently emerged for use in the home as well as the office, including:

— Integration of television, telecommunications, and computers through digitization and compression techniques.

— Reduced costs and more flexible use and application of telecommunications through developments such as ISDN, fiber optics, and cellular radio.

— Miniaturization (tiny cameras, microphones, and small, high-resolution display screens).

— Increased portability through the use of radio communications and miniaturization.

— Expanded processing power through new microchip development and advanced software.

— More powerful and user-friendly command and software tools, making it much easier for users to create and communicate their own materials (Bates, 1995).

The commoditization of ultra-high technology opens spellbinding opportunities for new knowledge-exchange products. British Telecom, for example, believes that future generations of portable phones could be installed right in your ear. While talking, the user could also glimpse images or data that are pulled invisibly off the Internet and projected onto a magnifying mirror positioned beside one eye.

The technology of the future will respond to our voices and extend our senses. It will stimulate complex phenomena—weather patterns, stock market crashes, environmental hazards—solving problems and predicting outcomes at a price anyone can afford. Computers—or networks of them—will become ubiquitous as they are invisibly imbedded in other things. These machines will reconfigure themselves when new applications are required. A whole new metaphor for computing is taking shape, patterned on the natural resilience and elegance of biological organisms. They will learn to diagnose, repair, and even replicate themselves (Gross, 1997).

The impact of technology on organizations, on management, and on the community is mind-boggling. And it has only begun. The emerging power and applicability of technology will turn the world of work on its head. Organizations will become more virtual rather than physical because of technology. People will be more linked to customers in Kuala Lumpur than to co-workers across the hall because of technology. Thus, the twenty-first century leader will need to appreciate and understand the power and purposes of technology.

3. Radical Transformation of World of Work

The world of work and the workplace is being dramatically transformed. Workers no longer work in an office. Corporations collaborate and compete with one another at the same time. Customers provide supervision as well as dictate services. Fellow employees work closely with each other while never having met one another. Companies have temporary, part-time CEOs and permanent full-time janitors. Corporate headquarters staff may consist of less than 1% of a company's workforce, if there is a headquarters.

Organizations have moved from the quality efforts of the 1980s, through the reengineering processes of the 1990s to the radical transformation of the workplace itself as we enter the twenty-first century. They have moved from focusing on reducing of defects and streamlining business processes to totally new forms that enable organizations to manage continuous, white-water change. They now work to create "high performance work organizations" in which work is reorganized, redesigned, or reengineered to improve performance.

Decades of breaking work into ever-smaller tasks are coming to an end. Instead, teams of employees will be responsible for key business processes from beginning to end. Impatience with the rate of change will cause many organizations to reengineer (start from scratch) their key processes.

Companies will focus on and organize around what they do best. Therefore, they will structure according to core competencies instead of according to product or market. The organizational architecture of companies will evolve around autonomous work teams and strategic alliances. In such companies, "noncore" work will be outsourced or done by temporary and contract workers as needed.

Advances in information technology described above are providing faster transmission of data and expanded storage capacity as well as clearer, more complex links among users and greater computer power. Such innovation will permit greater control of more decentralized organization, while permitting the information flow needed to give local managers substantive decision-making authority.

Because of this technology, corporations will become cluster organizations or "ad-hoc-racies"; groups of geographically dispersed people—typically working at home—that come together electronically for a particular project and then disband, having completed their work. More organizations will comprise a minimal core of permanent employees supported by independently contracted professionals.

As more companies realize that the key resource of business is not capital, personnel, or facilities but rather knowledge, information, and ideas, many new ways of viewing the organization begin to emerge. Everywhere companies are restructuring, creating integrated organizations, global networks, and leaner corporate centers. Organizations are becoming more fluid, ever shifting in size, shape, and arrangements.

Organizations are also becoming more and more virtual. A virtual organization is a temporary network of independent companies, suppliers, customers, and even rivals linked by information technology to share skills, costs, and access to one another's markets. In its purest form, a company decides to focus on the thing it does best. Then it links with other companies, each bringing to the combination its own special ability. It will mix and match what it does best with the best of the other companies. For example, a manufacturer will manufacture while relying on a product-design outfit to sell the output.

The virtual corporation will have neither central office nor organization chart, and no hierarchy or vertical integration. Teams of people in different companies will routinely work together. After the business is done, the virtual organization disbands.

Technology allows for new strategic opportunities for organizations to reassess their missions and operations. It enables organizations to *automate* (which lessens the cost of production), to *informate* (which provides information that can be used to get a job done, generates new information as a byproduct, and develops new information), and to *transform*. Morton (1991) calls this a stage characterized "by leadership, vision and a sustained process of organization empowerment." Twenty-first century leaders will need to understand how to restructure, to connect, and to think in a new paradigm characterized more by interdependent systems than by independent entities.

4. Increased Power and Demands of the Customer

Global communications and marketing have increased consumers' awareness about possible products and services. Global competition has offered customers a more varied and higher quality of choices. What has been created is a "convergence of consumer needs and preferences." Consumers are now able to choose the products and services they want based on the best:

1. Cost—What is the least expensive, most economical choice?

2. Quality—No defects; meeting and exceeding the customer's expectations.

3. Time—Available as quickly as possible.

4. Service—Pleasant, courteous, and available; products are reparable or replaceable.

5. Innovation—New, something not yet envisioned by the customer (e.g., Sony Walkman).

6. Customization—Tailored to very specific needs.

Jorma Ollila, CEO of Nokia, adds that twenty-first century customers will be much more accustomed to information, technologically more connected, more culturally conscious, and more international by nature.

Customers will more and more determine how organizations set strategies and carry out operations. Customers, rather than workers, will become the focus of leadership-attention organizational priorities. How to better serve customers through continuous innovations will become a prime focus of twenty-first century leaders.

5. Emergence of Knowledge and Learning as a Company's and Country's Greatest Assets

Technology and globalization has led to a global economy based on knowledge. Knowledge workers now outnumber industrial workers by 3 to 1. The workforce has moved from manufacturing (working with the hands) to mentofacturing (working with the mind). Continuous learning and knowledge production provides the key raw material for wealth creation and has become the fountain of organizational and personal power.

The wealth of nations will depend increasingly on knowledge-based, high-tech industries, in areas such as biotechnology, health, environmental products and services, tourism and hospitality, telecommunications, computer software and software applications, financial services, and entertainment (film, television, games). These are all highly competitive global industries. Keeping even a few months ahead of the competition, in terms of innovation and knowledge, is critical to survival.

Information—processed by human brainwork into knowledge, integrated and intuited into wisdom—has quite suddenly become the world's most important resource. Knowledge will be playing the prime role in world history that physical labor, minerals, and energy once played.

Brainpower is becoming a company's most valuable asset and is what conveys a competitive edge in the marketplace. Stewart (1997, p. 44) asserts, "Brainpower . . . has never before been so important for business. Every company depends increasingly on knowledge—patents, process, management skills, technologies, information about customers and suppliers, and oldfashioned experience. . . . This knowledge that exists in an organization can be used to create differential advantage. In other words, it's the sum of everything everybody in your company knows that gives you a competitive edge in the marketplace."

Increasingly, work and learning are becoming the same thing. Zuboff (1988) sees "learning as the new form of labor." Because the new global economy is based on knowledge work and innovation, there is a convergence between work and learning. While you perform knowledge work, you learn. And you must learn minute by minute to perform knowledge work effectively. Learning is becoming a lifelong challenge as well as a lifelong process. Most knowledge has a shelf life of three years or less, and knowledge continues to double every 18 months!

Simply put, knowledge has become more important for organizations than financial resources, market position, technology, or any other company asset. Knowledge is seen as the main resource used in performing work in an organization. The organization's traditions, culture, technology, operations, systems, and procedures are all based on knowledge and expertise. Knowledge is needed to increase the abilities of employees to improve products and services—thereby providing quality service to clients and consumers. Knowledge is necessary to update products and services, change systems, and structures, and communicate solutions to problems.

In the new knowledge economy, individuals at every level and in all kinds of companies will be challenged to develop new knowledge, to take responsibility for their new ideas, and to pursue them as far as they can go. Leaders themselves will need to learn continuously as well as to create an environment that allows workers to increase knowledge.

6. New Roles and Expectations of Workers

Need for knowledge and higher-order cognitive skills

As society moves from the industrial era to the knowledge era, job requirements are changing. Employees are moving from needing repetitive skills to knowing how to deal with surprises and exceptions, from depending on memory and facts to being spontaneous and creative, from risk avoidance to risk taking, from focusing on policies and procedures to collaborating with people. Work will require higher-order cognitive skills—the ability to analyze problems and find the right resources for solving them, often with both limited and conflicting information.

The workforce is rapidly changing. As of the year 2000, over 80% of all jobs in the United States are in knowledge and service industries. Many of the new jobs require a much higher level of technical skill than the jobs they replaced, especially in manufacturing and resource-based industries. People retain existing jobs only if they were retrained to higher standards.

Twenty-first century workers, according to Drucker (1992), will be composed more and more of knowledge workers. A fascinating aspect about knowledge workers is that they do, in fact, own the means of production, and they can take it out of the door with them at any moment. Therefore, managers have to attract and motivate; reward, recognize, and retain; train, educate, and improve; and, in the most remarkable reversal of all, serve and satisfy knowledge workers. Organizations must provide a structure in which knowledge workers can apply their knowledge.

Growing importance of emotional intelligence

Emotional intelligence, according to Goleman (1997), involves both social competencies (empathy and social skills) and personal competencies (self-awareness, self-regulation, and motivation). It includes areas such as self-confidence, the need to get results, constant improvement, influence, service orientation, conflict management, drive for achievement, optimism, initiative, and teamwork.

Only recently have managers begun to realize how important emotional intelligence is to a worker's success. But as research by Goleman (1998) has shown, emotional intelligence-based competencies affect performance for jobs of all kinds, being twice as important as cognitive and technical expertise combined; and the higher one goes in an organization, the more critical are these skills. A work world engulfed with competition, technology, and speed requires workers with ever increasing social and personal competencies.

Increase in temporary workers

Another new element of today's and tomorrow's work environment is the presence of temporary and part-time workers. More and more companies are depending heavily on temporary help, and their employment is rising annually at 17% and over $50 billion in revenue. Businesses have made "temp" help an integral part of the hiring process as well as overall human resources policy. The hiring of temporary workers allows organizations to be more flexible, but at the expense of worker loyalty and knowledge retention.

Telecommuting workers

Telecommuting, thanks to digital phone lines, affordable desktop videoconferencing, and wide ranging cellular networks, is out of the experimental stage. By means of local phone companies offering Integrated Services Digital Network (ISDN) lines that can transmit voice, data, and video simultaneously, telecommuting has become easy and highly productive.

The over 15 million telecommuters in the United States represent the fastest growing portion of workers. The entire 240-member core sales staff at American Express Travel Related Services are telecommuters. Ernst & Young has implemented "hoteling," in which up to 10 people share a single desk in a fully equipped office on an as-needed basis. Employees must reserve space and equipment in advance. Over the past three years, the accounting firm has slashed its office space requirements by about 2 million square feet, saving roughly $25 million per year.

In addition to reducing air pollution and cutting down on office space and equipment purchases, telecommuting enables corporations to hire otherwise unavailable key talent. For example, Northern Telecom in Memphis was able to hire someone from Philadelphia who did not want to move to Tennessee.

How to attract and retain knowledge workers, to build the emotional intelligence of staff, and to motivate temporary and telecommuting employees will be a critical skill of the twenty-first century leader, one that will require the ability to be a "servant" as well as a leader.

7. Biotechnology

Just as information technology undergirds today's booming economy, biology may drive tomorrow's. In fact, biology could transform information technology through such developments as DNA-based computers and software that repairs flaws as nature does.

The twenty-first century will "start the century of biology," says J. Craig Venter, president of the Institute for Genomic Research and pioneering gene finder (Carey, 1998). Corn yields could double and science could eventually find ways to stave off heart disease and cancer. Already, research centers such as Venter's have read the entire DNA codes for the bugs that cause cholera and tuberculosis, opening the door to better treatments and vaccines, leading to possibly finally winning the war against bacteria.

Biotechnology is widely forecast as being the dominant factor of the twenty-first century. Bioengineered products—the products of biomanufacturing—will fuel the new bioeconomy. Major advances in the genetics of DNA will lead to much longer, more productive lives. People will soon be walking around with chips in their bodies that will monitor and assist activities.

New research technologies are vastly accelerating the pace of discovery in biology, driving forward not only medicine but also industry, environmental cleanup, and agriculture. Scientists are unlocking biochemical pathways in cancer, clogged arteries, and Alzheimer's disease. Not only are they understanding life, they're manipulating it. They are slipping new genes into people to treat disease and genetically engineering plants and animals to boost yields or transform them into bio-factories of plastics and drugs.

Some of the new possibilities on the horizon include a so-called retinal display that "paints" pictures directly on the eye by modulating a stream of photons from light-emitting diodes and scanning them across the retina. The mind perceives these scans as vibrant color pictures. British Telecom's "homo cyberneticus" shows off its artificial retina and a pacemaker that sends warning signals to the doctor, as well as a vest that turns body heat to electricity (Carey, 1998).

Advances in genetics and other areas of biology are bringing an unprecedented wave of innovation. Here's what's already being developed in the fields of agriculture, medicine, and industry:

Agriculture

— Salmon and trout engineered to grow twice as fast as normal.

— Soybeans, cotton, corn and other crops engineered to resist pests and withstand bad weather, as well as to produce increased nutritional value.

— Cows, pigs, sheep, and goats that make drugs in their milk.

Medicine

— Bacteria genetically engineered to lap up underground spills of toxic chemicals.

— Natural hormones that stimulate growth of new blood vessels, bypassing clogged vessel.

— Capacities to make people healthier and to live much longer.

Industry

— Plants that produce biodegradable plastics.

— Computers that harness the information storage capacity of DNA.

— Enzymes that reduce the need for environmentally harmful chorine in papermaking.

The powerful developments in the field of biotechnology expand the power of organizations but raise significant ethical issues for leaders.

8. Speed of Change—Moving from a Newtonian to a Quantum World of Chaos

For nearly three centuries the world and the workplace have been built upon Newtonian physics—the physics of cause and effect, of predictability and certainty, of distinct wholes and parts, of reality being what is seen. Newtonian physics is a science of quantifiable determinism, of linear thinking, and of controllable futures, in sum, a world that does not change too fast or in unexpected ways.

In the Newtonian mindset, people engage in complex planning for a world that they believe is predictable. They continually search for better methods of objectively perceiving the world. This mechanistic and reductionist way of thinking and acting dominates life even though it was disproved over 70 years ago by Albert Einstein and others who introduced the scientific community to quantum physics in the 1920s. Margaret Wheatley (1992), author of *Leadership and the New Science,* rightly notes, however, that in today's world this old, disproved mindset is "unempowering and disabling for all of us."

Quantum physics, on the other hand, deals with the world at the sub-atomic level, examining the intricate patterns out of which seeming discrete events arise. Quantum physics recognizes that the universe and every object in it are, in reality, vast empty spaces filled with fields and movements that are the basic substance of the universe. Thus, relationships between objects and between observers and objects are what determine reality. The quantum universe is composed of an environment rich in relationships; it is a world of chaos and process, not just of objects and things. Quantum physics deals with waves and holograms, with surprises rather than predictions.

In understanding quantum physics, organizations realize that they cannot predict with certainty, that chaos is part and parcel of reality. It forces us to change the way we think, the way we attempt to solve problems, the way we deal with order versus change, autonomy versus control, structure versus flexibility, and planning versus flowing. Leaders will need new ways of seeing the world, new visions for leading their people.

New Forces Demand New Leaders

In this chapter, we have explored the eight most significant factors that have emerged in the world of work factors that will totally transform the relationships and dynamics that leaders must exhibit both internally and externally to the organizations they manage. Each of these eight factors forces leaders to have responding attributes in order to successfully navigate in the twenty-first century. In chapter 2 we will explore these eight attributes.

CHAPTER TWO

Attributes and Competencies of the Twenty-First Century Global Leader

New times demand new kinds of leaders with new attributes and competencies. As we noted in chapter 1, eight significant forces have transformed the world of work as we conclude the twentieth century, namely, (a) globalization, (b) technology, (c) radical restructuring and reengineering of the world of work, (d) increased customer power and demands, (e) the emergence of knowledge and learning as the organization's must valuable assets, (f) changing roles and expectations of workers, (g) biotechnology, and (h) ever more rapid change and chaos. Leaders must now operate in a dramatically transformed world with new kinds of workers and customers, within new global marketplaces and highly technologized environments.

As Table 2.1 displays, each of the transforming forces creates the need for a special competency or attribute for the twenty-first century leader.

Table 2.1

Leadership Competencies Necessitated by Workplace Transformations

World of Work Transformations	New Global Leadership Attributes
Globalization	Global mindset and competencies
Knowledge era	Teacher, coach, mentor, and model learner
Changing workers	Servant and steward
Organizational restructuring and chaos	Systems thinker and polychronic coordination

Leadership Competencies Necessitated by Workplace Transformations (continued)

World of Work Transformations	New Global Leadership Attributes
Biotechnology, environment	Spirituality and concern for ethics
Technology	Technologist
Customer expectations	Innovator and risk-taker
Future speed of change	Visionary and vision-builder

The successful twenty-first century leader will need to develop each of these competencies or attributes. Let's now explore in greater detail what are the essential elements of these attributes and why they are so important.

I. Global Mindset and Competencies

A key leadership attribute of twenty-first century leaders will be the ability to see the world and the workplace with a global mindset. A global mindset is defined as "a predisposition to see the world in a particular way that sets boundaries and provides explanations for why things are the way they are, while at the same time establishing guidance for ways in which they should behave" (Rhinesmith, 1993). Mindset is a filter through which we look at the world. Rhinesmith compares domestic and global mindsets as shown in Table 2.2.

Table 2.2

Comparison of Domestic and Global Mindsets

Domestic Mindset	Global Mindset
Functional expertise	Bigger, broader picture
Prioritization	Balance of contradictions
Structure	Process
Individual responsibility	Teamwork and diversity
No surprises	Change as an opportunity
Trained against surprises	Openness to surprises

Global mindsets are not exclusive, but inclusive. People with global mindsets seek to continually expand their knowledge, have a highly developed capacity to conceptualize the complexity of global organizations, are extremely flexible, strive to be sensitive to cultural diversity, are able to intuit decisions with inadequate information, and have a strong capacity for reflection. A global mindset thinks and sees the world globally, is open to exchanging ideas and concepts across borders, and is able to break down one's provincial ways of thinking. Emphasis is placed on balancing global and local needs, and on being able to operate cross-functionally, cross-divisionally, and cross-culturally around the world.

Key global competencies for twenty-first century leaders will include the abilities:

— to describe clearly the forces behind the globalization of business.

— to recognize and connect global market trends, technological innovation, and business strategy.

— to outline issues essential to effective strategic alliances.

— to frame day-to-day management issues, problems, and goals in a global context.

— to think and plan beyond historical, cultural, and political boundaries, structures, systems and processes.

— to create and effectively lead worldwide business teams.

— to help the company adopt a functional global organizational structure.

The key to globalizing an organization, according to David Whitwam, CEO of Whirlpool, is for the leaders to get everyone in the organization to think globally, not just a few. "You must create an organization where people are adept at exchanging ideas, processes, and systems across borders" (Maruca, 1994, p. 137) To do this Whitwam believes that the leadership must build upon a unifying global vision and philosophy to help create a global mindset—and unless leaders can globalize their organizations, their organizations will die.

2. Teacher, Coach, Mentor, and Model Learner

Jacques (1989) asserts that leaders must have the "learning how to learn" skill, the opportunity to learn, and the capacity to learn. Marsick (1987) notes that top executives seldom take the opportunity to learn through organized learning programs, yet must continually learn to remain successful in their positions.

Self-learning is critical to executive success. Dechant (1990) discovered in her research that the ability to learn might be the "most salient" competency for leadership. And no task is more important for the new leader than encouraging and inspiring learning!

Cohen and Tichey (1998) note "the scarcest resource in the world today is leadership talent capable of continuously transforming organizations to win in tomorrow's world." Thus, for companies to survive in the future, they must become not only learning organizations, but also teaching organizations. Everyone, especially leaders, must pass his or her learning on to others. In teaching organizations, leaders see it as their responsibility to teach, coach, and mentor so that people throughout the organization are developed to efficiently and effectively apply knowledge to the business of the organization. Since learning is critical for the success of the business, leaders find ways for their people to do it every day.

Leaders can help others learn through a variety of approaches—as a teacher, coach, and mentor. The choice among these roles will depend on the focus of help, timespan, approach, and activities, as shown in Table 2.3.

Table 2.3

Leader as Teacher, Coach, and Mentor

DIMENSION	TEACHER	COACH	MENTOR
Focus of help	Task	Person's job	Development
Timespan	A day or two	A month or year	Career or lifetime
Approach to helping	Show and tell; give supervised practice and set up opportunities to try out new skills	Explore problem together	Act as friend; listen and question to enlarge awareness
Associated activities	Analyze task; give clear instruction; supervise practice and give feedback on results at once	Jointly identify the problem; create development opportunities and review	Link work with parts of life; clarify broad and long-term aims and purpose in life

Great leaders are great teachers and co-learners. Institutions that succeed over the long term do so because they continuously regenerate leadership at all levels (not just because of their core competencies or use of modern management tools). Twenty-first century leaders will thus be involved in building "information-structures" as well as infrastructures.

Leaders benefit just by preparing to teach others. Because the teachers are people with hands-on experience within the organization—rather than outside consultants—the people being taught learn relevant, immediately useful concepts and skills. Leaders help to create the next generation of leaders by teaching people about the critical issues facing their business and by teaching them how to anticipate changes and deal with them.

Leaders look for creative ways to find teaching and learning opportunities; they try to turn every interaction with their people into a learning and teaching event and often set aside time to teach leadership outside of scheduled activities. The leader should be a devoted learner, one who takes time to learn and demonstrates a love for learning. Practicing action learning, taking risks, seeking innovative answers, and asking fresh questions all exhibit solid learning practices and skills to employees.

Since the new twenty-first century organization will consist more and more of knowledge specialists, it will be an organization of equals among colleagues and associates. No knowledge or area will necessarily rank higher than another; each will be judged by its contribution to the learning and success of the organization.

This information-based, more egalitarian company will need a leader who can motivate and assist colleagues in the collection, storage, and distribution of knowledge within and outside the unit. He or she will help determine what knowledge is important for organizational memory, assure that mechanisms exist for gathering and coding the knowledge, and encourage people to transfer and use knowledge.

An analogy might be that of a coach of a soccer team who transforms individuals into a cohesive unit in which every member is responsible for the success of the team, and all players can see how their individual play affects the whole game. The manager motivates, implores, inspires, and promotes each team member so that each is able to successfully play the game with minimal input from the sidelines.

3. Servant and Steward

The words *servant* and *leadership* are usually thought of as opposites. When opposites are brought together in a creative and meaningful way, however, a powerful paradox emerges, a paradox that is critical for leadership success in the twenty-first century. Servant-leadership emphasizes increased service to others, a holistic approach to work, a sense of community, and shared decision-making power.

The 'servant-leader' concept was introduced in the 1970s by Robert Greenleaf (1977), who had been an AT&T manager for over 30 years. His essay on "The Leader as Servant" quickly sparked a radical rethinking of leadership. Influential business theorists such as Senge (1990) and Block (1996) now cite this attribute as one of the most critical for the twenty-first century leader.

Greenleaf's insight was inspired by his reading of Herman Hesse's short novel *Journey to the East,* about a mystical journey by a group of people on a spiritual quest. Leo accompanies the party as the servant who sustains them with his caring spirit. All goes well with the journey until one day Leo disappears. The group quickly falls into disarray, and the journey is abandoned. The group cannot manage without Leo. After many years of searching, the narrator of the story stumbles upon Leo and is taken into the religious order that sponsored the original journey. There, he discovers that Leo, whom he had known as a servant, was in fact the head and guiding spirit of the order—a great and noble leader.

Great leaders, according to Greenleaf, must first serve others, and this simple fact is central to their greatness. True leadership emerges from those whose primary motivation is a desire to help others. Serving others—including employees, customers, and community—must be a leader's number one priority. The first concern is to make sure that other's highest priority needs are being served. The best test is to ask these questions: Do those served grow as persons? Do they, while being served, become healthier, wiser, freer, more autonomous, more likely themselves to become servants?

Servant-leaders must be willing to suspend their need for control. In order to process multiple levels of experience, they must be able to see their own values, backgrounds, and experiences and to recognize that thinking that one's own background or area of experience is superior to others' can be a fatal flaw.

Spears (1995) has identified 10 fundamental characteristics of the servant-leader:

1. Listening—Leaders must have a deep commitment to listening intently to others and thereby be better able to identify and clarify the will of a group. The leader listens carefully to what is being said and not being said.

2. Empathy—Workers need to be accepted and recognized for their special and unique personalities. One must assume the good intentions of co-workers and not reject them as people, even when forced to reject their behavior or performance.

3. Healing—Many people have broken spirits and have suffered from a variety of emotional hurts; servant-leaders help make whole those with whom they come in contact.

4. Awareness of self and others—The leader helps others understand issues involving ethics and values.

5. Persuasion—Rather than using authority to coerce, the servant-leader seeks to convince and effectively builds consensus within groups. The leader recognizes the need to create strategy democratically.

6. Conceptualization—To be able to dream great dreams and think beyond day-to-day realities requires discipline and practice. A servant-leader's thinking must stretch to encompass broader-based conceptual thinking.

7. Foresight—Servant-leaders must be able to foresee the likely outcome of a situation; they learn lessons from the past, perceive the realities of the present, then predict the likely consequence of a decision for the future. This ability is deeply rooted within the intuitive mind.

8. Stewardship—A servant-leader holds the organization in trust for the greater good of society.

9. Commitment to the growth of people—Because the servant-leader sees people as having an intrinsic value beyond their tangible contributions as workers, the servant-leader is committed to the personal, professional, and spiritual growth of each and every individual. This commitment includes staff development, personal interest in employees' ideas and suggestions, encouragement of worker involvement in decision making, and active assistance for laid-off workers to find other employment.

10. Building community—The servant-leader creates a community of people within and outside the organization who care for and support one another.

The capabilities of a servant-leader mesh well with the concept of emotional intelligence-based competencies as defined by Goleman (1997). In his more recent research, Goleman (1998) discovered that such competencies account for close to 90% of what distinguishes the most outstanding leaders from average ones. The emotional competence framework includes:

1. Social competencies (how one establishes relationships)

— Empathy—Awareness of others' feelings, needs and concerns.

— Social skills—Adeptness at obtaining desirable responses in others (communication skills, change catalyst, conflict management, building nurturing relationships, collaboration and cooperation).

2. Personal competencies (how one manages oneself)
    — Self-awareness—Knowing one's strengths and weaknesses, self-confidence
    — Self-regulation—Self-control, trustworthiness, conscientiousness, adaptability, and innovation.
    — Motivation—Achievement drive, commitment, initiative, and optimism.

Harlan Cleveland (1997), one of the great leadership theorists of the twentieth century, notes, "As we near the end of the twentieth century, we are beginning to see that traditional autocratic and hierarchical modes of leadership are slowly yielding to a newer model—one that attempts to simultaneously enhance the personal growth of workers and improve the quality and caring of our many institutions through a combination of teamwork and community, personal involvement in decision making, and ethical and caring behavior." This new model of leadership is one of being a servant.

4. Systems Thinking and Polychronic Coordination

Today we are living in an age of intensive global interdependence, one where the old way of seeing the world as a predictable, independent mechanism no longer fits. Building on the new quantum physics of the twentieth century, a new model must emerge where the whole organizes and even partly defines the parts. Within organizations, the new framework requires that we pay attention to the relationships between people, to the validity of each person's unique reality, and to the multiple creative possibilities that exist at any moment in time.

Effective leadership in the twenty-first century will require the ability to be a systems thinker. Senge (1990), Wheatley (1992), and numerous others have begun pointing to this attribute as absolutely essential for today's and tomorrow's leaders.

Systems thinkers have the ability to see connections between issues, events, and data points, to see the whole rather than just its parts. Systems thinking requires the ability to frame structural relationships that result in dynamic networks as opposed to staid, patterned interactions or relationships predicated on one's position in the hierarchy.

Leaders must shift their perspective from mechanistic and reductionist ways of thinking and action to a perspective that encourages attention to the whole. Since the seventeenth century, managers have operated on the premise that by analyzing single parts they can understand the whole. This was the basis of Newtonian physics. Hobbesian policies and Adam Smith's free market economics took their lead from this mechanistic approach, and Taylor's scientific management stressed internal competition, control, predictability, and relativity.

A twenty-first century leader must think in terms of whole systems, seeing the business as part of a wider environment. This new leader views business opportunities not simply from the perspective of a solo player, but as one player among many, each coevolving with the others. This attitude is sharply different from the conventional idea of competition, in which companies work only with their own resources and do not extend themselves by capitalizing on the capabilities of others. In the global market, you want to make use of the other players—for capacity, innovation, and capital.

Leaders must help people see the big picture with its underlying trends, forces, and potential surprises. They need to think systematically and be able to foresee how internal and external factors might benefit or destroy the organization. The ability to decipher and analyze massive amounts of sometimes contradictory information demands patience and persistence. Some key elements needed to accomplish this way of thinking include:

— Avoiding symptomatic solutions and focusing on underlying causes.

— Distinguishing detail complexity (many variables) from dynamic complexity (when cause and effect are distant in time and space, and when the consequences over time are subtle).

— Seeing processes, not snapshots.

— Focusing on areas of high leverage.

— Seeing interrelationships, not things.

— Seeing that you and the cause of your problems are part of a single system.

— Balancing inquiry and advocacy.

— Distinguishing what is espoused from what is practiced.

— Recognizing and defusing defensive routines.

— Seeing and testing leaps of abstraction.

Walter Kiechel (1990), managing editor of *Fortune* magazine, predicts that "tomorrow's managers will to be simultaneously and consecutively specialists and generalists, team players and self-reliant, able to think of themselves as a business of one and plan accordingly." The new leader is internetworked rather than a practitioner of the old-style, brilliant-visionary, take-charge approach. They will need to possess both analytic and strategic thinking skills.

In the changing organization with its increased use of project teams, managers will more and more likely be leading and coordinating 3, 5, even up to 10 different task-focused teams, each carrying out a variety of activities on totally different time schedules. The ability to quickly enter into and become a trusted partner of these teams is a taxing challenge. To plan, manage, balance, and juggle these many balls requires an agile, systems-thinking, and well-organized leader.

5. Spirituality and Concern for Ethics

Twentieth century cost-cutting, downsizing, and reengineering have cut the soul out of many companies. Workers are feeling unfulfilled, unmotivated, and finding little meaning in their work. Too often people are seen as disposable. Thus, many cutting-edge leaders are helping their companies set off on spiritual journeys that are attempts to create a sense of meaning and purpose at work and a connection between the company and its people. They recognize that combining head and heart will produce a competitive advantage.

Galen and West (1995) note how spirituality is becoming an important tool for corporate success, that spirituality can "enlighten the bottom line." Many companies are beginning to "take the road less traveled" and focusing on bringing meaning and values back to the workplace. Boeing leaders recognize that for their company to be truly alive they need more creative, vital, and adaptable workers, and that such creativity, vitality, and adaptability reside in the soul. AT&T believes leadership training requires development of values. A "soul" committee at Lotus Development makes sure the company lives up to its stated values. Medtronic motivates workers by appealing to their inherent desire "to be something bigger than themselves." Tom Chappell, CEO of Tom's of Maine, sees the company's aim as one of "serving our customers and serving our community" by abiding by certain values such as supporting the environment and treating workers, suppliers, and customers with respect. Tom's gives 10% of its pretax profits to charity, and employees are encouraged to donate 5% of their time to volunteer work.

Leaders must weave ethics into the fabric of the organization's culture. Actions include:

— Institutionalizing ethics throughout the organization via a proactive ethics program.

— Setting the organization's ethical tone by tying ethics to shared company values and goals. Employees are more likely to follow the corporate ethics programs and policies when senior management proactively endorses and practices them.

— Exhibiting high ethical standards by leaders who set the example for all employees.

— Creating an ethical climate in the organization that accommodates differences in cultures worldwide.

— Developing a reward system that encourages good ethical behavior, empowers employees, equates ethical behavior with success in business, and treats ethics programs as a continual learning process.

In 1994 the Caux Roundtable in Switzerland developed what is believed to be the first international code of business ethics (Curtin, 1996). Business leaders from around the world advocated the following seven principles:

1. Responsibility of businesses to look beyond their shareholders and economic growth toward stakeholders by improving lives, sharing wealth, and shaping the future of the global communities in which they operate.

2. Economic and social responsibilities of businesses to contribute to the social advancement, human rights, education, and vitalization of host nations and the world community.

3. Need for trust and sincerity in business behavior to facilitate business transactions on the global scale.

4. Respect for international and domestic rules.

5. Protecting and improving the world environment.

6. Support for multilateral trade systems worldwide.

7. Avoiding participation in and not condoning unethical and illegal business practices.

Shell Leader Promotes Ethical Principles and Profits

Mark Moody-Stuart, the new CEO of Royal Dutch/Shell, is proud of a recent corporate success story. In a West African nation, a Royal Dutch/Shell manager had been stopped by a police officer demanding cash. A second police officer said, peering into the car, "This lot's from Shell. You're not going to get any money." Moody-Stuart beams, "Word must be getting around: no bribes paid or accepted by Shell workers." In fact, the actions of these Shell employees are in harmony with Shell's "Statement of General Business Principles, Principle 4: Business Integrity," which states:

> Shell companies insist on honesty, integrity and fairness in all aspects of their business and expect the same in their relationships with all those with whom they do business. The direct or indirect offer, payment, soliciting and acceptance of bribes in any form are unacceptable practices. Employees must avoid conflicts of interest between their private financial activities and their part in the conduct of company business. All business transactions on behalf of a Shell company must be reflected accurately and fairly in the accounts of the company in accordance with established procedures and be subject to audit.

Moody-Stewart also expects all of the Shell companies to "express support for fundamental human rights in line with the legitimate role of business and to give proper regard to health, safety, and the environment consistent with their commitment to contribute to sustainable development." The company embraces the UN Universal Declaration of Human Rights. They have pledged to set up "Social Responsibility Management Systems" and to develop training programs and procedures to help management deal with human rights dilemmas as part of the steps they are taking to implement their statement of principles. In 1998, Shell broke from many of its competitors by quitting an industry group that was fighting efforts to limit global warming by reducing emissions from fossil fuels such as oil and gas. (See chapter 6, where John Browne of BP Amoco has also taken this position.)

The company has also committed to report on its performance in living up to these ethical principles and to allow for independent auditing of its results. In 1997 Shell's mandate against bribery led to the firing of 23 employees. The company had rules against bribes in the past, but the company now tracks and reports its enforcement, allowing the world to watch over its shoulder (Hamilton, 1998).

6. Technologist

Technology enables the organization to "stretch," to democratize the strategy-creation process by tapping the imagination of hundreds, if not thousands, of new voices in the strategy process. Technology forces and enables leaders to lead their organizations through a complete transformation process, a process that creates the organizational shifts listed in Table 2.4.

Table 2.4

Dimension Differences between the Old and New Organization

DIMENSION	OLD ORGANIZATIONS	NEW ORGANIZATIONS
Critical tasks	Physical	Mental
Relationships	Hierarchical	Peer-to-peer
Levels	Many	Few
Structures	Functional	Multidisciplinary teams
Boundaries	Fixed	Permeable
Competitive thrust	Vertical integration	Outsourcing and alliances
Management style	Autocratic	Participative
Culture	Compliance	Commitment and results
People	Homogeneous	Diverse
Strategic focus	Efficiency	Innovation

Technology adds considerable capability to the functions of scanning and environmental monitoring. This effective scanning of the business environment—to understand what is changing—is necessary for an organization to proactively manage its way through a global environment made so turbulent because of technological changes.

The technology-driven networks and databases will replace the multit-iered hierarchy with a wide breadth and depth of knowledge that is the sum of employees' collective experience. The new organizational architecture will evolve around autonomous work teams and strategic alliances.

Technology demands the recreation and redefinition of organizations and leadership as we know them. It permits the redistribution of power, function, and control to wherever they are most effective, and according to the mission, objectives, and culture of the organization. The twenty-first century leader needs to know the power as well as the limitations of technology.

7. Innovator and Risk-Taker

Einstein stated that "imagination is more important than information." Hamel and Prahalad (1994) note that in today's world, it is "imagination and not resources that is scarce." Tichey and Cohen (1997) write that "leadership is about change. It's about taking people from where they are now to where they need to be. The best way to get people to venture into unknown territory is to make it desirable by taking them there in their imaginations." Jack Welch, CEO of General Electric, believes that efficiencies in business are infinite, a faith grounded in the belief that there are no bounds to human creativity. "The idea flow from the human spirit is absolutely unlimited," Welch declares. "All you have to do is to tap into that well" (Byrne, 1998).

Leaders must continuously look for "white-space opportunities," new areas of growth possibilities that fall between the cracks because they do not naturally match the skills of existing business units. They also look for "strategic intent," a tangible corporate goal or destiny that represents a stretch for the organization.

Often, new ideas are not allowed to occur in an organization because they might conflict with existing, established, mental models or ways of doing things. The new leader has the task of confronting these existing assumptions without invoking defensiveness or anger. Thus, a leader must be able to un-cover and test the mental models and basic assumptions of colleagues.

Twenty-first century leaders must be willing to take risks. And not only should they themselves be creative, they should encourage and reward creativity around them. New leaders must be truly open to the wide range of perspectives and possibilities essential to identify trends and to generate choices.

For Jack Welch and leaders of other world-class companies, the generation of new ideas is the lifeline to continued success. Although everyone is encouraged and expected to be creative, it is the leaders who can best create this environment, who can challenge the old ways, who can encourage risks as well as protect and encourage those whose risks have not been successful. The new leader should be at the forefront of trying new things.

8. Visionary and Vision-Builder

The twenty-first century leader must be able to help build the company's vision and to inspire workers, customers, and colleagues. The leader must envision together with his or her fellow employees the type of future world the company desires, one that is exciting and challenging enough to attract and retain the best and brightest of know-how workers. To the extent that the leader is able to build a shared, desired picture for the organization or unit, people are willing and committed to carry out the vision. Leaders should attempt to:

— Blend extrinsic and intrinsic visions

— Communicate their own vision and ask for support

— Encourage personal visions from which emerge shared visions

— Keep visioning as an ongoing process

Byrne (1998) notes that "the idea of rising above the tumult of day-to-day-business to ponder the complexity of markets with visions and strategic thinking is looking attractive again. Reengineering consultants with stopwatches are out. Strategy gurus with great visions of new prospects are in." Kotter (1996) makes the following distinction between the manager and the leader:

> Leadership is about setting the direction, which is not the same as planning or even long-term planning. Planning is a management process, deductive in nature and designed to produce orderly results, not change. Setting a direction is more inductive. Leaders gather a broad range of data and look for patterns, relationships and linkages that help explain things. The direction-setting aspect of leadership does not produce plans; it creates vision and strategies. These describe a business, technology, or corporate culture in terms of what is should become over the long term and articulate a feasible way of achieving this goal.

Trying to get people to comprehend a vision of an alternative future is also a communications challenge of a completely different magnitude from organizing them to fulfill a short-term plan. "It's much like the difference between a football quarterback attempting to describe to his team the next two or three plays versus his trying to explain to them a totally new approach to the game to be used in the second half of the season" (Byrne, 1998).

The ability to conceptualize complex issues and processes, simplify them, and inspire people around them is essential for the twenty-first century leader.

Leaders create stories about the future of their organizations. These stories create a case for change, a vision of where the organization is going, and an understanding of how to get there.

Global Leaders with Twenty-First Century Leadership Attributes

Having explored the transformative forces and the leadership competencies needed to lead in the twenty-first century, let us now look at 12 global leaders who can serve as models for twenty-first century leadership.

CHAPTER THREE

John Chambers:
Leading Cisco Systems,
the World's Largest Company

Under the dynamic leadership of President and CEO John Chambers, Cisco Systems has quietly become the worldwide leader in networking for the Internet, a success story that has been compared to that of Microsoft and Intel in their respective markets. Yet it remains "the most important company no one's ever heard of." *Upside* magazine called Cisco "the most invisible major company in high tech" (Marshall, 1997).

Although few Internet users ever see or hear of the products Cisco provides, investors know the company well. Cisco is among the 20 highest valued companies in the world. In fiscal 1999, the San Jose–based company racked up over $12 billion in sales. This represented an increase of 200% over 1995 revenues. Since 1995 its share price has increased by nearly 3000%, giving Cisco a market value of over $400 billion only 10 years after going public—the fastest a company has ever risen to this level. It is the second-largest company on Wall Street and the fastest growing technology firm in history.

Much of Cisco System's success stems from President and CEO John Chambers' drive and business savvy. Those who know him best—including his toughest competitors—praise him as a leader with few peers. "He's done a phenomenal job," said Eric Benhamou, CEO of rival 3Com Corp. of Santa Clara. "He owes his success to skill, not luck" (Marshall, 1997). The Internet's twenty-first century global leader attributes his astonishing achievements to the "power of networks—both personal and high-tech ones" (Corcoran, 1998).

Chambers' achievements have led to many honors and awards. In January 1998, Chambers was one of two business leaders worldwide to receive a special Trade Award from the Prime Minister of Japan in recognition of Cisco's success as the worldwide leader in networking and for using innovative strategies for developing its business in Japan. He was also selected as *Electronic Business* magazine's "CEO of the Year" for 1997 by a poll of industry executives. In addition, *BusinessWeek* voted him one of its top 25 managers in 1996; *Network World* has listed him among the top 25 most powerful people in networking; and *Upside* rated him ninth in its "Elite 100" list.

Early Years

Chambers worked as a marketing manager at IBM in the late 1970s and early 1980s, before joining Wang Laboratories in 1982. He spent eight years at Wang, the last two as Senior Vice President of U.S. Operations.

He joined Cisco Systems in January 1991 as Senior Vice President of Worldwide Operations, at a time when the company had $70 million in annual sales and a market cap of $600 million. He was promoted in May 1994 to Executive Vice President with responsibilities for R&D, manufacturing, worldwide sales, marketing, and support.

Since he became President and CEO in 1994, Chambers has grown the company from $1.2 billion in annual revenues to its current run-rate of over $12 billion by establishing leadership in key technology sectors of the networking industry and aggressively pursuing new market opportunities.

Cisco Systems—Worldwide Leader in Networking the Internet

Cisco's core business is making the essential "plumbing" of the Internet: routers, hubs, and switches. Its networking solutions connect people, computing devices, and computer networks, allowing people to access or transfer information without regard to differences in time, place, or type of computer system. Cisco provides end-to-end networking solutions that customers use to build a unified information infrastructure of their own or to connect to someone else's network.

Routers account for almost half of Cisco's revenue, but local area network (LAN) and wide area network (WAN) switch sales are increasing. The company is first in the backbone LAN switching, high-end router, mid-range router, and low-end router markets. It is number two in the WAN switching and workgroup LAN switching markets. And it is gaining in the remote access dial-up market, where it currently holds the number three market-share position. (LaPlante, 1997)

Cisco's $55 billion market capitalization exceeds that of Ford or GM and is at least 50% greater than its six largest rivals combined. Based on its market capitalization, the market value of Cisco increased by over $180 billion in 1999 alone. Since Chambers arrived, the San Jose-based company has jumped from being a one-product business with revenues of $70 million and 400 employees, still recognizable from the days when it was run by its Stanford University founders, to a public company with $12 billion in revenues and 21,000 employees in 54 countries.

The company continues growing at a sizzling pace because of its central position in a fast-growing industry in the midst of enormous change. Cisco dominates the $20 billion data networking equipment market, and with Internet traffic doubling every four months, demand for newer and faster systems is intense. In 1998, *Forbes ASAP* designated Cisco as the country's most dynamic company and *Fortune* calls Cisco one of the 25 best companies to work for in the U.S. And it is about to take on new markets and, inevitably, new competitors.

Let's look at the leadership attributes that Chambers has displayed in guiding Cisco Systems into becoming a leading company for the twenty-first century.

Maintaining Vision in a Dull Business

For years, building routers was considered a steady but unexciting business. "Five years ago, the majority of technical people thought that Cisco had the wrong model," said Eric Schmidt, chief executive of Novell Inc., a major software company. Routers, which depend heavily on software to provide the "intelligence" that helps them carry out complex tasks, were useful for connecting companies together. But switches were considered more powerful, capable of swiftly handling rivers of information, including traditional voice signals, although limited to the relatively small local area networks. (Corcoran, 1998)

Cisco and others recognized, however, that some of the technology used in switches could be used to make larger and faster routers. Today, top-notch routers are so fast that they can carry voice signals along with data, albeit with varying levels of quality. Such technology has led people to dream of the Holy Grail of networking: a single network that fuses data, voice, and video information. In fact, every networking company wants to create technology that will join the traditional telephone network with the Internet technologies.

Despite his impressive accomplishments so far, Chambers knows that in the high tech world, he must constantly keep his eye on the bigger picture. For him, this means not just dominating a particular market but changing the way the world works and plays. "The technology revolution currently going on will rival the Industrial Revolution in terms of the impact on our society," he says. "At Cisco, we have the chance to be at the very forefront, driving these changes—if we do our job well."

Chambers foresees the future of technology as far more than increased computing power—it will be about communicating. The electronic gadgets that people will use to talk to one another will be "as varied and unique as trinkets on a charm bracelet" (Corcoran, 1998). But they will all use standardized communications networks. And in Chambers' vision, Cisco's technology will reside at all the critical junctures, moving data from one place or device to the next.

New Way of Doing Business

Eschewing the "Old World thinking" of companies such as IBM that have difficulty in adapting to new environments, Chambers has helped fuel the Internet revolution, "rushing into technologies and markets that speed communications." He has orchestrated numerous acquisitions and developed critical partnerships, turning Cisco Systems into "the world's most comprehensive end-to-end supplier of networking equipment" (Brandt, 1998).

As Cisco's management works on putting together the pieces for that grand network, it takes full advantage of the communications systems available today to handle its business. According to Carl Redfield, Cisco's senior vice president for manufacturing and logistics, 80% of Cisco's annual $2 billion in materials purchases are handled via electronic networks, in which computers at either end communicate directly with one another. The rest are handled via the Internet. In essence, he believes that no one should consider being a supplier to Cisco unless they do business over the Internet (Corcoran, 1998).

Chambers, according to his peers, has "managed to pull together a seamless strategy for the company, and that's something most networking firms have failed to do" (LaPlante, 1997). For example, during fiscal 1997, Chambers quickly reorganized Cisco's operations into three business units to better focus on customer needs and become a leader in each market area.

Cisco's strategic initiatives illustrate its ability to systematically align customer needs, employee care, and organizational processes LaPlante.

1. Become a leader in providing end-to-end networking solutions.

2. Succeed in each individual line-of-business segment targeted (service provider, enterprise, small and medium businesses).

3. Forge strategic partnerships.

4. Spearhead data, voice, and video integration efforts.

5. Recruit, retain, and develop the top 10% of technology employees.

6. Become number one in sales of high-end networking products.

7. Promote Cisco's Internet Operating System as the leading network services architecture.

Nice Guy in a Cutthroat Marketplace

With a reputation for being a nice guy in a cutthroat marketplace, Chambers has earned a reputation as being an ethical contender, not a predator, in the high-tech arena. Even when the stakes are high, he acts like a gentleman. He recognizes that to have a healthy business does not require destroying the competition: "You don't need to drive a stake through a company's heart and let the whole world see it bleed. I don't think it's necessary, and I don't think it's constructive" (LaPlante, 1997).

In the words of Peter Swartz, a Salomon Smith Barney analyst, "Chambers is a West Virginia choirboy, soft-spoken, articulate." His manner is humble, disarming, boyish, and self-effacing, a leader who really cares about people. Chambers describes his priorities this way: "The two things that get companies into trouble is that they get too far away from their customers and too far away from their employees" (LaPlante, 1997).

His experiences at IBM and Wang have influenced Chambers in several ways. For one thing, he is determined to avoid the arrogance that can make big, successful technology firms remote and unresponsive to their customers.

In fact, Chambers is obsessed with customer relations at Cisco, undoubtedly a result of watching firsthand as IBM threw away its well-earned reputation for outstanding customer service. "They didn't want to hear from customers, and top management would tell customers they were wrong," Chambers recalls (Banm, 1998).

When it comes to customer service, Chambers is the first to "walk the talk." On his way to his first board meeting as chief executive at Cisco, he overheard a colleague taking a call from an irate customer. Chambers insisted on first working through the customer's problem before arriving, more than half an hour late, at the board meeting.

Regardless of where he is, Chambers goes through voice-mails every evening from managers dealing with customers on the "critical list" so that he "can hear their emotion." A critical account is defined less by the number of dollars, or sales volume, at stake than by the fact that someone associated with the account—the client perhaps, or the sales rep, or an engineer servicing the account—is concerned about a problem, about instability or a chance for a buying decision to go against Cisco.

As Chambers explains, "I'm probably the only CEO in the world in a company of this size who does this. But the fact that I pay attention to these issues at this level means that the whole company has to" (LaPlante, 1997). And he stays close to his customers and employees, spending more than 40% of his time on the road, meeting with customers during the day, and then taking local Cisco employees out for pizza and beer.

Perhaps the most solid evidence of his customer focus is the fact that every manager's compensation is directly tied to customer satisfaction. Cisco surveys clients extensively each year, polling them on approximately 60 performance criteria, from product functionality to service quality. "If a manager improves his scores, he can get a fair amount. But if the scores go down, we'll take money out of the manager's pocket," says Chambers. Strategies of this kind contributed to the annual increase in the number of completely satisfied end users (Baum, 1998).

As Chambers sees it, Cisco is just a few steps ahead of many other companies in grabbing the savings that come from becoming an Internet company. So he came up with a method to help Cisco create lasting bonds with its customers. As Cisco becomes a one-stop shop for everything a customer needs to be an Internet company, Chambers is also exploring ways that Cisco can pump up its name recognition through national advertising—a tactic aimed at making a decision to "buy Cisco" easy to explain.

Beyond partnering with customers, he has also struck important strategic alliances with other high-flying companies, such as Microsoft, Intel, and

Compaq—companies that Cisco relies on to provide the technologies that it either cannot or will not create on its own. Cisco believes that such deals should deliver both it and the partner $500 million to $1 billion in revenue that they wouldn't have won on their own. With 10 such deals so far, Chambers is eyeing a few more. He concedes that some will not pan out. But because they let Cisco tell a customer it can arrange for all the necessary technology to create an end-to-end network, Chambers calculates that the deals are worth the effort (Scouras, 1998).

Ethics and Service

Chambers' road to success has included plenty of bumps. When he joined Wang in 1982, the company controlled a near-monopoly in the word-processing business. Chambers was in charge of half of the company's overseas businesses when chairman An Wang asked him to take over U.S. operations. "I figured he meant me to start at the New Year," says Chambers. "But he said, 'No, I mean tomorrow.' I knew we were in trouble." One of his first tasks in his new post was to fire 4,000 people. "It damn near killed me," he says. (Marshall, 1997) As a company, Wang had ignored the rise of personal computers, bringing about its own demise.

After spending eight years at struggling Wang, Chambers packed up his belongings and quit in disgust without any place to go—and that was during a period when job prospects in the computer business were not bright. "There were a lot of feelings at that point of what a gutsy move that was, when you need to support a family. He stood by what he believed, and he didn't believe that Wang was headed in the right direction and that his place was there," according to one source. "Rather than look for a job while he was trying to run a worldwide sales force, he chose to openly share what he was doing and put his money where his mouth was, so to speak. I think I admired that quite a bit, and I'm not sure that I could do the same thing." (Kupfer, 1998) After becoming CEO at Cisco, he vowed never to order mass layoffs, and at one point when Cisco had to cut costs, he did so without firing anyone. He also makes sure that the company's business practices are squeaky clean.

Despite the heavy demands of his position, Chambers finds time to devote to community and political events. Impressed by Chambers' involvement, Hewlett-Packard's Platt speaks highly of his efforts: "Very often CEOs of younger, smaller companies say they don't have time for these things. John has shown that he is personally committed to his employees as well as his community, and he has encouraged others in his company to get similarly involved" (LaPlante, 1997).

His ethical stance and all-around business talents have not gone unnoticed. In its quest for the CEO of the Year, *Electronic Business* looks for "a quintessential well-rounded executive: someone with outstanding business sense, a passion for his job, the highest degree of integrity and ethics and someone who commands respect from his peers" (LaPlante, 1997). Through a complex process of nominations and research supported by qualitative and quantitative data, a CEO is chosen each year. This includes an evaluation of the integrity, innovation, and respect that the candidates have among their peers, other senior industry executives, and analysts. Chambers' selection in 1997 "was not that difficult. He scored highest among the nominees in the survey, has delivered consistently high financial results for Cisco's shareholders and is held in high regard by the industry" (LaPlante, 1997).

Attracting and Retaining Top People

As the pioneer in internetworking, Cisco Systems has a huge head start on the rest of the industry. It has "assembled so much scarce engineering talent that it can design new generations of products faster than anyone else" (Schlender, 1997).

A crucial factor in Cisco's success will be its ability to retain talent in the hottest technology employment marketplace in history. Cisco has only a 6% voluntary attrition rate among employees. A full 40% of all Cisco stock options are in the hands of individual employees without managerial rank. "Not line managers, not vice presidents, not directors," Chambers says, "but individual contributors" (LaPlante, 1997).

Chambers understands the importance of keeping good people. During the numerous acquisitions that Cisco has made, Chambers has stressed the need to retain the people who come with the deal. After all, what Cisco is generally buying is not market share, but people and next generation products. When employees, often entrepreneurial engineers, are lost, a deal loses much of its value. That they usually want to stay is a tribute partly to the lure of Cisco stock options and partly to Chambers' policy of buying only firms in the area, so that families do not have to uproot. But the Chambers style of decentralized management is also a key factor. People who do well are given a lot of freedom; people who do not, leave. "It's called accountability," says Chambers (LaPlante, 1997).

Assuring Global Success in a Technological Age

It goes without saying that a leading company in the Internet world such as Cisco must have a global focus. With products sold in 115 countries, Chambers recognizes the importance of understanding the unique needs of customers around the world.

Every day, Cisco and its customers are demonstrating that networking and the Internet can fundamentally and profitably change the way companies do business. Cisco describes this change in the "Global Networked Business" model. A Global Networked Business is an enterprise, of any size, that strategically uses information and communications to build a network of strong, interactive relationships with all its key constituencies.

The global networked business model opens the corporate information infrastructure to all key constituencies, leveraging the network for competitive advantage. It employs a self-help approach of information access that is more efficient and responsive than the traditional model of a few information gatekeepers dispensing data as they see fit. Cisco itself is a leading example of a global networked business. By using networked applications, the Internet, and its own internal network, Cisco is saving at least $500 million a year in operating costs, while improving customer and partner satisfaction and gaining a competitive advantage in areas such as customer support, product ordering, and delivery times (Nec, 1996).

Innovation

In contrast to many technology companies, Cisco does not insist on the use of one technology over all other alternatives and impose it on customers as the only solution. The company's philosophy is to listen to customer requests, monitor all technological alternatives, and provide customers with a range of options from which to choose. Cisco develops its products and solutions around widely accepted industry standards. And in some instances, technologies developed by Cisco have become industry standards.

Chambers also insists that no technology should be rejected because it was not invented in-house. He takes a pragmatic approach, preferring to buy innovative startups rather than fight them. And if a useful technology can be more quickly or cheaply bought than developed by Cisco's own engineers, Chambers does not shy away from making a quick purchase. This approach is unusual for Silicon Valley. As one expert explains, "At a lot of technology companies, it's a sign of weakness to have to look outside for technological help. John has instilled a culture in which it's not a sign of weakness but a sign of strength to say, 'I can't do everything myself. I will find a partner and trust myself to be able to manage the process.'" (Corcoran, 1998)

In addition, Chambers has embraced an outsourcing strategy, having modeled Cisco after Hewlett-Packard when he took the helm. Cisco itself largely does only the final assembly of its routers. Cisco seeks to maintain control over the intellectual property of manufacturing, not the bricks and mortar, and thus gives its suppliers intricate orders on how to build its components and then computerized scripts for testing those parts.

In some cases the most efficient means to bring in new capabilities is to acquire whole companies. Cisco's first acquisition was the purchase in 1993 of Crescendo, an Ethernet-switching company. The purchase was prompted by an important customer, Boeing. About to lose Boeing's business, Chambers asked what Cisco had to do to keep it. The response was to make this new technology a core competence, right away. Last quarter, Crescendo's Catalyst switches earned more than $600 million. He also uses acquisitions to complete the company's product offerings, most notably the $4 billion stock deal to buy StrataCom. This deal gave Cisco a bigger presence in the asynchronous transfer mode (ATM) market and rounded out its line of routers, hubs, and switching products. To date, Cisco has acquired over 40 companies for a total price tag of more than $16 billion.

Cisco also leads the world in the use of Internet technology to revolutionize business processes and to gain a sustainable, competitive advantage. Practicing what it preaches, the company has moved much of its sales and technical support effort to the World Wide Web. Cisco's Web site, the Cisco Connection Online, is the world's largest electronic commerce site. Cisco executives say they are booking as much as $20 million a day through the Web. The goal is to link Cisco's ordering and production system so closely that a customer's order triggers component suppliers to ship their parts. That makes products more tailored to customer needs and reduces inventories. Internally, Cisco now handles all employee expenses and a growing number of customer service and support tasks via Web page applications. Proxy voting for shareholders is another candidate for the Internet. Chambers believes that this innovative use of the Internet alone saves the company at least $360 million a year, "which is more than our major competitors spend on R&D" ('Mr. Internet,' 1998).

Learning and Listening

Chambers realizes the dangers of complacency; he never underestimates the potential of new competitors to strike a surprise blow against Cisco. As he explains, "Paranoia allows us to stay on top." (Kupfe, 1998) He learned not to take market share for granted after his devastating experience at Wang Laboratories, after the once mighty word processing company was upended by the PC revolution. The convergence of the Internet with the telephone and television will bring Cisco new markets with unfamiliar requirements. Chambers knows better than to be caught off-guard.

In the speed-of-light pace of the high tech world, Chambers must constantly learn to stay ahead of the game. And he has learned the value of learning by attentive listening. He has a keen ability to listen, and he expects his team to develop that same level of skill. So what will make Cisco Systems, in Chambers' own words, "a kinder, gentler and ultimately much more successful IBM"? By understanding what really matters to the customer, by truly listening to them.

Cisco is the first successful company Chambers has worked for, and he knows what happens to companies that become mired in old ways of thinking and computing. He also realizes what will happen to Cisco if he fails, if he doesn't make the company a formidable competitor that can stay ahead of the Lucents and the up-and-coming companies that keep bringing out new technologies that could revolutionize the business of networking. Chambers recognizes that he must be flexible and quick on his feet.

For example, Cisco made a characteristically fast change of direction in response to customer feedback in the Ethernet versus ATM debate. "We were pushing ATM for workgroup and desktop applications," says Chambers. "But our customers came forward and made it clear they were going with routers and fast Ethernet," he recalls. To make a long story short, "we moved from a non-player in that market to a billion-dollar revenue stream." Today, Chambers says, fast Ethernet outsells ATM at the desktop and workgroup level at a rate of 10 to one.

In January 1996, Chambers began hearing from his large accounts that they wanted single-vendor servicing in the networking arena—what Chambers now calls "end-to-end coverage"— that allowed them to reduce the total cost of ownership of an entire network by including calculations for installation, maintenance, and support, not just the cost of the individual components. "I said, 'Well, I don't think that's what you want,'" Chambers recalls. "I said, 'That sounds like the IBM of 20 or 25 years ago. And look where they are now.'"

His customers disagreed. Chambers listened. And it began to make sense. "They were quite clear that the IBM of 20 to 25 years ago was exactly what they wanted," he says. Why? Because of the newness of networking technology, companies need the same kind of help in understanding, implementing, and managing it as they did in the early days of the computer revolution.

Eventually, customers will acquire enough internal knowledge and expertise to feel comfortable loosening ties to Cisco. Chambers is fully aware of this, although he predicts that it won't happen for three or four years in the networking arena. "That's the mistake that IBM made: They stayed at the same level of competency, while their customers' knowledge grew and grew and grew," he says. "They focused on the politics of the account and the control of the account, rather than asking themselves whether they were adding value." Chambers believes in learning from such mistakes.

Entering the Twenty-First Century with Confidence

Now Chambers is pushing Cisco into its most dangerous territory yet. He believes the Internet is about to undergo a dramatic change, merging with the telephone and cable TV businesses, thus creating "one mammoth voice-video-data network worldwide" (Brandt, 1998). Chambers is also aware that the Internet economy will reach nearly $1 trillion worldwide by 2002 (Schmit, 1998). But when recently asked what kind of a company Cisco will be in the year 2002, Chambers confidently responded: "We will be the leader in data, voice, video, and in all major segments of the market" (Chambers, 1998).

Thus, Chambers is readying Cisco to compete in a much bigger league. As data traffic mushrooms, phone companies are building new networks, phasing out the century-old system designed to carry only telephone calls and replacing it with one that can carry information of all kinds—voice, video, and computer files. Selling new versions of its equipment into this bigger market means that Chambers must challenge more powerful rivals than before, such as Nortel, which is twice as large as Cisco; Lucent, over three times as big; and even Siemens, with seven times Cisco's sales. Chambers must also win new customers, the big phone companies, with which Cisco has had only limited dealings.

What does Chambers think of Cisco's chances in this new universe of fused voice, video, and the Internet? "I want Cisco to be a dynasty," he says. "I think it can be a company that changes the world." And he means it (Kufner, 1998).

CHAPTER FOUR

Ricardo Semler: Semco and the World's Leading Maverick

In the coming years, maverick men and women whose vision is different from everyone else's will break out of the corporate pack. No blueprints exist for maverick management. By its very nature, maverick thinking is off the diagonal, cannot be premeditated, and defies conventional wisdom. Maverick managers stand apart by taking notions like a flexible workplace or open-book management to unprecedented extremes.

—Jaclyn Fierman, *Fortune,* 1995

Ricardo Semler is generally recognized as the world's leading maverick, a Brazilian who has helped Semco not only survive but thrive in a country that in recent years barely blinked at an annual 3000% inflation rate. He has taken Semco from an autocratic company to one where employees run the operation—they wear what they want, choose their own bosses, and come and go as they please. Semler, who shares the title of CEO with 5 other people on a rotating basis, relies on the market to police both his employees and his own far-out ideas. Professor Charles Handy, one of the world's top authorities on organizational leadership, says of him: "The way that Ricardo Semler runs his company is impossible: except it works, and works splendidly for everyone" ('Man Who Drives,' 1993).

Although some theorists have felt that Semler may have taken the doctrine of employee involvement to ridiculous extremes, it has been successful despite overwhelming obstacles. Since becoming CEO, Semler has seen the company experience tremendous increases in growth, in profits, and market share—all during frequent, massive national recessions.

Semler's so-called "ridiculous" concepts are attracting worldwide attention—from management guru Tom Peters, who spotlighted Semco in *Liberation Management,* to the venerable *Harvard Business Review,* which says Semler's "Managing Without Managers" article, published in 1989, is one of its most frequently requested reprints. Mobil, IBM, and hundreds of other U.S. companies have made the pilgrimage to Sao Paulo to witness the Semco operation firsthand. His book *Maverick,* the English-language version of Semler's own management memoirs, penned at the decrepit age of 28, has sold over a million copies and counting.

Semco—The Company

Founded by Semler's father in the 1950s, Semco manufactures a variety of products: pumps that can empty an oil tanker in one night; dishwashers capable of scrubbing 4,100 plates an hour; cooling units for air conditioners that keep huge office towers comfortable during the most sweltering of heat waves; mixers that blend everything from rocket fuel to bubble gum; and entire biscuit factories, with 6,000 separate components and 16 miles of wiring. Although close to financial disaster in 1980, Semco S.A. is now one of the fastest growing companies in Brazil. 1997 revenues were over $100 million, up from $35 million in 1990, and profits were $8.2 million (Wheatley and Blount, 1997).

Early Years at Semco

Semler was 20 when he joined his father's company, fresh from the University of Sao Paulo, where he had graduated in law. Around 90% of Semco's turnover was in marine products during an economic slump when Brazil's shipbuilding industry was among the hardest-hit sectors. He believed Semco's only chance was to broaden its product line, but it was over a year before his father could be persuaded. "Better make your mistakes while I'm still alive," he said and handed him the company to run.

When, at age 21, Ricardo Semler took over the family business from his father, Semco looked much like any other old-line Brazilian company. Fear was the governing principle. Guards patrolled the factory floor, timed people's trips to the bathroom, and frisked workers as they left the plant. Anyone unlucky enough to break a piece of equipment would replace it out of his or her own pocket.

At first the young Semler carried on the autocratic ethic, working a relentless schedule. But the pressure was literally killing him. One day, while visiting a pump factory in upstate New York, he collapsed on the shop floor. The doctor pronounced him basically healthy but more stressed out than any 25-year-old he had ever seen. After that experience, Semler resolved to remake his company into "a true democracy, a place run on trust and freedom, not fear." The revolution at Semco was ready to be unleashed.

During the 1980s, Semler made Semco a laboratory for unusual but successful management practices as the company became one of the most progressive and democratic workplaces in the world. All regulations were replaced with the rule of common sense. Dress codes and complex company rules about travel expenses were scrapped. Throughout this period of democratization, company performance improved dramatically. Sales went from $11,000 per employee in 1979 to $135,000 in the early 1990s, more than four times the average figure for Semco's competitors (Fierman, 1995). Semco increased productivity and sales tenfold in just over 10 years and held its own in the midst of various national economic recessions.

Visionary Leader in Good Times and Bad

Semco is constantly evolving, building new visions and ways of getting things done. When the Brazilian economy took a turn toward chaos in 1990, empowerment, profit sharing, self-set salaries, and other innovative policies were no longer enough to ensure survival. Sales plummeted, workers took a voluntary pay cut, and Semco held on by its fingertips. The only solution was to cut permanent staff and contract out more work. But Semler saw a better way to do just that. Instead of contracting work to strangers, the contracts were given to Semco workers who were set up in business with generous severance settlements and an offer to lease company equipment. Fifty or so satellite companies have sprung up on the premises since then.

In 1990, Semco had about 500 employees. Today, it has some 200 workers, with that many more in these company satellites, in what can be called a radical experiment in unsupervised, in-house, satellite production of goods and services for sale to Semco and to other manufacturers by employees, part-time employees, and ex-employees. "The threat of competition keeps us all on our toes," says Semler. "This program has made us leaner and more agile, and given them [the employees] ultimate control of their work lives. It makes entrepreneurs out of employees" (Semler, 1994a).

Semler has also developed a new "hierarchy" of leadership. The Semco bureaucracy has been whittled from 12 layers of management to 3 and replaced with a new structure based on concentric circles to replace the traditional, and confining, corporate pyramid. There are still leaders in Semco. Instead of a pyramid hierarchy, though, there's a more complex geometry: a ring of "Counselors," including Semler, who handle Semco's general policies and strategies; a slightly bigger circle of Partners, who head up Semco's seven business units; a large pool of Associates, which comprises most of the workers; and all sorts of triangular, coordinating configurations in between. "Circles free our people from hierarchical tyranny; they could act as leaders when they wanted and command whatever respect their efforts and competence earned them. There is no single boss, but rather an informal group of six top managers who take turns acting as chief executive, rotating every six months" (The New Mavericks, 1993).

Innovations Built on Trust

Semler's vision is based on his trust and confidence in people. As he notes, "Most of the rigorous procedures and systems introduced by companies are ways of saying to employees 'we don't trust you.' Basically, I couldn't imagine working with people I didn't or couldn't trust. These are responsible adults who, theoretically at least, should be trustworthy. So it didn't take any courage to do it but it had always been a basic belief of mine. Now some people I'm sure abused the situation, but I'm sure no more than if you took the other approach; and why penalize and constrain the overwhelming majority—at vast expense—when the real benefits of all the controls are essentially non-existent" (Lloyd, 1994).

As a result of Semler's numerous innovative changes, Semco has been revolutionized, moving from Dark-Ages style management practices to practices that would challenge the thinking of even the most progressive organization. The key thrust of Semler's vision is founded in his faith that when people say they will do something, in general they do. He has thus sought to create a company that is free from fear and insecurity and characterized by freedom, trust, and commitment. He has brought new dimensions to the term *empowerment*.

Building trust and teams is essential for any organization to be innovative, according to Semler. Thus, Semco does away with the formalities that discourage team development. "We encourage movement between projects and areas within the organization which help team creation and recreation. Because we work on six-month operations budgets, there is a tendency to have to rethink things every couple of months. Then there is the transparency—the fact that every one knows what is going on. Also we do balance sheet training programs and these include the janitors. That helps trust. There is no classified information whatsoever in the company" (Lloyd, 1994).

Semler presents himself as the questioner, the challenger, the catalyst, as the person who asks basic questions and encourages people to bring things down to the simplest level in making key decisions shaping their work performance. By challenging the status quo at every turn and allowing people to come up with appropriate solutions, the attack on bureaucracy and conventional styles of management has become more dramatic over the years. Numerous innovations have resulted, such as the spinning off of factories and other business units into separate self-regulating units, widespread profit-sharing, the hiring and firing of managers by their employees, and the idea that to stay employed you have got to find a way of adding visible value so that your team will continue to want to include you as part of their six-month budget. As a result of these innovations on the part of his employees, Semler prides himself on the fact that he is now completely dispensable.

Systems Thinking

In restructuring Semco, Semler notes that he has picked the best from many systems. "From capitalism we take the ideals of personal freedom, individualism, and competition. From the theory, not the practice, of socialism we have learned to control greed and share information and power. The Japanese have taught us the value of flexibility, although we shrink from their family-like ties to the company and their automatic veneration of elders. We want people to advance because of competence, not longevity or conformity" (Semler, 1993).

When you eliminate rigid thought and hierarchical structure, things usually get messy, which is how Semco's factories tend to look. Instead of machines neatly aligned in long, straight rows, the way Henry Ford would have wanted them, they are set at odd angles and in unexpected places. That's because the workers typically work in clusters or teams, assembling a complete product, not just an isolated component. This approach gives them more control and responsibility, which makes them happier and the resulting products better. Nearly all of the workers have mastered several jobs. They even drive forklifts to keep teammates supplied with raw materials and spare parts, which they have been known to purchase themselves from suppliers.

The Metalworkers' Union at first resisted this flexibility. Long ago, organized labor was forced to adopt narrower and narrower job classifications as a defense against giant corporations that pushed ever harder for higher productivity and profits. Eventually the unions realized that they could turn the system against the corporate masters by refusing to allow any deviation from the rules without extra pay. With time, the system became more beneficial to labor than to management—but it really wasn't serving either side. When the union realized that Semco had no intention of dismantling its power—that the higher profits its factories would generate would mean higher pay for its members and that upper management was intent on giving workers a meaningful say in the business—obstructionism eased. The Semco climate allows employees to innovate. As a result, all employees, both management and nonmanagement, are freer.

As Semler notes, "Common sense in business is by far the most revolutionary thing you can think of. Few things are as far from the way things are actually run as common sense" (Semler, 1994a).

Global Mindset and Cultural Dexterity

"Up until now," Semler points out, "it has been easy enough for the First World to keep its distance from the Third World and view the Southern Hemisphere as very far away. But technology is drawing everyone and everyplace close." Most organizations are unprepared for this New World order. Their impulse is to try to homogenize everything. To survive in modern times, however, they must do just the opposite—relish diversity, learn from each other's differences, and let cultural differences thrive.

According to Semler, we have always lived in tribes and always will. Whether these groups are ethnic, religious, political, or vocational, they serve as our anchors. He believes that we must redesign our organizations to let tribes be. Since different tribes will never fully integrate, we must develop systems based on coexistence, not on some unattainable ideal of harmony. "By all means establish and promote a common goal, but recognize diversity and let people determine their own ways of achieving it," he urges (Muehrcke, 1998).

Democracy in the Workplace

One reason the revolution in employee involvement at Semco occurred was that Ricardo Semler was bored. It was 1980, and 20-year old Semler had "discovered the depressingly narrow range of my musical ability," dropped his quest to be Brazil's answer to Les Paul and caved in to his father's demand to take over as CEO of Semco, the family's hydraulic pump business in Sao Paulo. But when he showed up for work the first day, he was immediately itchy. His discomfort with the company's environment is clear as he describes his early days there: "I tried to fit in, I really did," he says. "I even went to a trendy men's store and acquired a complete corporate outfit—navy blue suit with white pinstripes, white shirt with French cuffs, black shoes. I didn't wear the suit—the suit wore me." Semler was not just hemmed in by his suit; Semco's very structure oppressed him. "It was a prison atmosphere—people were searched coming in and out of the plant; you were docked for tardiness. It all seemed rather silly," he says. "I couldn't imagine spending the next 40 or so years of my life like this" (The New Mavericks, 1993).

Semler is convinced that the freedom he had enjoyed as a teenager, both as a student and playing in a rock band for eight years, was an important influence in the radical changes implemented over the years at Semco. He was used to the freedom of doing what he wanted to do. "The transfer to a highly structured world with classic systems just didn't make sense to me," he says. "Why do people have to wear business suits, why do they have to come in at 8 a.m. in the morning instead of 8:05 a.m.? There were no good answers" ("Man Who Drives," 1993). And he rebelled. As he explains, "Thousands of rules work fine for an army or a prison system, but not for a business. And certainly not for a business that wants people to think, innovate, and act as human beings" (Semler, 1993). The maverick's ideas to reshape Semco were beginning to emerge.

With his father's rather wary endorsement, Semler was given the green light to make changes. He committed himself to removing the sources of stress at work, democratizing Semco and creating a corporate culture based on trust rather than fear. Semler's first step was to remove the most visible signs of corporate oppression: dress codes, reserved parking spaces for executives, time clocks, and the like. In the next few years, the new CEO got rid of "poppy-cock" regulations altogether, completely upending the corporate pyramid to let democracy—and workers—rule. Semler has worked hard to abolish blind, irrational authoritarianism and encourage employees to be self-governing and self-managing.

The organization has none of the usual trappings of a successful business. There are no security desks, receptionists, secretaries, or personal assistants. Everyone at Semco, even top managers, fetches guests, stands over photocopiers, sends faxes, types letters, and dials the phone. There are no executive dining rooms, and parking is strictly first-come, first-served. Unnecessary perks and privileges that feed the ego but hurt the balance sheet and distract everyone from the crucial tasks of making, selling, billing, and collecting have been stripped away.

The company seems to thrive on its freedom. The factory workers set their own production quotas and sometimes come in on their own time to meet them, without prodding from management or overtime pay. They help redesign the products they make and formulate the marketing plans. There are virtually no manuals or written procedures—the policies of the company are in a 20-page booklet with lots of cartoons. The basic rule is "Use your common sense."

Employees now work in flexible, ever changing teams. They set their own working hours and carry out their own quality control inspections. Staff may work at home, and if they want to put their feet up on the desk or shift their machinery to a different position in the factories, they are encouraged to do so. Their bosses can run the business units with extraordinary freedom, determining business strategy without interference.

Semco employees truly run their own company. A third of them actually set their own salaries, with one crucial hitch: they have to reapply for their jobs every six months. All leaders are scrutinized, undergoing evaluations by peers and subordinates once every six months. If a manager's grade is consistently low, he or she steps down. "It's a good check on performance," says Semler, "and surprisingly free from office politics." He elaborates, "Workers may like a nice guy, but if the tougher guy leads to more profits, it doesn't matter how nice the other guy is."

In addition Semco has a system where all strategic or long-range planning is done through a series of meetings in which these decision-making discussions are open to anyone who wants to attend. As one union representative has noted, "Only at Semco are workers treated like responsible people." For major decisions, such as buying another company, everyone at Semco gets a vote (and they have even vetoed Semler's ideas a few times). Even though Semler's family still owns the company, his vote carries no more weight than anyone else's. Says Joao Vendramin, who runs the durable goods division and is one of the rotating CEOs: "Ricardo will say, 'If you want to know my opinion, I can give it to you now or later. But it's just another opinion. And I watch while they sometimes elect a manager I would never want to work for. But I trust my employees. They're looking for success as strongly as I am' " (McNerney, 1995).

Semco has absolute trust in its employees and, in fact, partners with them. The company has a profit-sharing plan that is democratic. Managers and workers negotiate over the basic percentage to be distributed—about a quarter of the corporate profits—and they hold assemblies to decide how to split it.

No one earns more than four times as much as any other worker. The open books stop flagrant abuse. "I like to think it is because everyone at Semco is reasonable and honest," he says. "Maybe, but I'm sure our transparency had a lot to do with it—public salaries are a strong disincentive to be conspicuously greedy" (Semler, 1993).

For Semler, the only real source of power within an organization is information, and "the real test of an organization's approach is whether this is really shared and open. By the democratization of information, you can take out layers of management and it really encourages teamwork." Sharing power "grows responsibility and encourages people growth and trust" (Semler, 1994b).

Semler explains his commitment to workplace democracy and trust this way:

> We treat our employees as adults. We trust them. We get out of their way and let them do their jobs. We don't condone symbols of power or exclusivity such as executive cafeterias or reserved parking places. We give people an opportunity to test, question, and disagree. We let them determine their own training and their own futures. We let them come and go as they want, work at home if they wish, set their own salaries, choose their own bosses. We let them change their minds and ours, prove us wrong when we are wrong, and make us humbler. (Semler, 1993)

"It's time to really involve employees," continues Semler. "The era of using people as production tools is coming to an end. Participation is infinitely more complex to practice than conventional corporate unilateralism, just as democracy is much more cumbersome than dictatorship. But there will be few companies that can afford to ignore either of them." As Semler has often stated, "Only the respect of the led creates a leader."

Semler believes that Semco thrives chiefly by refusing to squander its greatest resource, its people. The bottom line is an important means to an end, but only a means. If a company were directed toward the profit goal alone—especially if it is short-term—it would undo some other "long-term considerations, such as quality of the product, quality of life of the people, and quality of the organization as a whole."

Still, the rewards have already been substantial.

> We've taken a company that was moribund and made it thrive, chiefly by refusing to squander our greatest resource: our people. Semco has grown sixfold despite withering recessions, staggering inflation, and chaotic national economic policy. Productivity has increased nearly sevenfold. Profits have risen fivefold. And we have had periods of up to 14 months in which not one worker has left us. We have a backlog of more than 2,000 job applications, hundreds from people who say they would take any job just to be at

Semco. As a matter of fact, our last help-wanted newspaper ad generated more than 1,400 responses in the first week. And in a poll of recent college graduates conducted by a leading Brazilian magazine, 25 percent of the men and 13 percent of the women said Semco was the company at which they most wanted to work. (Semler, 1993)

Taking an Ethical Stand

Semler notes that corruption may not have been "invented in Latin America, but is prevalent. There is a phrase often heard in Latin America, 'You can run a successful business or be ethical. Take your pick.' " However, one of what Semler describes as his idiosyncrasies is "proving that business can be conducted without blind obedience to established but anachronistic rules and traditions, including corruption." Over the past 20 years, there have been numerous circumstances when he has refused to pay bribes to inspectors. His actions have resulted in shipments being held up for ages at airports and docks, trucks being stopped at state borders for inspection, and certificates, approvals, and forms of all kinds taking forever to be issued. But as Semler says, "It is the price of doing business honestly."

Among the Semco values are the following (Semler, 1993):

Quality

It's only worth working at a place of which you can be proud. Create this pride by insuring the quality of everything you do. Don't let a product leave the company if it's not up to the highest standards. Don't write a letter or a memo that is not absolutely honest. Don't let the level of dignity drop.

Honesty

Semco and its people must strive to communicate with frankness and honesty. You must be able to believe fully in what is said to you by your co-workers. Demand this transparency when you are in doubt.

Job Security and Age

Anyone who has been with us for three years, or has reached the age of 50, has special protection and can only be dismissed after a long series of approvals. This doesn't mean Semco has no layoff policy, but it helps to increase the security of our people. Any person being laid off has a chance to try another position.

Semler prides himself on developing a new way of running an organization, one that is not socialist or pure capitalist, but "a new way, a third way, a more humane, trusting, productive, exhilarating, and in every sense, rewarding way."

Technology as Appropriate

Semler is a twenty-first century leader who recognizes the value and importance of technology in creating corporate success but also has seen how computers have often become an end rather than a means. Instead of helping to organize data, computers are "drowning us in it" (personal correspondence, March 19, 1999). Many leaders who have limited understanding of technology have thus been wrapped around the fingers of computer professionals, who have leveraged their special knowledge into a sort of priesthood.

Semler's philosophy is to make sure the technology is simple and helpful. Whoever and whatever department needs computers can buy what they need but must be sure it is efficient.

Learning and Sabbaticals

Semler believes that everyone in Semco needs to be constantly learning. Employees can take what Semler calls "hepatitis leave," a sabbatical to recharge and "do what you would do if you had hepatitis and couldn't come to work for a month or so." This sabbatical allows associates to take a few weeks or even a few months every year or two away from their usual duties to read books or articles, to learn new skills, or to redesign their jobs.

Semler gets regularly "infected" himself. Semler now spends at least a quarter of his time traveling, speaking at conferences, and exchanging experiences all over the world. His wife Sofia (whom he married in 1988) accompanies him. "There is a chunk of time we spend trying to decipher what the world is all about, which often means travelling to distant places and doing strange things. If you are in the middle of China or the North Pole, there is a little bit of something that you understand better." Semler is always reading, always trying to learn new ways of leading. He notes that he "has been almost compulsive reading management books, including ones on psychology, sociology, and anthropology."

Another way in which Semco people are forced to learn quickly is through regular job rotations (similar to what Jorma Ollila does at Nokia). People stay in jobs for a minimum of 2 years and a maximum of 5 years. This change obliges people to learn new skills, which makes life interesting for them and makes them more valuable to the organization. It also discourages empire building and gives people a much broader perspective of the company. This form of organizational learning also forces the company to prepare more than one person for a job and generates opportunities for those who might otherwise be trapped in the middle of the pyramid. A final value of job rotation is that it encourages the spread of diverse personalities, outlooks, backgrounds, and techniques, thus injecting new blood and fresh vision throughout the company.

The company also encourages contact between people in different jobs. At Semco, "we encourage everyone to mix with everyone else, regardless of job. In our offices the purchasing and engineering departments have been scrambled so that everyone sits together, near the factory. The idea is that we all can learn from one another. Nearly all of our workers have mastered several jobs, which has caused conflict with unions' need for narrow job classifications, but is critical for our company's survival" (Semler, 1993). Over a period of years, however, Semco has develop a "learning trust" with the labor unions, a trust that has been helped by a course that teaches everyone, even messengers and cleaning people, to read balance sheets and cash flow statements.

Semler attributes the company's success, despite some of the harshest economic conditions imaginable, to its ability to keep on learning, to continuously recognize and adapt to change. As he puts it, "We have learned to see the need for change and have been smart enough to seek our employees' help in making change happen" (Semler, 1993).

The Leader of the Mavericks

Richard D'Aveni, a professor of business strategy at Dartmouth's Amos Tuck School, declares that leaders who have mastered "entrepreneurial judo," mavericks "whose vision is different from everyone else's" will enable their companies to break out of the "pack of competitive parity." "This is not an age of castles, moats, and armor where people can sustain a competitive advantage for very long," says D'Aveni. "This is an age that calls for cunning, speed, and enterprise" (Fierman, 1995)."

Great mavericks don't all think alike; indeed, their ideas can be diametrically opposed at times. But they do share an ability to stun the competition with their own personal brand of can-doism. Unconventional leaders can be irritating, threatening, and disruptive for employees and competitors alike. But they're exactly what's called for at a time when all leads are only temporary. Says Mark Hochman of Rath and Strong consulting group in Lexington, Massachusetts: "Mavericks are no longer oddities; they're necessities" (Fierman, 1995). Ricardo Semler has proven to be the leader of the mavericks.

CHAPTER FIVE

Kofi Annan: Leading the United Nations into the Twenty-First Century

When Kofi Annan began his term of office as Secretary-General of the United Nations on January 1, 1997, he assumed one of the most difficult leadership positions in the world. In the words of one writer, speaking of the secretary-general position: "It is really two jobs—administering one of the most politically sensitive, not to say neurotic, bureaucracies in the world, and providing the world with moral leadership" (Shawcross, 1996). In fact one of his predecessors called this post "the most impossible job in the world."

In addition, Annan was the first black African and first international civil servant to lead the UN. He has faced a mixture of controversy, criticism, and praise since he became Secretary-General. But while debate about Annan's policies and decisions will inevitably continue to surface (as they would for any leader of the UN), few would deny his stature as an articulate, ethical, international statesman and leader.

Early Years

Annan's father was a provincial governor and a chief of the Fante tribe in Ghana, where he was born in 1938 and grew up (Keen, 1998). Annan began his studies at the University of Science and Technology at Kumasi, Ghana, where he was also a track star (Ratnesar, 1998), but completed his undergraduate work in economics at Macalester College in St. Paul, Minnesota, in 1961. He went on to graduate studies in Geneva, Switzerland, at the Institut Universitaire des Hautes Études Internationales and later received a Master of

Science degree in management as a Sloan Fellow (1971–1972) at the Massachusetts Institute of Technology (MIT).

During his long and varied career at the United Nations, Annan's postings have included Under-Secretary-General for Peace-Keeping Operations (1993–1997); Assistant Secretary-General for Program Planning, Budget, and Finance and Controller (1990–1992); Assistant Secretary-General in the Office of Human Resources Management and Security Coordinator (1987–1990); Director of Budget in the Office of Financial Services (1984–1987); and Deputy Director of Administration and Head of Personnel at the Office of the UN High Commissioner for Refugees (UNHCR) in Geneva (1980–1983). Special assignments have included Special Representative of the Secretary-General to the former Yugoslavia, and Special Envoy to NATO (November 1995–March 1996). In addition to his official duties, Annan has served as chair of both the Appointment and Promotion Board and the Senior Review Group for the UN staff.

He has contributed to the work of the Administrative, Management and Financial Board; the Secretary-General's Task Force for Peace-Keeping; and the United Nations Joint Staff Pension Fund. During a brief absence from the United Nations (1974–1976), Annan served as the Managing Director of the Ghana Tourist Development Company and served on its board as well as the Ghana Tourist Control Board. He is married to Nane Annan, an artist and former lawyer, and the niece of diplomat Raoul Wallenberg, who rescued scores of Jews from the Nazis during World War II.

The United Nations—An Organization of 185 Sovereign Nations

Created in 1945, the United Nations is an organization of 185 sovereign nations dedicated to finding solutions to international problems or disputes and to dealing with pressing concerns that face people throughout the world. Within the UN, representatives of almost all countries of the world—large and small, rich and poor, with many different political views and social systems—have a voice and vote in shaping the policies of the international community. About 80% of the work of the UN is devoted to helping developing countries build the capacity to be self-sufficient.

The UN has six main bodies: General Assembly, Security Council, Economic and Social Council, Trusteeship Council, International Court of Justice, and Secretariat. All are based at UN Headquarters in New York except the

International Court of Justice, which is located at The Hague, Netherlands. In addition, 14 specialized agencies (such as the World Health Organization and UNICEF), working in areas as diverse as health, finance, agriculture, civil aviation and telecommunications, are linked together through the Economic and Social Council. The UN employs approximately 53,300 employees worldwide, with operating expenses for the entire system—including the World Bank, IMF, and all UN funds, programs, and agencies—totaling about $18.2 billion.

Creating a New Vision and Sense of Purpose for the UN

What makes Annan a successful global leader? One of his most impressive characteristics is his ability to provide the vision and inspiration required to revive the United Nations, an organization badly in need of a new sense of purpose and accomplishment. Although perhaps most strongly criticized by the United States, numerous countries have pointed out the need for reforms at the UN. For several years complaints have included overstaffing and keeping "parasites" within the ranks, bureaucratic bloat, ongoing inefficiencies, and lack of consistent results. The resulting downsizing and job insecurity brought on by reform have left many UN employees demoralized and fearful. Under Annan's leadership, however, morale has gradually improved. One of his staff member admits, "We haven't felt this good in years." A senior official adds that the difference between Annan and his predecessors is "night and day" (Ratnesar, 1998).

While some argue that his reforms are not extensive enough, Annan has begun the difficult task of what he calls "a sweeping process of reform throughout the United Nations system, with the aim of consolidating, streamlining, and reorganizing wherever possible with three central aims in mind—efficiency, transparency and accountability." He candidly recognizes the mistakes and triumphs of the UN in the past: "The past decade has seen the United Nations pass from cold war deadlock and low expectations through a time of high ambition and great euphoria, then to crisis and disillusion and finally to what is now, I think, a mood of sober optimism." From this sober optimism he hopes to reform and rebuild the UN, to fulfill his mission of moving "into a new era of political clarity and organizational stability" (UN, 1999, April 23).

He speaks often of his somewhat lofty and idealistic vision of the UN. In an address to the General Assembly, for example, he said:

> This is the age of the United Nations. Unfettered by ideological conflict and empowered by technology and global prosperity, we can envision like never

before the realization of our noble aims. We owe it to all succeeding generations that this moment of promise becomes a new beginning for all nations and
peoples alike. There is a light at the end of our century's dark and dangerous
tunnel, and it is brightened by the hopes and dreams of all the world's peoples.
The United Nations remains the one, true and universal vessel of those dreams.
Reinvigorated, reformed and recommitted, it can carry those dreams into the
next millennium, and make them reality. (UN, 1997, July 16)

Such eloquence from other leaders or politicians might be interpreted as
empty rhetoric. But when spoken by Annan, these words take on a deeper
dimension of truth and inspiration. As Brian Urquhart, a key UN official,
explains, "He really does believe in what he is doing. He's not an egomaniac.
He's a genuine public servant. It's very refreshing" (Shawcross, 1996).

According to Annan, "The United Nations is a living testament of hope."
In more concrete terms, he explains that the role of the UN is to work "to
end violence and promote tolerance; advance development and ensure equality; protect human rights and alleviate poverty. The United Nations, at its best,
enables the achievement of those highest of human aspirations." Some of the
steps he suggests to achieve this level of service include reform, transformation
of the organization's mission, greater responsiveness to the needs of people and
Member States, improved work in development, more effective promotion of
human rights and good governance, quicker responses to crises, creation of
new partnerships, and "re-imagining its promise and remaking its role" (UN,
1997, October 24).

Can Annan lead others to share in his vision and work toward it? Although this is clearly one of the most difficult of the "daunting responsibilities"
of his job as secretary-general, his team-oriented approach and inclusiveness
build support from within the UN. Addressing the UN staff, he points out the
need for teamwork: "For we are above all a team. I do not think anyone who
achieves success in the Secretariat can rightfully claim that he or she has done
it alone. I have always believed that success is possible only when it is built on
the support and cooperation of others." As he concludes his remarks he reit-
erates the need for team commitment: "My mission, however impossible, is
your mission too. . . . There is no alternative to the United Nations. It is still
the last best hope of humanity. That is our collective challenge. Now let us get
on with the job" (UN, 1997, January 9).

Annan's sense of teamwork goes beyond the internal workings of the
United Nations. He reminds the member states that neither he nor the UN
staff alone can accomplish the mission of the UN: "The United Nations is
your instrument for peace and justice. Use it; respect it; defend it. It can be

no wiser, no more competent and no more efficient than those Member States that now comprise and guide it." He emphasizes the collective nature of his vision of the UN in the years to come: "There is no lack of blueprints for a new, post-cold war United Nations. There is no lack of ideas or debate. What we need is consensus and commitment. Our task now is to find common ground, to shape together the changes that will move this Organization forward" (UN, 1996, December 17). In his speeches, he often reminds his audiences of the Charter of the United Nations, which begins, "We, the People of the United Nations."

Although he fills one of the most visible leadership positions in the world, Annan retains a warmth and humanity that have made him a popular UN staff person for years. Instead of using the elevator reserved for the Secretary-General, he often chooses to wander through the offices, talking with employees and asking about their families. A close friend from college, describing Annan's ability to transcend his role as an international leader and identify with ordinary people around the world, notes that "he's a human being, a real person" (Ratnesar, 1998). Annan emphasizes the need to "demystify the United Nations and not make it so bureaucratic and distant from the average person." One of his goals is to bring the organization closer to everyday people, "to show that this Organization deals not in dusty abstractions, but in crucial life-and-death matters affecting the well-being of all women, men and children, every citizen of this planet" (UN, 1997 May 27). His warm smile and notorious sense of humor undoubtedly contribute to his popularity as well.

Global Big Picture

If any leader needs to have a global mindset, surely the secretary-general of the UN must. One of Annan's greatest strengths is his ability to see the international big picture, a product of his keen intellect and his international education and experience. From his youth in Ghana to his studies in the United States and Switzerland to his extensive work-related travels, Annan has had the opportunity to see the world from many perspectives.

During his more than 30 years at the United Nations, Annan has had plenty of opportunity to experience international cultures, values, and work styles firsthand. He speaks fluent English, French, and several African languages, and his resumé includes work experience in Addis Ababa, Cairo, Geneva, Ghana, and New York, among others. He has, of course, benefited from the continuous international exposure gained when working at the UN in any location (UN Department of Public Information, 1997. June 13). During his career with the United Nations, his responsibilities have involved a variety of issues, including management of various kinds (administration, budget, finance, and personnel), refugee concerns, and peace-keeping. He has led several critical diplomatic assignments, including the release of Western hostages in Iraq and repatriation of international staff following the invasion of Kuwait in 1990, initiation of "oil-for-food" talks to provide humanitarian aid to Iraq, and coordination of the transition from the UN Protection Force (UNPROFOR) in former Yugoslavia to the multinational Implementation Force (IFOR), led by NATO, following the 1995 Dayton Peace Agreement.

Education and work experience in various countries do not ensure, however, that an individual will develop the knowledge and skill necessary for cultural agility and a global mindset. Annan seems to have been able to apply his experiences to his growth as a truly global person. His speeches resound with references to international justice, peace, and economic development. While many people loosely use the terms *global* or *globalization,* Annan seems to have a deeper understanding of the meaning and consequences of global interdependence:

> Today, we live in an interdependent, global village. We face new realities. We must accept change as an essential condition of life. The challenges that face humankind today cut across all borders and they involve all aspects of human security, but human understanding has not yet grasped them. Issues before the United Nations, such as the environment, drugs, pandemics, sustainable development, are issues that carry no passports. This is the message we are trying to send to the world. Yet the public is still thinking in local terms. (UN, 1997, November 19)

Annan appeals to people of all nations to recognize that "global threats and opportunities alike require concerted action across borders and beyond traditional categories" and that conflict, economic stability, and the consequences of social injustice no longer respect national boundaries. In the face of global crises, he states, "Never has it been more important for Member States to act as united nations—not just in name, but in reality—in order to cope with such cross-border problems. The key, I believe, lies in pursuing a goal of good governance" (UN, 1997, December 3). The objective of the UN, according to Annan, is "to create an enabling environment which can foster the growth and prosperity to which all human beings aspire" and " to ensure a brighter future for all the human race" (UN, 1997, January 9).

Annan recognizes that the world has changed dramatically in the last few years. The cold war, for example, "signaled, in many ways, the end of the political universe in which the United Nations had emerged and developed." In this new world, he says,

States need united action perhaps more than ever, but not so much against armed aggression by States as against other, insidious global dangers. These new threats are global in nature. . . . They include the great environmental challenges, like global warming, and atmospheric and marine pollution; new epidemics and pandemics, like HIV/AIDS; international terrorism; and transnational drug trafficking and crime, such as money laundering. They require a global response. (UN, 1997, May 27)

Under Annan's quiet, soft-spoken demeanor lies a steely determination that earns him respect throughout the globe. He is able to work effectively with representatives from countries with widely diverse political, economic, religious, and cultural systems. Saddam Hussein of Iraq has called him "a courageous man." Boris Yeltsin of Russia was "very pleased" with his election as head of the UN and announced that he supported Annan's "energetic work to carry out organizational reform in the UN." Because of his gentle manner, some wondered if he would be "easy to push around—if not by foreign tyrants, then perhaps by the Americans who had engineered his victory." After tough negotiations with Iraq in 1998, one writer concluded, "Last week's events proved that Annan can play tough with both" (Ratnesar, 1998).

Although Annan appreciates the need to win the United States' support, he is careful to emphasize the global nature of the UN. Admitting that there have been "numerous and persistent misunderstandings" between the US and UN, he seeks constructive solutions: "The time has come to clear the air, to speak frankly between friends. An open, sincere, and constructive dialogue is always healthy" (UN, 1997, January 24).

Sense of Spirituality and Stewardship

Perhaps a major part of Annan's appeal as a leader is his deep commitment and the sense of spirituality that he exudes. Despite 30 years as a civil servant at the UN, his reputation and soul "seem still to sparkle" (Shawcross, 1996). Bill Richardson, a U.S. ambassador to the United Nations, has said of Annan, "He's an enormously skilled tactician with a great human touch. He projects a real moral force." As longtime friend and former Ghanaian Finance Minister, Kwesi Botchwey, describes him this way: "He is a very calm, composed person. But at the same time, he is very tenacious. He has a lot of spine." In American diplomat Richard Holbrooke's words, "He has an anticharismatic charisma. He has tremendous dignity and self-control." Assistant Secretary-General John

Ruggie adds, "He does not allow his ego to get in the way of what he is trying to accomplish" (Ratnesar, 1998).

Among friends and professors who knew him in college, Annan is described as "a man of precision, competence, tenacity, humor, patience, and deep moral character." His college speech and debate coach at Macalester, Roger Mosvick, notes, "There's nothing bombastic, flamboyant or selfish about this man. . . . He's in the business of politics not for himself but to serve the public. He's a public man in every respect, very soft-spoken and understated. . . . He reeks of honesty. . . . He's immediately trustworthy and carries with him a sense of credibility, and that lends a lot of authority to his demeanor"(Berg, 1998). Italy's ambassador to the UN, Francesco Paolo Fulci, comments, "This man is an immense moral force. It's a sort of inner force." One of the reasons he has been able to make progress in repairing the United Nations is because "his commitment is unquestioned." Co-workers note that "they have never seen him lose hope and have never seen him angry." In Annan's own words, "I'm a patient, persistent, and very hopeful person. We all have moments of doubt, but it is not something that weighs me down" (Keen, 1998). His wife describes him as a "doting husband" and "deeply patient man," adding that she has never heard him raise his voice. To unwind from the tensions of his work, he reportedly listens to jazz, walks in the country, smokes his daily cigar, and enjoys the company of his wife (Ratnesar, 1998).

Annan himself describes his recognition of his inner direction during his first term at MIT. In the midst of intense competition among the bright and talented students at MIT, he reflected,

> How could I possibly survive let alone thrive in this group of over-achievers? And the answer came to me most emphatically: not by playing according to their rules. Follow your own inner compass, I said to myself, listen to your own drummer. To live is to choose. But to choose well, you must know who you are and what you stand for, where you want to go and why you want to get there. My anxieties slowly dissolved. (UN, 1997, June 5)

He also brings to his position a belief in positive change. This is evident in his description of the ability of the nations of the world to bring about global change:

> The global response to these recent developments has, to an alarming degree, been one of despair and resignation. It is said that these State failures and the civil and ethnic wars that too often have followed in their wake are inevitable,

and that the difficulties occasionally faced by international interventions confirm precisely the intractability of these problems. I wish to propose a different view. And that is that these failures, these wars, these problems are political problems and economic problems with political and economic solutions. There is nothing inevitable about conflict in one part of the world, or tyranny in another. Freedom and human rights are concepts as universal as they are political, amenable to human agency of any color or creed. (UN, 1997, June 5)

Speaking of his goals to the UN General Assembly, he says,

I intend to lead an international civil service that will be honest, efficient, independent and proud of its honorable contribution to the improvement of life on this planet. Finally, I intend to stress not only our legal obligations, not only our fiscal limitations, not only our political and diplomatic considerations, but above all, the *moral dimension* [emphasis added] of our work in this Organization. (UN, 1996, December 17)

Annan also reminds us that while a market economic system has great powers, it also implies moral responsibility:

As powerful and as progressive a bond that market rationality constitutes, it is not a sufficient basis for human solidarity. It must be coupled with an ethic of caring for those whom the market disadvantages, an ethic of responsibility for the collective goods that the market underproduces, an ethic of tolerance for those whom the market pits as your adversary. (UN, 1997, June 5)

His deep convictions about global, universal spiritual beliefs are also reflected in the following discussion of the role of international public service:

We do what we do in the realm of international organization because we strive, in our own fashion, to give expression to universal truths. What might these be in so contested an arena as international affairs? I believe that they include the truths of human dignity and fundamental equality, whereby a child born in the smallest village of the poorest land is valued as much as one born on Beacon Hill. I believe they include a yearning for peace, the awareness that we are but stewards of this extraordinary only one earth, the understanding that even though the world is divided by many particularisms we are united as a human community. (UN, 1997, June 5)

When he speaks of the values of the UN, "values of peace, of freedom and of justice, of progress and development, of generosity and solidarity, and of respect for human rights," the listener senses that these are the values that he stands for in his own life, as well.

Dedication to Learning

As a world figure, Annan must constantly learn in order to keep up with the rapid changes occurring all over the globe. Described by college friends as "both humble and brilliant," he has displayed his capacity and desire to learn since youth. His fellow students at Macalester found his curiosity about American culture and life "endearing." Roger Mosvick, a speech and debate coach at the college, tells of his endless questions about culture at a traditional Thanksgiving dinner (Berg, 1998).

To accomplish his vision for the UN and for the world, Annan recognizes the key role that information, knowledge, and education must play: "information has a great democratizing power waiting to be harnessed to our global struggle for peace and development." He speaks out strongly against ignorance: "It is ignorance, not knowledge, that makes enemies of men. It is ignorance, not knowledge, that makes fighters of children. It is ignorance, not knowledge, that leads some to advocate tyranny over democracy. . . . The challenge now is to make information available to all" (UN, 1997, November 19).

Well-educated, Annan describes the learning he took away from his years at MIT as "not only the analytical tools but also the intellectual confidence to help me locate my bearings." While admitting that MIT is more likely to produce Nobel laureates in physics, chemistry, and economics, or business leaders or engineers than a United Nations Secretary-General, he skillfully ties the process of international organization to the fields of science and engineering: "Science and international organization alike are constructs of reason, engaged in a permanent struggle against the forces of unreason. Science and international organization alike are experimental; both learn by trial and error and strive to be self-correcting. Lastly, science and international organization alike speak a universal language and seek universal truths" (UN, 1997, June 5). His leadership of all nations in the "struggle against forces of unreason" exemplifies his belief in the importance of learning and information.

Annan demonstrates his dedication to education and learning through service to a variety of educational institutions. His posts have included Chairman of the Board of Trustees of the UN International School in New York (1987–1995), Governor of the International School in Geneva (1981–1983), member of the Board of Trustees of Macalester College, which in 1994 awarded him its Trustee Distinguished Service Award in honor of his service to the international community, and member of the Board of Trustees of the Institute for the Future, in Menlo Park, California.

Innovation and Systems Thinking

As the leader of the reinvention of the UN, Annan has already demonstrated his innovative and entrepreneurial spirit. He may not be able to innovate as quickly as a corporate CEO might—after all, the UN is essentially a political structure that emphasizes consensus among member states. But he has enthusiastically stepped up to the challenge: "We at the United Nations are working hard to firm up the grounds on which the project of international organization rests. And we are doing so by recognizing its experimental nature and embracing the imperative of inventiveness that this implies" (UN, 1997, June 5). The Secretariat staff alone has been cut by 25% since 1984–1985, and tougher standards have been set for staff performance.

Annan's version of reform involves much more than simply cutting staff and reducing budgets. He emphasizes that he is leading a reform at the UN, not as an end in itself, or as a way to please certain constituencies, but "as a means to better carry out our mission of peace, development and human rights" (UN, 1998, April 27). His reform initiatives reflect an understanding of the criticality of coordination, communication, and cooperation throughout the sprawling UN system. Since his appointment, communication and information flow have reached unprecedented levels. His weekly cabinet meetings, started in 1997, serve as a model for the entire UN system. Such meetings enable dynamic interaction so that common policies and initiatives are understood and can be carried out around the world with a much higher degree of coordination and shared commitment.

Starting with a clearly articulated vision and sense of purpose, Annan has begun to streamline, realign, and restructure the organization to accomplish its mission. The Secretariat's work, for example, is now organized around four core missions of the UN: peace and security, economic and social issues, development cooperation, and humanitarian affairs. This restructuring has helped clarify areas of responsibility and reduce duplication of effort. While he acknowledges the need for ongoing, continuous reform and improvement, Annan is anxious to finish his main administrative and managerial reforms, so that the UN can focus on defining its vision for the future. "We have taken the first vital step towards transformation," he points out in his annual report. "But we have a way to go before becoming a truly effective twenty-first century organization. To move forward we need to create new visions and devise new ways to achieve them" (UN Department of Public Information, 1998).

Technology Required for Global Organizations

For Kofi Annan technology is not an option; it is a way of doing business in a global organization. Each Wednesday morning all senior UN officials gather at the Secretariat for his cabinet meetings. Those who are traveling use a special phone system to join the discussions. Others located in Vienna, Geneva, Rome, and Nairobi join the group by satellite feed to a split-screen monitor. While teleconferencing and related technologies are relatively new to the UN, the real innovation is the use of that technology to allow far-flung members of the organization to participate in strategic planning and real-time decision-making. Annan's reform efforts rely heavily on the ability to share information, coordinate operations, and communicate a more unified sense of purpose—technology provides the means to do so effectively.

He recognizes the tremendous power of technology and its crucial role in today's, and tomorrow's, world. In his words,

> Issues before the United Nations, such as the environment, drugs, pandemics, sustainable development, are issues that carry no passports...this is where we need to rely on the possibilities of technology. We at the United Nations are convinced that information has a great democratizing power waiting to be harnessed to our global struggle for peace and development . . . New technology that is simpler to use at a fraction of the cost holds out the possibility of a new, truly global information order. (UN, 1997, November 19)

Calling as a Twenty-First Century Global Leader

Annan's understanding of leadership at the UN and for future roles in the twenty-first century can be summarized in his comments in a recent interview:

> Service with the United Nations is more than just a job. It is a calling. No one joins the Secretariat to become rich and famous, to be appreciated and applauded, to live a life of ease and comfort. We join the United Nations because we want to serve the world community; because we believe this planet can be a better and more secure place; and because above all, we want to devote our time, our intellect and our energies to making it so. (UN, 1997, January 9)

CHAPTER SIX

John Browne: Energizing BP Amoco toward World-Class Status

Today BP Amoco is one of the top corporations in the world, with strong positions around the world, growing output, and extensive reserves. The person widely credited with turning British Petroleum (now BP Amoco) from a "crisis-ridden behemoth into the world's most profitable oil company" is CEO Sir John Browne (Reed, 1997). And at a youthful 51 years of age, he will clearly be a top global leader for the next century.

Early Years

Browne has been associated with British Petroleum (BP) in some way for most of his life. His father worked for BP, and John followed in his footsteps, joining BP as an apprentice petroleum engineer in 1966. Browne gained his early experience primarily in exploration and production, working at facilities in Alaska and elsewhere in the United States, Canada, and the UK. In 1984 he became group treasurer and chief executive of BP Finance International, and in 1986 he moved to Standard Oil of Ohio, in which BP had a majority stake. He progressed quickly through the BP system, becoming managing director and CEO of BP Exploration in London in 1989, a managing director and member of BP's Board of Directors in 1991, and Group Chief Executive in 1995.

He is also a director of SmithKline Beecham and of Intel, and a trustee of the British Museum. Browne earned a degree in physics from Cambridge

University and a master's in business from Stanford University. He is a fellow of the Royal Academy of Engineering and the Institute of Mining and Metallurgy.

Descriptions of Browne paint a complex, multidimensional portrait of an extraordinary man. He is "soft-spoken," a collector of pre-Columbian art, and an opera enthusiast (Reed, 1997). Yet he is also a courageous innovator, willing to "break from the pack" on controversial issues such as the environment, a risk-taker, and a savvy competitor.

BP Amoco Today

BP Amoco, formed by the merger of British Petroleum and Amoco in December 1998, is the United Kingdom's largest company, the world's second largest publicly traded oil producer, after Exxon, and the world's third largest natural gas producer, behind Gazprom and Exxon. Its main focuses are exploring for, developing, and producing oil and natural gas and producing chemicals. A dynamic global organization, BP Amoco markets its chemicals in more than 60 countries and its petroleum products in more than 50 (Hoover's, 1998). While not the largest oil company, it is the most profitable. The company's debt has been cut from a 1992 peak of $16 billion to $7 billion, its output is growing at about 5% each year, and yet its exploration and development costs are among the lowest in its industry (Prokesch, 1997, p. 148).

In a 1997 survey sponsored by the *Financial Times* and Price Waterhouse to determine Europe's most respected company, BP tied with Nestlé for second place, behind ABB, and John Browne was chosen as the most respected business leader in the oil and gas sectors (Price Waterhouse, 1997).

BP Amoco is a dramatically different company today than it was a decade ago when its businesses included everything from coal and minerals to animal feed. Its main oil fields were beginning to decline and its exploration and development costs were much higher than its competitors. The business was unfocused and performance was mediocre. Over the last few years, Browne and his predecessor, David Simon, have led the efforts to simplify and streamline the organization. As a result the number of employees has decreased from 129,000 to 53,000, processes that encourage learning and the creation of value have replaced a bureaucratic system of procedures, and teams and informal networks encourage knowledge sharing. Let's look at how Browne's leadership skills have transformed BP Amoco into one of the top global companies entering the twenty-first century.

Importance of Learning at
Individual and Organizational Levels

Perhaps one of the most remarkable of Browne's leadership tenets is his solid belief in the importance of knowledge, ideas, and learning, at both the individual and organizational levels. According to him, "Learning is at the heart of a company's ability to adapt to a rapidly changing environment . . . a company has to learn better than its competitors and apply that knowledge faster and more widely than they do" (Prokesch, 1997, p. 148).

Along with his belief that the people of BP Amoco, their skills and experience, are a key competitive advantage in the industry, he also supports the development of that asset by encouraging learning. The company distinguishes itself through "a process of education which will enable all the leaders of BP both to keep up to date in their own subjects and to acquire a breadth of knowledge—in finance and public policy and in the art of coaching staff" (Browne, 1998, January 27). Browne believes that a key role of top management is "to encourage learning, and to make sure there are mechanisms for transferring the lessons" and that "leadership is about catalyzing learning as well as better performance" (Prokesch, 1997).

One of Browne's core philosophies captures this focus on learning in simple terms: "Every time we do something again, we should do it better than the last time" (Prokesch, 1997, p. 148). He cites the example of drilling, which accounts for over half of the $3.8 billion in capital expenditures on exploration and productions. If each drilling operation is more efficient than the last, the company stands to make a great deal more money. Indeed, since 1995 the average time spent to drill a deep-water well has decreased from 100 days to 42.

For Browne learning comes from many sources—experience, contractors, suppliers, customers, and other industries. But the real value of information is to leverage it "by replicating it throughout the company so that each unit is not learning in isolation and reinventing the wheel again and again" (Prokesch, 1997, p. 148). The company's virtual team network provides one of the best examples of the company's belief in and financial commitment to the sharing of information. BP Amoco has also adopted an experimental approach to the application of new, sometimes radical, ideas. Innovative concepts are first tried out on a small scale, studied and evaluated, and, if successful, applied on a wider basis.

Browne also asserts that the organizational structure—very flat and team-based—is designed to promote learning. The headquarters operation employs

350 people, down from 4,000 in 1989. Decision-making has been pushed down to the individual business units to allow learning to flow more freely. One of the reasons the company was divided up into numerous business units was to allow individuals to see the impact of their work and experience a sense of ownership not often available to those in large organizations. Since the company is organized around processes, not hierarchies, employees can see how work actually gets done and understand the role they play in accomplishing results. And by focusing on one clear process within the complex workings of the organization, individuals can develop a deep understanding of that process and more easily share information and innovative approaches for improvement. This aspect of the structure also allows people to work face-to-face and to form deep personal relationships, which are critical in a learning organization (Prokesch, 1997, p. 162).

Browne has encouraged the formation of "learning communities" in which peer groups work on problems they have in common and learn together as equals. He observes that working as peers helps avoid the politics inherent in any hierarchical structure. Peers are more open with one another, freer to communicate, share knowledge, and openly disagree (Prokesch, 1997, p. 164). Recognizing that no one person or organization can solve huge problems such as limiting gas emissions, Browne canvassed 350 leaders with the BP Group concerning their ideas and views in this area. To his surprise he received 200 pages of workable suggestions. He uses this as an example of how difficult challenges can be sources of "real creativity and positive energy" (Browne, 1998, February 2).

A difficult question for many executives is, Just how does a company develop its learning capabilities? Browne suggests that people first must believe that producing value is central to everyone's job and that competitive performance matters. As he points out, "BP is not a collection of *financial* assets. It is a combination of assets and the activities, people, and learning needed to extract maximum value from those assets" (Prokesch, 1997, p. 157). Employees must understand that they control the future of the company and that they are expected to constantly monitor and improve the competitiveness of the business. BP Amoco promotes learning by making sure that individuals and teams understand the critical performance measures of their business, constantly benchmark those measures, set increasingly higher targets, and strive to meet them.

Browne's commitment to learning is illustrated by the selection and support of a knowledge management team, led by Kent Greenes. Since 1997 the team has implemented activities that have saved the company about $700 million. Simple tools, such as peers assisting peers, "after-action reviews," a shared database of internal knowledge and experience, and enhanced virtual connections (through desktop videoconferencing, multimedia e-mail, and a real-time shared whiteboard, for example) provide an atmosphere conducive to organizational learning (Stewart, 1999).

Perhaps most important of all, Browne believes that the top management of a company must demonstrate their own involvement in sustaining a learning organization. As he explains, "You can't say 'Go do it' without participating . . . Learning is my job, too" (Prokesch, 1997, p. 168). And he admits, "I still have a lot to learn" (Browne, 1998, February 27). Known for his intellectual curiosity, Browne often becomes an expert in whatever interests him. His research into financial markets and investment banking, for example, led Ron Freeman, European co-chief of Salomon Smith Barney, to remark: "Calling on John was like taking an oral exam before a very tough professor" (Guyon, 1999).

Global Mindset

Browne acknowledges that we are rapidly moving into a new era of globalization—global trade, investments, competition, and so on. He calls the liberalization of markets and international economic relationships the "single dominant characteristic of the 1990s." As a result corporate responsibilities have changed as well. In his words, "Companies are considered to be actors on the international stage in their own right, if not directors of the play" (Browne, 1997, November 13).

As the leader of a company with operations throughout the world and a frequent traveler, he has had firsthand experience with both the positive and negative effects of this trend. While globalization holds tremendous potential for growth and new opportunities, it also brings with it a concern for the impact on individuals. According to Jeffrey Garten (1998, p. 26), one of the key challenges for the leaders of global organizations is "finding a balance between the relentless pressure for short-term profits and broader social responsibilities." He cites John Browne as an example of a leader with "a clear philosophy and strategy" to accomplish that task.

Part of the success of any global organization must be a commitment to understand diverse customers and their needs. Browne remarks, "I think there's a great prize for companies which can make themselves distinctive by understanding and responding to the changing global market place" (Browne, 1998, February 27).

It is difficult to discuss globalization without referring to advances in information technology that are requisite to doing business worldwide. Concerning advances in communications technology that allow people working in an oil field in the North Sea to share experiences with others working in the Gulf of Mexico, he notes, "It is that sort of ability to transfer learning from one part of the company to another which makes a global business into something more than the sum of its parts" (Browne, 1997, October 28).

Difficulty of Innovation in a Giant Corporation

Operating innovatively within a large organization sometimes seems to be an impossible task. However, Browne encourages individuals and teams within the organization to be creative and to take risks. He has attempted to build a culture that encourages and inspires entrepreneurship. He speaks, for example, of the fundamental changes in the world and the opportunity that provides for creating "a radically new future." As one interviewer observes, "Browne is the kind of person who never accepts that something can't be done and who is always asking if there is a better way or if someone might have a better idea. Under his leadership, BP is becoming the same kind of company" (Prokesch, 1997, p. 148).

Browne's comments on breakthrough thinking provide clues to his own entrepreneurial nature. For example, he disputes the conventional belief that break-through thinking is more of an art than a science: "I think you *can* install processes that generate breakthrough thinking. We have" (Prokesch, 1997, p. 150).

He encourages BP Amoco's employees to constantly question the accepted methods and boundaries of projects to look for new approaches. The development of the Andrew oil and gas field in the North Sea provides an example of successful breakthrough thinking. Briefly, the company believed for years that the Andrew field could not be developed profitably. Browne took on this challenge and assembled a team of diverse people from inside and outside the local business group to try to solve this seemingly unsolvable problem. The team set an unattainable target and then did whatever necessary to meet it. They formed alliances with contractors, drilled horizontal rather than vertical wells, developed new purchasing strategies. As one participant described the project, "Every day, we challenged every assumption. We analyzed anything that might reduce costs and speed up the development time. And we made breakthroughs practically every day" (Prokesch, 1997, p. 157).

The project was a success, prompting Browne to call it a major watershed for BP Amoco. It set a whole new standard for innovation and teamwork within the company.

His explanation for the company's recent success also focuses on people: "The most important thing I have done is to play a part in building a team for today and for the future. We set strong goals and within that our people innovate to get the right answer" (Fagan, 1998). Browne has also been a leader in emphasizing the critical importance of learning and the education of its employees.

One of Browne's talents is to choose the right people and "galvanize them into action," according to Bruce Evers, an analyst at Henderson Crosthwaite (Fagan, 1998). BP Amoco does not attempt to mold everyone into a rigid corporate style, however. As he puts it, "We employ something over 50,000 people and we can't expect them to forget or alter their views when they come through the door every morning. And we don't want them to—because their individuality is what gives them the ability to produce ideas and to make a unique contribution" (Browne, 1997, October 28).

Ethics and Trust are Essential for Good Business

Beyond technology, markets, management processes, and other more technical aspects of succeeding in the petroleum industry, Browne promotes the need for more ethical and socially responsible actions on the part of business. He emphasizes that "in our pursuit of exceptional performance and sustained growth, there are certain . . . values we will not violate. The values concern ethics; health, safety, and the environment; the way we treat employees; and external relations" (Prokesch, 1997, p. 150). One area he has emphasized in particular is trust in the industry and its fair dealings with people and the environment.

He points out that genuine trust is needed for the industry to survive: "Trust in how we deal with people and with the environment. Trust that comes from a track record and from transparency, a willingness to be open and to share information rather than hide it away." His actions reflect his beliefs, as demonstrated by a controversial joint conference with Greenpeace. His explanation of such efforts is that survival requires trust-building by oil companies. While both sides will undoubtedly continue to experience conflict, Browne points out that the company must be open and explain what it's doing and why and must also listen to other viewpoints. In his words, "that is the way we have to work if we're going to retain trust and to keep public confidence" (Energy Intelligence Group, 1997).

He also talks extensively about the standards of ethics and business conduct, or the "standard of care." Within the "standard of care," he includes "the standard of care for the natural environment; the way companies work with the communities in which they operate, and the way companies deal with their employees and their families" (Browne, 1998, January 27).

Unlike some corporate heads, Browne sees taking an active role in improving the social climate of the localities in which BP Amoco operates as not only the right thing to do but as an essential ingredient in the primary goal of any corporation—making a profit. And making an impact on the community is not just a platitude from the corporate office; efforts to contribute to the community are reviewed and factored into performance measurements and compensation.

BP Amoco's results so far bear out the fact that profits need not be sacrificed for social responsibility. In fact Garten concludes that other companies would do well to consider Browne's global strategies: "Think long-term, invest heavily in the communities that you do business in, be obsessive about achieving profits, and fully integrate social responsibility into your policies on governance and compensation" (Garten, 1998, p. 26). In Browne's words, "However big we get, we are nonetheless made up of tiny parts. And the tiny parts matter," a comment reminiscent of the popular expression, "Think globally, act locally" (Fisher, 1997).

Protecting the Environment

What is John Browne's corporate stance concerning the natural environment? In the words of one *BusinessWeek* report, he has taken a "maverick position in his industry" by publicly stating that global warming is a real threat and by openly supporting alternative energy sources such as solar power (Reed, 1997, May 5). In fact, he believes that by improving the company's environmental performance, financial returns will actually improve (Arnst, 1997). As he points out, "people want to use energy without damaging our common environment and our job is to use our skills and technology to give the best possible choices." (Browne, 1998, February 2). Quite simply, BP Amoco's environmental goal is "not just to clean up damage but to create no damage at all in the first place" (Fisher, 1997).

In Alaska, for example, corporate scientists spent several months research-ing the effects on the atmosphere of compounds escaping from tankers during loading and unloading. The company proceeded to install protective equip-ment against leaks there and at a large facility in Scotland. While there was some pressure from regulatory agencies in the United States to take this action, the safeguards in Scotland were totally voluntary. Browne explains, "It's our way of saying to people, 'We're here to stay' " (Fisher, 1997). This concern for environmental issues has led one writer to comment, "On balance, BP is probably the environmentalists' preferred oil company, while Mr. Browne is definitely their favorite oil boss" (Lean, 1997).

Brown's maverick stance was also clear when he pledged in September 1998 to reduce the company's greenhouse gas emissions by 10% below 1990 levels, a goal that far exceeds those set during a summit of industrial nations in 1997 in Kyoto, Japan. And he plans to meet those goals without jeopardizing growth or profits. Browne expects each of its business units to reduce emis-sions, using strategies to improve energy efficiency, using new technology, and trading emissions. The company has already used technology that enhances oil flow on the Trans-Alaska Pipeline, resulting in the elimination of several pumping stations and 236,000 tons per year of carbon dioxide emissions. While admit-ting that these ambitious emission reduction goals alone will not solve all of the emission problems, Browne explains, "I hope we can show—in a small way—what can be done. And I hope we can help the process forward" (Hamilton, 1998).

Through scientific and technological advances, BP Amoco has been able to minimize the impact of its operations on the environment. For example, long-distance horizontal drilling has allowed the company to locate drilling sites where they cause the least disruption. The company has also minimized flaring, or burning of waste gas. While this attention to the environment might seem financially risky, the numbers tend to indicate otherwise. Over the last five years, the company's return to shareholders has exceeded 330%, nearly three times that of the healthy S&P 500 (Fisher, 1997).

Browne's comments on global climate change have been especially surpris-ing, coming from a major oil company executive. He admits that when he first spoke up about these issues, his actions were viewed as "breaking ranks with our colleagues in the oil industry, leaving the church as one particular commentator suggested." When BP resigned from the Global Climate Coalition, an energy-industry group opposed to efforts to control global warming, his stance shocked others in the industry. However, he has noted subsequent joint projects with other organizations and partners to develop practical solutions that will not hinder economic development. In his eyes, environmental commitment is not a public relations scheme or an idealistic dream; "It is our day-to-day business reality" (Browne, 1998, February 6).

Firmly grounded in this reality, he understands the difficulty some countries have in taking on problems such as global climate change when they do not even have clean drinking water. As a result he has championed measures that recognize these more immediate concerns (Browne, 1997, September 30). He strongly believes that organizations must meet problems not with "glossy public relations or expensive advertising campaigns. But with a willingness to engage in dialogue, and to contribute to the development of solutions" (Browne, 1998, February 2). Good environmental practices are also good business: "In each case it is worth noting that the environmental answer—the clean solution if you like—is also the best commercial solution. It is not a trade off" (Browne, 1997, October 28).

An unexpected supporter of alternative energy, BP Amoco has invested millions of dollars in solar energy development and is sponsoring a solar-powered Olympic village for the 2000 games in Australia. On January 30, 1998, he and U.S. Vice President Al Gore opened the first solar manufacturing facility in the United States, enabling California to take the lead as the world's top producer of solar technology. When operating at full capacity, the BP Solar Fairfield (California) plant will produce 10-15 megawatts annually, enough to power 3,000 new homes per year (British Petroleum, 1998). In his remarks, Browne affirmed that "BP is in the business of providing the energy consumers of the world the greatest amount of choice, and this is just one more step toward that goal." In a speech at Stanford University, he announced a goal for the company of $1 billion in sales of solar energy cells by 2007, a tenfold increase (Kemezis, 1997). Since its establishment 17 years ago, BP Solar has become one of the most successful solar energy companies in the world (British Petroleum, 1998).

Societal and Community Concerns

Browne's interest in environmental issues is just one aspect of his overarching belief in corporate social responsibility, globally and locally. He defines his view of social responsibility as more than "giving a few charitable donations or sponsoring the opera." In fact social responsibility is linked to power: "We can't deny reality. We do have power, and we have to use any power we have in ways which are responsive to the society in which we operate. We have to merge our interests with the interests of the wider community . . . In an open society all power implies trust and companies have to earn that trust" (Browne, 1998, February 27).

He has also spoken out on the issue of universal human rights, stating, for example, that "we will only have true development and full human rights when individuals have freedom from poverty and the freedom to develop their skills, as well as the freedom to express their views." This definition serves as a framework for action and the use of influence in the world on the part of BP Amoco. Browne makes clear that wherever it operates, the company attempts to contribute to civil society through its ethical standards, its actions to benefit the local community, and the infusion of positive energy into the community (Browne, 1997, November 13).

BP Amoco's work with NGOs (nongovernmental organizations) is one example of its social stance. As Browne points out, "Companies have an interest in development, in a clean environment and in the creation of an open society. Those are the conditions in which we can best pursue our business. We have no interest in repression, or pollution or poverty" (Browne 1998, February 2). Its community investments are substantial. The company assists many different groups around the world—Save the Children and other relief groups, church groups, environmental groups. Examples abound: providing computer-based technology to control flooding in Vietnam, financing replanting of forests destroyed by fire in Turkey, supplying solar-powered refrigerators to doctors in Zambia for storage of anti-malarial vaccines, supporting development of small business in Soweto (Garten, 1998, p. 26).

He describes a project in Colombia in which waste rock cutting from drilling operations has been made into bricks for the construction of homes and buildings in the area. This creative use of waste rock costs no more than disposal and in fact has been so successful that it has become a side business. In his candid style, Browne notes, "Those are not acts of charity but of what could be called enlightened self-interest. They represent good business" (Browne, 1998, February 2). Perhaps. But it has taken a leader like Browne to recognize this reality and begin taking actions that exemplify his beliefs.

Technology Critical to BP Amoco

Clearly, technology plays an important role in a large company such as BP Amoco—information and communications technology, drilling technology, seismic technology, alternative energy technologies—and the list goes on. While many people envision drilling for oil as a business of "dirt and drama . . . all about roughnecks and blowouts," automated equipment, remote sensing and advanced control systems have completely changed the nature of the business.

Much of the change in today's business world has been driven by scientific and technical advances, and "much of the gain [in performance] has come from great advances in technical productivity." Concerning the future of technology, Browne recommends that companies take a proactive stance: "Our success in building our relationships with the scientific community determines the extent to which we can control our own destiny, rather than being merely reactive, passive players." A corporate technical advisory board helps the organization keep in touch with new research both in the UK and internationally and has developed links with key institutions in the scientific arena. In his words, "Science and technology are central to strategy and performance" (Browne 1997, October 28).

An example of Browne's vision for the use of technology is the company's "virtual team network." The purpose of this computer network is "to allow people to work cooperatively and share knowledge quickly and easily regardless of time, distance, and organizational boundaries" (Prokesch, 1997). The network is made up of sophisticated personal computers with video-conferencing capabilities, scanners, faxes, groupware, and other features that allow users to hold virtual meetings and tap into an extensive central database of information.

Employees are encouraged to post their own home pages on an intranet to share technical expertise and experience, exchange ideas, and share projects and performance plans. As Kent Greenes, the BP Amoco virtual teamwork project director explains, "If it's easy for people to connect, communicate and share knowledge, they will do it. If it isn't, they won't" (Prokesch, 1997, p. 152). The network links teams throughout the world, connecting refineries and plants from Indonesia to Scotland. According to company sources, the virtual network produced at least $30 million in value during the first year, as well as less tangible benefits, such as the ability to look into the eyes of another person during a videoconference when he or she commits to something. Its benefits also include a decrease in helicopter trips to off-shore platforms, a drop in person-hours need to resolve problems, remote troubleshooting to avoid refinery shutdowns, reductions in rework, and many others.

What makes this technological advance even more significant is its focus on users, a rarity in many organizations. About a third of the cost of initial pilot program was spent on behavioral scientists, to help individuals learn to work together in a virtual environment, sharing information and building cooperative relationships. Browne's strategy was not to force the network on employees, but rather to demonstrate its benefits so that people would want to join in, a highly successful strategy (Prokesch, 1997, p. 153). Browne himself has two virtual team workstations, one at home and one at work. For a leader who believes in personal relationships and the need for dialogue and frequent communications, technology of this type is essential.

Contemplating advances in science and technology, he admits, "I still find the extent and pace of the change a source of wonder. Not least because it makes me wonder—what's next?" (Browne, 1997, October 28). To continue to find a sense of wonder in the world is a refreshing attribute in a corporate leader.

Importance of a Corporate Vision for Long-Term Success

Browne's commitments to the environment, social and community responsibility, and to employees and customers suggest some of the main factors in his vision and sources of his ability to inspire others. In fact, his vision was an important factor in his selection for EIG's Petroleum Executive of the Year Award in 1997. His unanimous selection for this award by chief executives and other senior managers from 100 of the world's largest oil and gas firms reflects the high regard in which his peers hold him. Examples of his visionary leadership as recognized by his peers include his pioneer alliance in Europe of BP with Mobil Oil Corporation, his innovative financial and technological approaches, and successful risk management in newly opened areas such as Algeria and the Caspian Sea (Energy Intelligence Group, 1997).

Despite the fact that BP Amoco is currently a highly respected company, such perceptions are often short-lived. For BP Amoco to continue to earn respect, he foresees the need for a number of corporate traits, one of which is "a sense of the long-term." By that he means that the company must recognize that business is cyclical and position itself to "thrive even in hard times." He clarifies that while he is certainly in favor of short-term profits, he believes that the planning process should never get "carried away by short-term trends or by over-enthusiasm which comes with short-term success" (Browne, 1998, January 27).

Systems Thinker

Another attribute of Browne is his ability to be a systems thinker and his "willingness to think radically." Success is constantly eroding, according to Browne, and a company must "have a culture which not only embraces change but which goes out and looks for it." BP Amoco must constantly question its technical assumptions, look for new opportunities, and constantly adjust to a drastically changing market, created by events such as the upheavals in Russia, the gradual unification of Europe, and the deregulation and privatization of gas and electric utilities. He cites the possibility of eventually building a gas pipeline, perhaps 4,000 km long, from Siberia to China, where the energy is badly needed. Such projects mean that "we have to work in circumstances which are beyond prediction," implying the need for radical thinking (Browne, 1998, January 27).

According to Browne, the role of the top management is to "stimulate the organization, not control it" (Prokesch, 1997, p. 158). He believes that the role of a leader at any level is to demonstrate to individuals that they are capable of achieving much more than they may think and encourage them to constantly grow and improve. The role of the leader is not to enforce the existing procedures but to challenge people's creativity.

Leading BP Amoco into the Twenty-First Century

One of the most important characteristics of successful companies and people, exemplified by Browne, is a sense of positive energy even in the face of challenges that can seem daunting. We should look for a constructive way to move forward, based on a determination to treat problems as challenges that we can resolve. "Optimism is the guiding star of business," according to Browne. "Without optimism you never would take the risks which go with investment. But it isn't naïve optimism. It has to be optimism based on the magical combination of the ability to conceive of new possibilities and the simultaneous ability to deliver the practical reality" (Browne, 1997, September 30).

His positive outlook on life and his determination to take what may look like a constraint and convert into an opportunity are exactly the type of leadership needed by BP Amoco as it faces the monumental challenges of the twenty-first century.

CHAPTER SEVEN

Carol Bartz: Taking AutoDesk to the Top

Perhaps less well-known than some of her high-tech counterparts, Carol Bartz, chairman, CEO, and president of AutoDesk, has earned a reputation as a twenty-first century leader. According to *Forbes* magazine, Carol is "one of high tech's most important players of either gender and is its most powerful woman" (Leadership, 1996). Beyond her renowned ability to lead corporations to financial success, Bartz embodies other aspects of leadership that organizations will need to survive in the future.

Bartz graduated from the University of Wisconsin with honors in computer science. She also holds honorary doctoral degrees from the Worcester Polytechnic Institute and William Woods University. She started her career in product line and sales management positions at Digital Equipment Corp. and 3M. In 1983 she joined Sun Microsystems, moving up quickly to vice president of marketing, president of Sun Federal, vice president of customer service, and finally vice president of world wide field operations. In 1992 she left Sun to become chairman of the board, CEO, and president of AutoDesk, Inc.

Bartz serves on the boards of Cisco Systems, Inc., AirTouch Communications, Cadence Design Systems, Network Appliances, California Chamber of Commerce and the Foundation for the National Medals of Science and Technology. She is also a member of President Clinton's Export Council, the California Business Roundtable, and the Business School Advisory Council of Stanford University. She is an active member of the International Women's Forum, the Committee of 200, and other groups and is an advocate for women's health and education issues.

AutoDesk—World's Leading Supplier of PC Design Software and Multimedia Tools

To the average person, the company name AutoDesk may not ring a bell—unless that person happens to be an architect, engineer, geographic or mapping specialist, or 3-D computer animation professional. AutoDesk is the world's leading supplier of PC design software and multimedia tools, including well-known products such as AutoCad and 3D Studio. The fourth largest PC software company in the world, AutoDesk has 3.5 million customers in over 150 countries, and in 1998 the company shipped its 1 millionth copy of AutoCad. The company counts 90% of the Fortune 100 firms among its clients. Headquartered in San Rafael, California, it employs over 2,500 people worldwide.

Systems Thinker

Bartz has a history of improving corporate financial performance. Before joining AutoDesk, as president of worldwide field operations and executive officer at Sun Microsystems, she oversaw an increase in revenues from $2.6 billion to $3.6 billion. And prior to that accomplishment, she led a dramatic increase in revenues at Sun Federal—from $21 million to $124 million in two years. Bartz joined AutoDesk in 1992, and in just seven years the company's revenue grew from $285 million to over $700 million. In 1995 alone she pushed net income up 40% to $1.40 per share.

When Bartz arrived at AutoDesk, it was a 10-year-old company without "the discipline required of a swiftly growing public corporation" (Computer Captain, 1997). By one account, decisions were made erratically by an "inner circle of leaders, and designers [who] were more concerned with entering new product areas than with profitability or organizational fit." Drawing on her 25 years of business experience, she took bold, decisive steps to lead the company in a new direction. She abandoned products, such as network and workgroup software, that did not complement AutoDesk's focus, while looking for new ways to leverage its existing, strong customer base. At the same time, she led the diversification of the company into new but related operations, such as its 3-D Studio software, used to design 70% of all computer games. She also helped the company redefine its market more broadly to incorporate mechanical design and geographic information systems customers, previously untapped by the company. In her words, "people in different jobs use the same tool differently. I had to convince our people that they needed to see our technology as a geometric platform that can be expanded" (Verespej, 1996).

To align the organizational structure with these changes in market and products, she reorganized AutoDesk into five market groups: architectural, engineering, construction, and facilities management; data management; geographic information systems; mechanical computer-aided design; and multimedia. She also consolidated several product development sections into one group to produce a more holistic focus on developing new markets and technologies. Under her leadership, the company has adopted a more effective fiscal management strategy, reflected in its growing revenues. As she explains, "We truly understand our balance sheet and revenue expectations, and we work hard to keep the company managed that way, rather than just chasing growth for growth's sake" (Verespej, 1996). Today AutoDesk is a professionally run, globally competitive company.

Bartz's Vision for AutoDesk

Part of AutoDesk's success stems from Bartz's ability to articulate a broader vision and provide the leadership to pursue it. How does she see the future of AutoDesk? "I want AutoDesk to be the design center of the universe—in both multimedia and traditional design . . . AutoDesk has the potential to transform how business is conducted around the world. We can usher in a new age of personal creativity and expression where people are limited only by their imaginations. It is an environment that will deliver a wealth of alternatives to business and consumers" (Bartz, 1997c).

Bartz has inspired AutoDesk's employees to move toward her vision for the company. She has encouraged them to realize that the company "is not a one-product—design-automation software—company, but rather one with a core-technology software that can move into countless markets." This more diversified vision of AutoDesk's products and markets is becoming reality. When Bartz first came to the company, AutoCad design software accounted for 90% of sales; three years later, 25% of sales came from new products and markets, and the trend continues.

Bartz envisions 3-D technology software as a key to AutoDesk's future growth and success. As she explains, "We will leave behind the flat world of lines, dots, and circles for 3-D visual development that will relay information in a way never before imagined. . . . We will be able to think better in 3-D because that's the world we live in." Not surprisingly, Bartz is committed to making AutoDesk the leader of the 3-D software market. Her vision of AutoDesk's role is clear: "We will create products that are a lot more intuitive, easier to use, and less expensive. We will put simplicity behind all the complexity that exists in 3-D technology to bring it effectively to all of us. We will be the leader in both product mix and volume" (Verespej, 1996). Her enthusiasm about the future of AutoDesk and her commitment to it are evident: "It's going to be so exciting that I want to savor every minute of it. We have great products; I think we have a great strategy from a technology and a marketing standpoint. We absolutely believe in our concept of being the design software company. Like Cisco being the networking company, Netscape being the Internet company, and Microsoft being the information company, AutoDesk is the design company" (Computer Captain, 1997).

Creating an Environment that Fosters Innovation

Along with a broader vision of AutoDesk's possible markets and products, Bartz has also created a more customer-focused, entrepreneurial work environment. As a result of restructuring, each product group is able to build partnerships with its specific customers, market in a way that makes sense for its own products, make its own decisions, and develop solutions to serve customers. In contrast to earlier practices of the organization, under Bartz AutoDesk holds an incredible amount of meetings with customers and partners to understand what they need and stay ahead of their needs.

Bartz also believes in the importance of shared decision-making and the need for an environment that fosters creativity. As she puts it, "The farther we can push responsibility down, the better we will be as a company. One of the things you learn as a CEO is to not have you or your executive staff make all the decisions. You have to have people feel involved in the company" (Verespej, 1996). She acknowledges that she must set the example by not micromanaging her staff, and that they, in turn, must not micromanage their employees.

Employee involvement is encouraged by a week-long leadership training program that emphasizes shared responsibility: "When you share responsibility with teams, it really gets people thinking about ownership." She admits that she can't possibly have all the answers, but wants to "provide an environment where smart people can find answers" (Verespej, 1996). She and her staff also try to make themselves accessible to employees, through efforts such as brown-bag lunches in which employees can discuss issues with executives, quarterly companywide meetings, and e-mail access. Another key to Bartz's success is her emphasis on hiring creative, intelligent, competent employees. As she puts it, "Casting accounts for 80% to 90% of a play's success" (Leadership Experts, 1996).

An Early Leader in Technology

Carol has worked in computer-related positions throughout her career. In her words, "I programmed my first computer in 1967 and for 30 years, I have never been more than an arm's length away from a computer." She explains that she chose to work at AutoDesk because, although it had "grown way ahead of itself," it had good technology and a good market position. She had also grown tired of the "'mine-is-faster-than-yours' side of the hardware business" (Computer Captain, 1997).

A key player in the development and marketing of innovative software, she understands both the critical role technology will play in the future and the current misunderstanding and misuse of technology. Concerning the misapplication of technology, she explains, "The thing that disappoints me the most about technology is that we've used it in the wrong ways. Technology may give you an extra 45 minutes, but we're not giving that back to our families. Instead we're doing 45 more minutes in meetings. We're way, way, way information overloaded" (Bartz, 1997b).

On a positive note, Carol points out that one of the greatest contributions of technology to education has been the enrichment of content. For example, when her daughter learned about caterpillars becoming butterflies by watching a CD, she was able to actually "see the butterfly exploding from the cocoon." What was once a "flatter, deader concept" conveyed through a series of pictures became a very powerful learning experience (Wolfson and Talitenu, 1997).

However, the overwhelming amount of information provided through computer technology and our inability to handle all of it are also serious concerns, ones that cannot be solved through "the simple search engine concept." In her words, "we're being abused by technology rather than using it" (Bartz, 1997b). However, she also believes that we will reach a happy medium, that technology "will allow us to have more legitimate free time because we can do things easier." The AutoDesk vision, "To create software tools that transform ideas into reality," reflects this interest in the productive and creative use of technology (AutoDesk, 1998b).

She seems to take special pride in the fact that at AutoDesk, "We're helping people do their work better, and we're helping to make it more fun" (Bartz, 1997b). As a concrete example, she describes how AutoDesk products allow an architect to focus on the creative process of designing a building, freeing him or her from much of the more mundane, boring work. Technology has also simplified and encouraged collaboration on major projects. For example, when building an office building, a Web site can be posted where everyone—the architect, structural engineer, electrician, and heating and cooling technician—can find information about the status of the project and up-to-date revisions of the plans.

Bartz's leadership in technology stems, in part, from this ability to realistically assess the effects of technology, positive and negative, and to provide a vision of the exciting possibilities for future technology applications.

Serving Employees and the Community

In Carol Bartz's world, leadership also entails community responsibility and considerate treatment of employees, and these two concerns are linked: "I think part of attracting great employees is that you have not only an exciting place to work because you have exciting technology, exciting markets, exciting industry, . . . but also that you're part of a community and that you would be proud to work here. And we want our employees, wherever they are in the world, to say, 'I work for AutoDesk and I'm really proud of that' " (Wylie, 1997).

Bartz connects corporate social responsibility and success: "we aren't just a commercial-oriented company. . . . to be successful we also have to be a successful part of whatever community we're in" (Wylie, 1997). In fact she believes that companies have "an enormous responsibility" to be active in the community. While billions of dollars have been made by companies and individuals in Silicon Valley, social responsibility has not always been a top priority. In her view too many people feel that "it's somebody else's responsibility to make a difference," a rationalization that she personally rejects. In her words, "we are all affected by society around us and we need to have a great living and a great work environment. And we have to help with that" (Wolfsen and Talitenu, 1997). Bartz herself has devoted considerable time, money, and energy as an outspoken advocate for women's health issues, a participant in the National Employer Leadership Council, a member of the Committee of 200 and the International Women's Forum, and a champion of the need to support and improve education, particularly in the areas of math, science, and technology.

Bartz also expresses sensitivity toward the company's customers. As she points out, "We spend a lot of time thinking about what our customers need." She spends time with customers—architects, engineers, designers of video games, map makers, and others—to see how products are used and what customers do and do not like. Her talent for dealing with people is reflected in her comment that "the most important part of meeting customers is the ability to listen" (AutoDesk, 1998c).

While technology may be the company's focus, she clearly considers the human factor as equally important. She admits that she doesn't use technology as much as we might think: "I don't sit with my head inside a monitor. . . . I've got to see people. . . . I think one of my big strengths is I'm a great reader of people. Technology doesn't allow me to do that" (Bartz, 1998c). The warm atmosphere at AutoDesk reflects her concern for people. Dress is casual, and in some locations employees can bring their pets to work or telecommute from home part of the time. Voted one of the 100 best companies for working mothers in 1998 (*Working Mother* magazine), AutoDesk provides a family-friendly environment with programs such as flex-time, six-week sabbaticals after four years of full-time employment, adoption assistance, dry cleaning services, and more. Individuality is both "honored and protected," and the company supports "direct, clear and ethical communications and actions, and speaking with honesty, courage and care. Teamwork is encouraged, as are flexibility and responsible risk-taking" (AutoDesk, 1998a). When asked how she was able to move AutoDesk forward so successfully, she responds, "Well, I would like to think I didn't do it. My employees have done a fabulous job" (CNBC, 1997). Under Bartz's leadership, an open, employee-friendly, socially conscious working environment has blossomed.

On a more personal level, she retains her own sense of priorities and values. She has openly criticized the popular notion of women keeping their lives in balance, a concept that suggests perfection and an ability to be able to do everything well all the time. "There are times when I am 80 percent dedicated to what's happening at AutoDesk," she explains, "and there are times when I have to be 80 percent dedicated to what's happening with my daughter." Her commitment to her family emerges often; speaking of certain events at her daughter's school, she admits: "I don't care if the largest customer and the Pope came to visit AutoDesk; I'd be with my daughter." When asked about the most fun she has ever had, her response relates to her family: "I think the most fun I've ever had is raising my daughter." She admits, "I love being a mom," a comment that of itself reflects a great deal of courage for a woman in a male-dominated business world (Wylie, 1997).

Her love of her family derives from her childhood in a "nice, small Wisconsin farming community." Her grandmother was, and continues to be, an enormous influence on her. Carol speaks warmly of this woman, in her mid-90s, who still works out on a treadmill and has always been courageous, determined, hard-working, and fair.

When asked about some of her most fundamental rules for success, she suggests three main beliefs: Do your best, be a logical person, and understand the consequences of your actions. She expresses her contentment in her current position: "I'm having fun and learning, surrounded by good people and making a difference" (Wylie, 1997). Her values once more come to the surface as she points out that she loves the people at AutoDesk, and "the market is exciting because it's meaningful—we help people create things." Her vision of success is "having whatever I'm doing at the time work for me and for the people around me." She believes that success is a series of small steps, and that if she focuses entirely on final outcomes, she will miss the opportunity to enjoy the process.

Need for More Women in Corporate Leadership

To meet the challenges of a fast-paced, ever-changing environment, leaders today and tomorrow need generous reserves of old-fashioned courage. While Bartz does not speak of herself as courageous, the evidence is clear. She has always dealt with a certain amount of isolation and lack of acceptance in a male-dominated field. She admits that as a student, she always loved math and was "a real nerd." She was one of only two women studying computer science in college. When she took over as CEO of AutoDesk, only one other female served as a CEO of a sizable tech company in Silicon Valley. How does she view the lack of highly placed women in this area? "It's pathetic. It paints a horrible picture of Silicon Valley." Others have made similar observations. Anita Borg, a senior researcher at Digital Equipment describes the indirect gender discrimination in the industry as "invisible-woman syndrome," in which women's ideas are "discounted or ignored." According to Borg, "You run into subtle sexism every day. It's like water torture. It wears you down" (Hamm, 1997).

Although Bartz feels comfortable with other high-tech executives, she notes that in groups of executives from other industries, they assume she must be somebody's wife. If 100 executives are in a room for a meeting, "it is still assumed that I am there for some other reason. They assume that there must be 99 executives and that person in a skirt." At a meeting she attended in Washington, DC, with Bill Gates, Andy Grove, and other high-tech executives and various senators, she recounts, "a senator turned to me and asked, 'So how are we going to start the meeting?' He thought I must be the moderator." While admitting that such incidents are annoying, her goal is not to change such individuals but rather "to try to change the environment so that my daughter has a place" (Bartz, 1997a). To survive and succeed in the high-tech world of Silicon Valley requires a great deal of stamina and tenacity, particularly for a female CEO.

She takes on a somewhat conciliatory tone, however, in suggesting that many situations would work better if we could find a middle ground between feminism and chauvinism. "If we allowed that, as women, there are wonderful things that we do well and wonderful things that males do well. . . . We could do the same things and not have to take these extreme positions" (Wolfman and Talitenu, 1997).

Bartz does acknowledge the importance for courage from within to turn ideas into reality. "I think you need the courage to bring your ideas to the surface. I think you need the courage to see many of your ideas fail. . . . A lot of your ideas aren't going to make it" (Wolfson and Talitenu, 1997). That internal courage also sustained Bartz through a battle with breast cancer, and the accompanying publicity and attention from reporters, shortly after she took the CEO position at AutoDesk

Supporting Learning

Since only 2% of technology company chief executives are women, Carol has automatically assumed a position as mentor to women in technology. She has often been mentioned by other women as a role model, and even if she wanted to, Carol "can't shake her position as a role model, leader and all around inspiration for women in Silicon Valley" (Wylie, 1997). In this unique and highly visible role, she has met the challenge of providing inspiration and mentoring, particularly to women and girls aspiring to succeed in technical fields.

As a result of her leadership, AutoDesk supports and encourages learning in many ways. In Carol's words, "AutoDesk has a real passion for education in general." The company invests a great deal of time with universities, technical colleges, and institutes worldwide, assisting them with engineering programs.

In addition Carol founded the AutoDesk Foundation, which fosters programs in math and science at local schools. One of the foundation's goals is "to work with primary and secondary schools to help them learn how to use technology in teaching."

Her support for technology in the schools goes far beyond simply getting hardware and software into classrooms and labs. She stresses that the emphasis must be on "How do you teach with technology, what is different? . . . We have to really help educators, both on the direct teaching and the administrative side, understand how technology is going to change the way they teach and the way they approach learning" (Wylie, 1997). The foundation emphasizes project-based learning that encourages children to take the initiative for their own learning and to learn to communicate, collaborate, and synthesize information in solving real-world problems. Other foundation activities include annual conferences for teachers, a free on-line newsletter about project-based learning, technical assistance for coaching, assistance in grant writing and curriculum writing, intern programs, and many other educational projects.

To further encourage support of education, Carol asks every AutoDesk employee to volunteer at their local schools on company time. Individuals work out with their managers how they will fit this volunteer work into their regular work schedules. She encourages those who have children to visit their schools, get acquainted with teachers, and help out. Employees without children can "adopt" a classroom and become involved. Carol encourages employees to pay attention to what is happening in the schools "actively and on AutoDesk time" (Wolfson and Talitenu, 1997).

Carol's passion for education undoubtedly stems, in part, from her views on the current status of schools. As she explains, "I think the education system in the United States needs to be dramatically improved. Are we lagging behind in technology? I think technology's one piece of it. I think that I'd like to start with how we lag behind in basic skills, like reading, mathematics, and sciences. I don't think we require enough of our students" (Wolfson and Talitenu, 1997).

Beyond her interest in improving general education in the United States, Carol expends a great deal of time and energy encouraging women and girls to pursue careers in math and science. She encourages girls to pursue math and science courses throughout their primary and secondary school years and to believe in their abilities, so that they have the choice to enter a technical field later on. She notes, "You can't decide you want to become an engineer or a biologist if you haven't had basic math or basic science." She also points to the need to consider more women for technically oriented jobs. "I think that it has to start with making sure that we have women prepared educationally and then I think that they have to be given more opportunity. I think it's still easier to hire and promote in your own image, and that's the default" (Wylie, 1997).

Not content to merely talk about women in technology, Carol actively participates in activities that promote her beliefs. She has participated in the NASA Women of the World program, an interactive, online forum for students and teachers. As a keynote speaker for the Girls and Technology Conference sponsored by the National Coalition of Girls' Schools in 1997, she urged corporate leaders to support parents and educators so that girls have every chance to succeed. Despite the typical demands on her time as a CEO of a major corporation, she supports women's success through speeches and appearances, e-mail connections, phone conversations, and "to some extent by just doing a great job so that I prove that women can be extremely successful." She believes that women need to be more supportive of one another than they currently are. "I think we should reach out and extend our hand, our advice, our limited time, as much as we can to make sure that we do help other women."

While Carol believes in women assisting other women in technology and business, she clearly feels that both men and women have a responsibility to work for progress. "Women need to jump out of their element, out of their comfort zone. And you have to ask the men, 'What are you doing at your company now so that your daughter or granddaughter can be a vice president or CEO of it?' " (WITI, 1997).

Given her interest in education, Carol also sees herself as a learner, especially through reading. As she admits, "I am a big reader. I always make it a point to read business magazines and technology journals as well as daily publications like the *Wall Street Journal* because it's very important to keep track of what's happening in the business and technology world. Because I have a good foundation it's pretty easy for me [to keep up with rapidly changing technology] as long as I keep active with my reading to stay abreast with what's happening." In her viewpoint "you learn relationships and you learn process throughout your whole life." Her response to setbacks and disappointments is to "Pick myself up; dust myself off, say, What in the world happened here? And keep going" (Bartz, 1997c).

Global Thinker and Political Idealist

As the head of a global company with sales and support offices and research centers throughout the world and products available in 19 languages, Bartz is keenly aware of the implications of a global marketplace. The pervasiveness and continued growth of products such as AutoCad throughout the world are evidence of the company's ability to appeal to a multinational market. She can chat just as easily about life in the former Soviet Union as she can about Silicon Valley.

International markets are not without their problems, however, especially for software companies. Bartz is quite vocal about the problems of software theft or piracy and the need for greater awareness of the legal restraints and ethical implications of software theft. It is an issue of enormous proportions—a Business Software Alliance study estimated that software companies lost about $6.5 billion in 1996 due to piracy.

As a major player in Silicon Valley, Carol has gradually realized the importance of political involvement. In her words, "I'm in my 40s and 50s here and if I don't start paying attention to what's happening politically and to our society and to the problems, who is? While we were all so busy in our 20s and 30s growing these companies, we always knew there was somebody else paying attention to the rest of this stuff. Now, it's us . . . it is part of our responsibility to not only carry our agendas forward, but to also make sure that this is a world that we want to live in" (Wylie, 1997).

She has actively participated in a group of CEOs who, although fierce competitors, are united in lobbying Congress concerning encryption, intellectual property, and Internet-based software theft (Bartz, 1996). Bartz, who has called the Internet, "the world's biggest software home shoplifting network," has called for support from the administration in Washington to extend copyright laws to the Internet (Levin, 1997). As she explains, "It's easy to be a closet politician, because you don't have to put your stands out publicly, but there comes a time when you have to go to the front lines and say 'I do believe this' or 'I believe that.' And I think we've all been able to be closet politicians."

Leader Is Like a Symphony Conductor

What is Carol Bartz's own concept of leadership? She describes it as "Motivating people to meet goals. Leaders help people believe in their goals and inspire them to deliver on their promises. Leaders instill a sense of purpose and urgency." Her leadership style at AutoDesk reflects this concept. She believes that the company must provide "an interesting, exciting place to work" and that the company leaders "need to define the visions and goals that inspire a motivated workforce. Without motivation, you might just as well not be there" (Leadership Experts, 1996).

Key characteristics for leadership, from her perspective, are intelligence, empathy, ability to inspire, judgment, charisma, and character. Because these traits are an integral part of an individual's personality, she does not believe that "nonleaders" can be trained to be leaders. She describes watching her own daughter and friends play and the way that a leader will naturally arise within the group. Some people are what she calls "discovered leaders"—they emerge "during tough times or when faced with the right challenges." In other words, "Leaders prove themselves when the opportunity arises."

Bartz includes A. P. Giannini, Jack Welch, Thomas Jefferson, and Margaret Thatcher on her list of role models. She also describes the difference between leaders of a previous era and those of the information age: "Fifty years ago leaders needed to excel in command and control. In today's fast-paced world, organizations must be flexible. Employees need more individual authority and responsibility. Leaders need to motivate and guide, like a symphony conductor" (Leadership experts, 1996). Carol Bartz clearly fits her own description as a leader for the twenty-first century.

CHAPTER 8

Felipe Alfonso: Visionary Director of the Asian Institute of Management

Rowena Figueroa

For the past 30 years, the Asian Institute of Management (AIM) has trained and developed many of the top professional, entrepreneurial, and socially responsible leaders throughout Asia and the rest of the world. Today, it boasts more than 23,000 master's graduates and executive education participants from 68 countries. These graduates manage the region's top private organizations, development agencies, and government institutions. In 1995, AIM was awarded the Ramon Magsaysay Award for International Understanding for "setting regionwide standards for excellence and relevance in training Asian managers for Asia's development" (Mendoza, 1995). That year, *Asian Business* ranked it as one of the world's top five MBA schools (Syrett, 1995). In the following year, it ranked third in *Asia Inc.*'s roster of the top 25 business schools in the Asia Pacific (Tripathi, 1996).

The person behind this burgeoning center for leadership development is Felipe B. Alfonso, known by people around him as a dapper, charismatic figure, tirelessly formulating new ideas and bringing people together. Verve, opportunism, limitless curiosity, and integrity have served this academic cum practitioner well. Few could lead one of Asia's top management schools while also serving as CEO of Manila Electric Company (Meralco), one of the region's best-run companies.

With the Asian crisis looming in the background, Alfonso's task has not been easy. Yet the years have proven repeatedly his ability to investigate, analyze, and influence. Whether advising a young professor or forming alliances between industry heads, he is in his element. Today, Alfonso is the consummate juggler. In addition to serving as AIM president and Meralco CEO, he also heads several organizations throughout the region.

Early Years

Several key individuals served as Alfonso's early role models. He attributes his strong sense of integrity to his parents. Apart from family, his Jesuit training provided him with several mentors whose legacies would have lasting impact. One was Father Blanco, who "transformed me, a boy from the provinces who hardly spoke English, to an orator. I remember how my father couldn't believe his eyes when he watched me" (Alfonso, 1998b). Alfonso considers the communication skills he developed to be "what has served me so well so far as my career is concerned." Then there was Father John, who inspired his social awareness. It is no wonder that part of AIM's mission has always been to develop "socially responsible leaders and managers." His philosophy teacher, Father Leo, honed his logical thinking to the extent that he learned algebra on his own.

Alfonso's dominating passion for teaching began in 1959 when he was a liberal arts instructor at a women's college. One can see his penchant for juggling multiple jobs in his decision to keep one foot in teaching while starting a career in law. True to form, he spent several years teaching while serving first as an associate in a private law office, and then as legal assistant and corporate secretary of four affiliated companies under the Tabacalera Group of Companies. He moved further into the business sector when he earned his MBA at New York University in the mid-1960s.

Although numerous options presented themselves to the new MBA graduate, Alfonso preferred to be a teacher. Straight from NYU, he taught at the Ateneo University MBA program while writing cases for the Harvard Advisory Group. In 1968, he landed a position on the AIM faculty, where he has found his academic home ever since.

As an adult, Alfonso developed close personal and professional relationships with two mentors. The first was Albrecht Lederer, once "management man of the year" in the United States. While a graduate student at NYU, Alfonso met with him weekly to discuss business issues. Shortly before Alfonso returned to the Philippines to start a new career, Lederer gave him a piece of advice he has never forgotten: "Whatever it is you do, never work for money. It will blind you and muddle your judgment. Work to serve others and the money will come your way" (Alfonso, 1998b).

AIM—Responding to the Emerging Needs of Asian Organizations

AIM was born out of a combination of two developments: (1) the Harvard School's mission to establish management programs in developing countries and (2) a movement in the country for Filipinos to take over management positions once held by expatriates. In 1968, AIM offered Asia's first case-method-based management education. Since then, AIM has added a series of innovative degree and non-degree programs to meet the needs of Asia's dynamic and fluctuating economies. 1974 and 1975 were watershed years for AIM. It introduced the Master of Management Program, a year-long program for experienced managers that centered on managerial rather than business functions; the month-long Basic Management Program for first-time managers; and the short-term Management Development Program patterned after Harvard's "Mini MBA." AIM's most radical program in those years, however, was the Rural Development Management Program, an offshoot of consulting arrangements and joint projects with government and nongovernmental organizations as well as AIM's response to the clarion call for effective development managers in Asia. A succession of specialized non-degree programs such as the Advanced Bank Management Program and the Advanced Marketing Management Program followed in later years.

By the early eighties, AIM's short-term programs had not only multiplied but also expanded abroad. At the same time, its local programs drew hundreds of overseas students each year. To meet a growing demand for a short-term program exclusively for senior executives AIM developed the Top Management Program (TMP). Since 1979, the TMP has gathered together 600 top executives, directors, and entrepreneurs from the region for a month-long knowledge-exchange on globalization, technology, and competition. Other programs followed and met with much success. Recently, AIM inaugurated what it calls its MBA for the twenty-first century, the Executive MBA (EMBA) program. This "cutting edge management program" bridges classroom learning and workplace realities with project folios and partnerships among faculty, students, and participating organizations.

Manila Electric Company

The Manila Electric Company (Meralco) provides more than half of the Philippines' total electric consumption and its franchise area produces 50% of the country's gross domestic product. The country's second most widely held company, Meralco was also the second biggest in terms of gross revenues in

1995. In early 1997, *Asianmoney Magazine* touted it as the country's best managed company for 1996. Established almost a century ago by Americans, Meralco has had an illustrious and eventful history. In 1961 ownership changed hands to Eugenio Lopez, Sr., and 600 other Filipinos. Under their administration, Meralco became the country's first billion peso nonfinancial corporation. This administration was disrupted between martial law in 1972 and 1986, when President Ferdinand Marcos took over the company. Shortly after Corazon Aquino's inauguration, ownership reverted to Lopez.

Under Alfonso's leadership, Meralco has striven to keep up with the times. In 1988, Meralco underwent a process of clarifying its vision and mission statement, "The Spirit of Meralco." This process initiated what became a much-needed transformation program for the company to survive industry deregulation and liberalization. These industry changes demanded that Meralco enhance old competencies and develop of new ones. With an eye to achieving world class status, Meralco has recently initiated business process reengineering, thoroughgoing training programs for its human resources, and a process of modernizing equipment and facilities. Equally important, it has diversified into businesses related to electrical distribution. Today, it is one of the top 200 emerging market firms worldwide.

Challenges of Globalization for Asian Leaders

Alfonso believes that the global environment has three main features. The first is increased international exposure. Part of the challenge to Asia's economies is to ride the changes wrought by this exposure. The current crisis marks a "transition to a new phase" that should give rise to more sophisticated commercial and financial structures in the region (Alfonso, 1997b). As a result of increasing exposure to competition, companies must "innovate or stagnate" and "achieve more with less." He notes:

> Globalization and liberalization have sent companies, both big and small, into an unending quest for better products and services, most cost efficient operations as well as leaner yet meaner work forces, all in an effort to improve corporate competitiveness. And spearheading this quest for competitiveness is the manager who must chart the course the enterprise will follow for the present and into the twenty-first century.

Alfonso sees the dominance of information technology as the second feature of the globalized environment. In the old economy, information flows were physical; today they are digital. "Our training and education sectors are all wired up to accommodate a generation that grew up with remote controls rather than rattles, with CD ROM's rather than dolls and marbles," he says.

The third feature of the globalized economy is the increasing cultural diversity of workplaces and of larger environments. To that end, Alfonso has worked to build AIM's international faculty, bringing in academics from the Philippines, Japan, China, Malaysia, India, the United States and Germany. Under his administration, AIM's foreign student population surged to more than half of its degree candidates. Moreover, the proportion of non-Filipino to Filipino residents in executive education programs rose from 1:1 in 1996 to 3:2 today (AIM, 1997).

Innovations in Learning

Globalization's expanding reach with the help of high technology has brought economies closer, raising new challenges for management and management development. First, one must view management development as a continuous learning process. Alfonso explains, "The most valuable skills a manager should have are learning skills. Development of managers must focus on teaching them how to learn more than just giving them information." Since information tends to have ever shorter life expectancies, all organizations must develop new learning methods, particularly those that enable quicker learning. He describes how AIM's efforts to design programs that meet the demands of busy individuals bear this out:

> Twenty-five years ago they said two years was too long, so we developed a one-year master's degree program. Now this is no longer enough. We recently launched an EMBA in Kuala Lumpur with a design that does not require students to leave work for more than two weeks at a time, three times a year for two years. Plus additional weekends for a total of 400 class sessions. Thus it has the same vigor as our one-year program. (Alfonso, 1998b)

The second implication for management development is the shared responsibility among individuals and organizations to learn. This mutual responsibility renders managers both as learners and mentors who provide no answers but who create a dynamic climate of inquiry and shared learning. Delivering the keynote speech at the 1998 Australian Institute for Training and Development Conference, Alfonso emphasized that "learning innovation is lifelong learning is learning to learn together" (Alfonso, 1998a). He also correlated the crisis with the absence of collaborative learning: "Some analysts have traced the Asian crisis to bad judgment or errors in judgment, miscalculations of management. If only 'learning to get ahead' had become 'learning to get together,' then maybe there would be better footholds for judgment calls and management risktaking."

Many of AIM's programs demonstrate the mutual benefits of learning together for all individuals and organizations involved. As Alfonso (1998c) explains, "We are a thirty-year-old management school, the first to introduce the case method in Asian graduate management education, the first to put under the same wing both business management and development management, among the first to push for centers of excellence of strategic research through our specialist thinktanks—the Policy Forum, the Center for Entrepreneurship, the Center for Banking and Finance."

Learning innovation enables stakeholders to benefit from each student's education. One prime example is the Master of Business Management (MBM) program's "Action Consultancy" (AC) co-curricular activity, which matches students with companies' needs. AIM, the student, and a participating firm discuss all learning and practical objectives—the student's, AIM's, and the firm's. The Master of Entrepreneurship program, still in its conception stages, further shows AIM's commitment to shared learning. AIM's Center for Entrepreneurship has forged an agreement with Clark Development Corporation to create a social laboratory in which AIM student-entrepreneurs can start-up their enterprise and learn from the entire process in a quasi-experimental manner. Clark's cybercity will provide the physical infrastructure, while AIM provides the intellectual infrastructure. Each enterprise project benefits the student, Clark, and AIM.

Alfonso envisions AIM's role becoming more like that of a "knowledge broker bringing together all stakeholders" for shared learning. According to him, learning will no longer be about "building skills" but about "changing mindsets" (Alfonso, 1998b). At the 24th ARTDO International Human Resource Development Conference he said, "This is the millenium of the possible, not the perfect. And the possible becomes real only by practice. The next millenium, after all, cannot be brave without managers brave enough to make a difference" (Alfonso, 1997b).

Building Bridges of Opportunities

Opportunities behind globalization are as numerous as its challenges. Negotiating across cultural gaps within and among societies compelled to work together requires more than communication savvy; a sharp eye for spotting potential synergies where no one else sees them is even more crucial. Alfonso leaps at opportunities to broker partnerships among stakeholders. During a signing ceremony between Yamaha and AIM, he discussed with Yamaha Philippines president Philip Yupangco the prospects of a musical instrument manufacturing industry in the Philippines. In the middle of the conversation, a former undersecretary of foreign affairs and current investment banker dropped by on his way to a meeting. Alfonso introduced both men. As it turned out, the banker had tried during his tenure in the government to help develop the musical instrument manufacturing industry. At the end of their conversation, arrangements were made to look at the industry's prospects with AIM students conducting the industry analysis (Alfonso, 1997a).

Linking people will be an important tool in the coming century. "When I go on trips on behalf of AIM," Alfonso explains, "I come back with many different potential things that can be done with people we've talked to. Many others come back and report, but that's it. Interfaces may have been staring at them in the face but they failed to seize opportunities because their minds were unprepared to see them" (Alfonso, 1998b). Spotting prospective interfaces often requires little more than the ability to listen empathetically. Those who "are so full of themselves that they can't listen to others" miss out on such valuable opportunities.

Importance of Spirituality and Ethics in Leadership Education

In the last decade, a growing number of management schools have been paying more attention to issues of spirituality and ethics. At a time when human interactions are becoming increasingly complex, more and more people are invoking values and ethics. Even businesses are adopting ethical terms in their avowed philosophies, values, and missions. For example, Meralco's company philosophy reads: "Service with integrity" (Manila Electric Company, 1996). Alfonso sees integrity as one of the most important qualities of a good leader. "It is not just honesty," he says, "but that I am who I am wherever I go." Those who have enduring success are those who have earned people's trust. "I do a lot of fundraising and in the process meet a lot of people. Often I only have 15 to 20 minutes of effective time with them. In that space of time, I have to be able to build rapport and get my message across," he explains (Alfonso, 1998b). That rapport must rest on a solid foundation of trust.

Alfonso believes management programs should give students more time for self-reflection and for a thorough evaluation of personal values. Yet how does one teach adults about values and ethics? "You can't, but they should be given the time to think these issues through and be given some inputs. In the last AACSB meeting in June in Chicago, corporate citizenship and ethics were at the forefront of discussions. Because in the end, it is who you are that matters. And it's the guy who can be trusted whom people will want to deal with" (Alfonso, 1998d).

Managing Technology

Quick and continuous technological advances have revolutionized the workplace. Organizations have responded by further upgrading workplace technology, often to the bewilderment and consternation of employees across ranks. The problem often lies in inadequate knowledge and skills to benefit from the new technology. In the last two decades, information technology (IT) has created a schism between technical specialists who have little idea about the business and managers who know little about IT.

According to Alfonso, insufficient knowledge sharing between both sides has resulted in waste amounting to "up to $3 trillion." "The challenge then," he says, "is to manage technology development so that it serves the business goals and not vice versa." Yet a large number of managers are reluctant to embrace new technology. For example, only 30% of mid- to senior-level managers who enter AIM's programs are computer literate. He describes how AIM updates its students' computer literacy: "All degree students have Internet addresses and can surf the net anytime of the day. IT is integrated into the curriculum, a literal hands-on training. And our newest facility, the AIM Center for Continuing Executive Education, houses an electronic library that serves as a gateway to the global information highway" (Alfonso, 1998c).

Serving Both Internal and External Customers

One of the most challenging yet exciting aspects of Alfonso's work is dealing with a variety of stakeholders each day. Rallying these stakeholders around one's vision requires the ability to distinguish between individual and organizational interests. At AIM, stakeholders include faculty, staff, students, donors, and partner organizations in industry and government. "All these have a claim on the Institute. Yet you have to balance their sometimes conflicting claims. In order to walk through this mine field of conflicting requirements, you have to be clear as to what their musts are," he says. (Alfonso, 1998b)

Each organization poses its own challenges. AIM's collegial structure makes lateral moves difficult, if not impossible. "Your power exists only to the extent that you respond adequately to your constituents' demands and to the extent that you're able to develop consensus on what needs to be done," he explains. One needs to respect the sense of ownership faculty have of AIM, where decisions are often made through democratic processes. He adds, "Leading this type of organization requires a different set of skills—the ability to communicate, listen, and hold judgment. You have to separate people's skills from attitudes and idiosyncrasies which make them difficult to work with. You've got to be able to live with those and see these people for the value they add to the organization" (Alfonso, 1998b).

The need to consider conflicting interests among different stakeholders has not been lost to Meralco's more hierarchical and bureaucratic structure. On one level are the employees—Alfonso sees the importance of moving internal stakeholders' skills in order to compete within an increasingly deregulated industry. On another level are the stockholders who must be provided greater shareholder value. Next are the customers who demand better service and better quality power at a lower cost. Equally important is the country, which also requires quality power, a major industrial input, at lower cost in order to gain international competitiveness. He explains, "The Company has to consider these national goals. But when you make specific decisions, occasionally the country's requirements might, at least temporarily, conflict with stockholder or staff requirements. So you have to keep your short-, medium- and long-term issues and goals separate" (Alfonso, 1998b).

Thus far, Alfonso has kept both organizations focused on their customers. Training programs at Meralco target "frontliners from security guards to telephone operators to all branch personnel." The company prides itself on the absence of the traditional dichotomy between management and employees, as 95% of all employees are co-owners through an Employee Stock Ownership Plan (Manila Electric Company, 1996). A thorough renovation of the distribution management system shortens response time to service interruptions by allowing a thorough analysis of each call. Improvements in the Customer Management System ensure world class customer service. At AIM, continuous improvement of all programs involves input from students, faculty, staff, and partner organizations.

Need for Holistic and Forward-Looking Thinking

Alfonso describes the manager for the next millenium as "holistic and forward looking." "Before money and machines," he says, "the emphasis should be on people. As one of our AIM professors notes, 'The Asian manager should fire the will of an organization's members with a vision larger than life, one that is well-thought and well-communicated.' " To "weave their images of the future," leaders will have "to act differently, think differently, and seek inspiration from different sources" (Alfonso, 1998b).

The Asian crisis has reinforced the important role perceptions play on all scales and levels of organization. "What brought about the exodus from Asia? It was perception. Economies can be volatile on the basis of perceptions." It is the visionary leader's role to shape an organization's image—how outsiders view it—as well as identity—how the organization views itself. He cites former Philippine president Fidel Ramos as someone who wove a new Philippine image and identity, which spurred the country's growth under his administration:

> The greatest contribution Ramos made to this country was to make people believe in it. He made us believe in ourselves, that we were not a defeated nation, that we could do it. That intangible was the driving force. So sometimes the softside of management is what's most critical. I can get a financial analyst anytime and even replace him with a computer program. But I cannot replace a manager who is able to secure the motivation and commitment of the people he is leading. (Alfonso, 1998b)

The ability to move people toward a vision requires emotional intelligence, which Alfonso defines as "the ability to sense, understand, and effectively apply the power and acumen of emotions as a source of human energy, information, connection and influence" (Alfonso, 1997a). "Emotions," he explains, "have long been considered to be of such depth and power that in Latin they were described as *motus anima*, the spirit that moves us." Successful leaders understand feelings—their own and others'—and acknowledge their power to inspire creativity, deepen relationships, and serve as an inner compass. Yet for all the advantages of honing emotional intelligence, practitioners as well as academics continue to either downplay the significance of emotional intelligence or ignore it altogether.

While Alfonso admits that business schools are just as guilty of perpetuating the primacy of intellectual ability, he advocates a system of mentorship in which emotional bonding between mentors and their pupils leads to successful learning. He cites a study on nearly 200 of the most successful Arab executives in the Gulf region. The study shows that, while education was the top indicator of future success, the second was early exposure to role models with whom individuals formed close relationships.

Twenty-First Century Leaders as Two-Way Communicators

The Greek term *dialogos* refers to the two-way flow of words or ideas. The term aptly describes today's dynamic exchange between leadership and learning. The complexity and unpredictability of today's business environment demands that individuals and organizations engage in a continuous learning process. This trend implies a blurring, if not joining together, of hitherto separate activities. On the one hand, leaders must learn as well as mentor. On the other hand, management academics must keep themselves profitable as well as relevant through alliances with industry. In short, continuous dialogue between the boardroom and the academy is key to the survival of both.

Commitment to an ongoing dialogue between management and education forms the crux of Alfonso's career. As globalization and technology make business environments more complex, an organization's capacity to learn in anticipation of new problems will determine its success. Today management and learning are interdependent activities within and among organizations. Therefore, organizational leaders must encourage their members to learn together, use their creativity, and form alliances. However, such climates require a great deal of trust on all organizational levels. To this end, leaders need to demonstrate their integrity by serving the needs of their internal and external customers. Moreover, they need to move others in ways that recognize people's intellectual and emotional capacities. Most of all, they need to weave visions that inspire others. Alfonso epitomizes the role of twenty-first century leaders should emulate.

Ken Chenault: Designated Leader for Guiding American Express in the Twenty-First Century

> I can say unequivocally that I admire Ken more than anyone else I've ever worked with. I think he will be our generation's Jack Welch.
>
> —Amy DiGeso, former American Express executive and CEO of Mary Kay, Inc.

BusinessWeek recently acclaimed Kenneth Irvine Chenault as one of the nation's top corporate executives, "particularly for those who are looking for all-around leadership capability." The recognition was gained for having demonstrated the ability to excel in managing technology and building relationships, in addition to having a "solid operating record" (Reingold and Byrne, 1997). Chenault was the only African-American on the list.

When he was named President and COO of American Express in 1997, Chenault became one of the highest-ranking black executives in corporate America. CEO Harvey Golub has openly stated that he has chosen Chenault to succeed him when he retires in 2001. Chenault would be the first African-American to control a company the size of American Express, ranked 65th largest in the United States by annual revenue according to *Fortune* magazine. Not one of the top 100 companies has a black CEO in this world of "glass ceilings and sticky floors" (Smith, 1997). As one observer has noted, Chenault, Barry Rand (Executive Vice President for Operations at Xerox Corp.), and others are "testing how high the glass ceiling really is." Chenault's appointment is seen by some as an affirmation that African-Americans are willing and qualified to take the lead and successfully run billion dollar corporations.

Early Years

Chenault is a native of Long Island, New York, and the son of a dentist who practiced in Hempstead, a mostly white, middle-class town. Even as a high school student, Chenault's capabilities as a leader were evident. He was class president of Waldorf school all four of his years of high school and captain of the basketball, soccer, and track teams. He graduated magna cum laude with honors from Bowdoin College in 1973 with a Bachelor of Arts degree in history, and earned a law degree at Harvard University in 1976 (Bowdoin College, 1996).

Although Chenault attended college during a turbulent period marked by Vietnam War protests and civil rights marches, Dan Levine, a history professor at Bowdoin recalls that at a time of race riots and antiwar protests, Chenault was "no wild-eyed radical." Instead, "he was a calm person who made his arguments by solid logic" (Dugas, 1997).

Before joining American Express, Chenault was an associate in the New York law firm of Rogers and Wells and a management consultant at Bain and Company. He was brought into Bain and Co. by W. Mitt Romney, son of the former governor of Michigan, who had been at Harvard Law School with Chenault. While Ken didn't have an MBA, Romney felt he was naturally suited to the world of business. In his words, "I'll take full credit for hiring Ken. He was able to process a lot of conflict and frenzy and still be able to cut through the confusion and arrive at very powerful conclusions and recommendations and then see them through to their implementation" (Pierce, 1997).

In 1981 at the age of 29, he was hired by client Louis Gerstner, then president of American Express and later IBM chairman, as director of strategic planning and began his swift rise to the top. Two years later he moved up to vice president of the merchandise services department, and after more than tripling revenues he was named department head. In 1986 he was promoted to executive vice president and general manager of the Platinum/Gold Card Division, leading record growth in that division. He rose to president of the Consumer Card Group USA in 1989, and took responsibility for marketing and operations for all U.S. consumer card products. In this capacity he led important re-engineering initiatives, addressed quality issues, developed new cardmember programs, and introduced a new vision of the credit card business for the future.

Based on his efforts and successful results, he was chosen as president of American Express Travel Related Services USA in 1993, and then vice chairman in 1995. On that occasion, Harvey Golub (American Express CEO) stated, "Ken is one of the outstanding leaders in our company. His leadership has helped us get our business back on track and restore confidence in American Express" (Lloyd, 1995). In February, 1997, he was named President and Chief Operating Officer.

During his tenure at American Express, Chenault has been involved in a variety of difficult efforts, including growing market share by expanding product offerings in key segments, globalizing the company, helping rethink the company's financial services strategy, improving employee satisfaction, managing brand extensions beyond traditional American Express products and services, and other initiatives. Since his appointment as President and COO, all of the company's business units report to him. He has also been nominated to membership on the board of directors. His success continues—Chenault and Golub were included on *BusinessWeek*'s list of the 25 top managers of the year for 1997, recognized as "strong-willed executives" who "muscled . . . [American Express] back into shape" (The 25 Top, 1998).

Chenault also serves on the boards of IBM, the Brooklyn Union Gas Company, the Quaker Oats Company, the National Collegiate Athletic Association, NYU Medical Center and NYU Downtown Hospital, Phoenix House, the National Center on Addiction and Substance Abuse, the Ronald H. Brown Foundation, and the Arthur Ashe Institute for Urban Health. He is a member of the Council on Foreign Relations and serves on the Dean's Advisory Board of the Harvard Law School.

American Express

Founded in 1850, American Express is a diversified worldwide travel, financial, and network services company, headquartered in New York City. American Express is one of the largest financial services companies in the United States and is the largest corporate travel agency. While it issues traveler's checks and publishes magazines (*Food & Wine, Departures* and *Travel and Leisure*), American Express (or AmEx, in common terms) is best known for its credit card which accounted for almost 20.7% of the U.S. credit card purchase volume in the first half of 1998. The company consists of three main units: Travel Related Services, American Express Financial Advisors, and American Express Bank. Ranked number 73 in the Fortune 500, its 1999 revenues totaled over $19.4 billion, with a net income of $2.48 billion. Its nearly 85,000 employees are stationed at locations throughout the world.

Vision and Systems Thinking

Chenault can be credited with providing vision to a company that was, in his words, "in very sharp decline." American Express's turnaround reflects "the revolution" brought about by Chenault and Golub. "We are by no means uncorking the champagne bottle. But we are very much in the game, which is a very different situation from three or four years ago," says Chenault (Greenwald, 1998). This reversal of fortune is due to significant improvements of their product line and growth of cardholders and volume.

"We've introduced more products in a period of 18 months than we did in the past decade," according to Chenault. Indeed, "American Express now offers 35 different consumer and business cards, many of them free and co-branded with other companies, up from just five cards a decade ago." As Morgan Stanley research analyst, David B. Hilder, explains, "Ken has a natural instinctive feel for what types of marketing strategies and propositions will work and the extent to which they need to be tested or don't need to be tested" (Pierce, 1997).

When Chenault discusses the future of American Express, he envisions one of the fastest-growing companies in the world, but not at all costs. "Against our vision of being the world's most respected service brand, I'd like to be one of the most admired companies in the world. That would mean that we would be perceived as one of the best managed companies, and we would, in fact, generate substantial growth in earnings."

While he may not see himself as a better human being than the next person, he is a better competitor than many. One observer speaks of his "fighting spirit shining through the friendly, gracious exterior, the signs of a fierce competitor who might be willing to lose a few battles but never the war." In a similar vein, another expert notes, "Ken is not afraid of challenges. He thrives on them. If he was on Wall Street, a trader, you would say he enjoys the kill." He describes his competitive edge in strategic terms: "You analyze the opposing team, the plays, the moves, what are the rules of the game, the weaknesses that can be exploited and the strengths that need to be dealt with" (Pierce, 1997).

Chenault has learned a great deal about management and leadership from AmEx CEO Harvey Golub and General Electric CEO Jack Welch. Describing Welch, he says, "He has demonstrated not only the importance of the vision, similar to Harvey, but the criticality of putting the tactics in place and setting very high performance standards," abilities that Chenault has also developed as a corporate leader (Pierce, 1997).

Globalist

One of American Express's main goals is to increase its international business to the point where it contributes about one-half of the company's earnings (excluding American Express Financial Advisors). Despite increased volatility in the global financial markets in 1998, American Express remains committed to that goal. As president, Chenault must keep a constant eye on conditions around the world that affect its international banking, card, and travel operations. With turmoil in Russia, unrest in Malaysia and Indonesia, economic ups and downs in Japan, and uncertainty in Latin America, Chenault has had plenty to watch lately.

The third quarter of 1998 saw a drop in stock prices of many banks and other financial companies, including AmEx. While the decline (41%) was not quite as sharp as that of some others in the business, such as Citicorp (51%), it was enough to spur the company to reevaluate its goals and global position. Under Chenault's leadership, the company developed a broad and diversified worldwide customer base that cushions some of the stock market blows. The company's performance targets were designed to apply over a range of economic conditions and market fluctuations, and AmEx has consistently met or exceeded its earnings and return on equity goals over the past five years.

Team Player and Steward

While performance may drive his success, Chenault recognizes the importance of working through people. According to one writer, he is "A warm, caring individual, he knows how to motivate people, how to criticize without humiliating, how to get people to do what they thought they couldn't, how to inspire through respect, even affection, rather than fear." Mitch Kurz, president of Y & R Advertising, describes him as "the most human of all chief executives I've worked with. He has extraordinary listening skills; he actively wants to hear our opinions. A senior executive can spend 15 minutes with Ken and be motivated for the next month without any more contact. Ken engenders a kind of loyalty which money can't buy" (Pierce, 1997).

Another writer describes him as "a born leader honing his skills, creating a vision for a company he loves, convincing people that they can win, and cheering them on as he plots the course" (Pierce, 1997). He is generally well liked and trusted by employees, and "his sunny personality and marketer's savvy are welcome contrasts to Golub's gloomy persona" (Grant, 1995). When Chenault was promoted to president, employees at the Fort Lauderdale operations center sent hundreds of congratulatory notes attached to three large banners. Employees cheered his promotion to president, according to Anne Busquet, president of American Express Relationship Services. "You would go in elevators and hear, 'Isn't it exciting about Ken? Can you believe that Ken got promoted? Isn't it fantastic? Oh I feel much better about the company now that Ken is president.' People wrote him notes; he was flooded with e-mail; there were flowers and calls from corporate and political leaders." As a leader, Chenault inspires loyalty and contributes "a sane, reliable voice in a fast-paced place" (Dugas, 1997).

Chenault's reputation as a mediator willing to listen to all sides dates from his college days. It was a time of turmoil, of riots and the Black Panther movement, of heated debate on a mostly white campus. He has been described as "deeply tied to the African-American students at Bowdoin and very much a part of the white student world," a bridge to many groups. As a college friend explains, "It was aggravating for us who were on the far right or far left. His style was to come in more the middle of the road, to say let's consider both sides here, and to look at it from the point of fact rather than emotion" (Pierce, 1997).

Drawing on his love of sports, Chenault recognizes the importance of coaching as a valuable leadership and instructional role. "The coach has to understand the capabilities of the different members of the team, to inspire people, to instill hope. The coach is accountable for the performance of the team." Chenault never loses sight of the need to be the leader of a team rather than its boss. As an example, he invites employees of different levels to brown bag lunches once a month. While this might be merely a superficial gesture on the part of some executives, he admits that he has gotten some of his best ideas from this process. However, he may not "push as much accountability into the next level in the organization" as he should, according to one observer. "Ken will share the credit when it goes well, but when it doesn't, he takes it on himself. Sometimes you can stick with players beyond their capability and it puts a tremendous stress on him" (Pierce, 1997).

An incident in 1991 provides a glimpse of his abilities to handle people and promote teamwork. As president of the Consumer Card Group, he was faced with a group of Boston restaurateurs who were threatening a boycott over the fees AmEx charged. In typical fashion, Chenault caught the first available plane and met personally with the individuals involved. He was able to defuse the situation and persuade the restaurateurs to remain with AmEx, saving the company from what could have been a major public relations fiasco. Although he was central to the effort to resolve the conflict, he comments that "it was a team effort" (Shook, 1997).

Another author describes him as "not one to make a fuss, least of all over himself." She also calls him "self-contained and firmly grounded," someone who "does not give the impression of having much of his ego tied up in a title" (Clarke, 1995). In his boss's terms, "he has earned the respect of the entire

American Express community." Golub adds, "Ken has a long and distinguished record of performance in continuously more challenging jobs. And he is the kind of leader whom people want to follow" (American Express, 1997)"

Ken revered his father, Dr. Hortensius Chenault, whom he has described as the most determined person he has ever known, overcoming every obstacle in his path. Descriptions of Chenault's work style depict a tactful hard worker, able to "get things done without hogging the limelight" and keep a low profile when necessary to get the job done. Chenault shares a personal moment from his early teen years that sheds light on this aspect of his personality. He accidentally ran across his father's dental board results, which showed that his father had gotten the highest score. When asked why he never mentioned this, his father noted that he had just done the best that he could do. Chenault's approach, which has been described as "Do your best and let the results speak for you," reflects his father's style (Shook, 1997).

Advancing Diversity
Rather than Adversity

While researching his senior thesis on the history of African-Americans at Bowdoin College, he discovered a devastating trend. Although Bowdoin boasted about having one of the nation's first black college graduates, Chenault found that for decades after, it had none. Race and poverty remain important issues for him. He finds time to raise money for the Rheedlen Centers and to talk to young people at the Centers about the importance of education and hard work. In a commencement address in 1996 at his alma mater, he stated, "I believe we all must be strongly committed to creating a more inclusive society." He continued by pointing out the important role of student diversity in education, stating that it has "for more than a century been valued for its capacity to contribute powerfully to the process of learning and to the creation of an effective educational environment" (Chenault, 1996). He sees diversity as "vital to the education of citizens and development of leaders."

Despite his recognition of race issues in the United States and the need to make improvements in this area, the expanse of his vision of society extends well beyond racial barriers. In his words, "I think it is unfortunate that we still live in a society where race becomes so defining. I'm very proud of who I am and I think that's important on an individual basis. But the reason why I got this job was my performance. And that's what I think should be focused on" (Dugas, 1997). He does not deny the issue of race, but keeps a balanced, realistic focus. As he told students at Howard University School of Business, "Remember we are very visible. Make sure when you speak up, you know what you are talking about. We have to be prepared. You need to understand eyes are on us. It may not be fair, but it's real. In business you have to be pragmatic" (Pierce, 1997).

The impression one gets is that Chenault takes a constructive, positive stance in all that he does. While many people have viewed the past few years of transformation and downsizing in corporate America as a backward step, particularly for minorities, Chenault has a different take on the situation. "The general view was that minorities would have a more difficult time. My feeling is that, at times of change, when results shine through, minorities fare better" (Clarke, 1995). Part of the reason for this viewpoint may be that because of corporate re-engineering and other recent trends, organizations tend to focus more on high performers, regardless of race and gender. While he is certainly aware of the pressures and high expectations of a person in his position, he remarks, "I feel very strongly that race has not been a factor in my career at American Express and I have been able to move forward based on my achievement. . . . I didn't have to go through the trials and tribulations Jackie Robinson went through. I've had a straightforwardly fair chance to get where I did on merit" (Authers, 1997).

Strong Work Ethic

While Chenault may be a charismatic, likable person, his success derives mostly from his strong work ethic. As Richard Parsons, president of Time Warner and a friend of Chenault's, explains, "He's done it the old fashioned way. People think there is some magic to it. But Kenny has just outworked all the others" (Dugas, 1997). Even his college friends remember him as smart and hard working. As his friend Geoffrey Canada says, "Ken was always smarter than anybody else. Ken could outwork and out hustle everybody. He was the kind of guy that while you thought you would get up in the morning and do it, he was doing it that night" (Pierce, 1997).

According to Earl Graves, publisher of *Black Enterprise* magazine and also a good friend, Chenault is "very focused and very direct in getting things done. He's responsible for much of the success of the company in the last couple of years" (Charkalis, 1997). Harvey Golub emphasizes Chenault's mature and balanced judgment and the fact that he always puts the interests of the company first. When asked to describe himself, Chenault's response is "focused on performance." In fact he has been called a classic overachiever. He "typically works 11-hour days and spends many evenings entertaining clients. Even when he steals some time to play golf or go to a basketball game, he seems to be thinking about work" (Dugas, 1997). Clearly, Chenault's success is "about accomplishment, hard work, drive, ambition, and being the best, about a man confident and secure, focused, above the crowd, but one of the crowd, about a man . . . being equal to the task" (Pierce, 1997).

Serving the Community

Chenault believes that it is possible to both make a profit and do good works. According to a former Bowdoin classmate, Geoffrey Canada, president of the nonprofit Rheedlen Centers for Children and Families in New York City, "He always believed you could be a successful businessman and still make a difference in the lives of poor Americans." And "he's compassionate, not the type who likes to step on others to get ahead"(Dugas, 1997).

The number and variety of honors and awards bestowed on Chenault illustrate his commitment to serving the community and society. He has received the Anti-Defamation League of B'nai B'rith Torch of Liberty Award, and in 1990 he was honored at the Black Achievement Awards for his business and professional accomplishments. He received the Candle in the Dark Award from Morehouse College for outstanding professional and personal achievements in February 1991 and the Corporate Patron of the Arts Award from the Studio Museum in Harlem in May 1993.

With an audience of more than 600 black managers in attendance, Chenault was honored in 1995 at the annual recognition dinner of the Executive Leadership Council and Foundation, a nonprofit organization of African American officers and executives from Fortune 500 companies, created to provide members a professional network and forum, to enhance the effectiveness of its membership, and to increase achievement of excellence. That same year, he was presented a Corporate Leadership Award by the Massachusetts Community Development Finance Corporation.

For his contributions to the community, he has also received the ROBIE Award for Achievement in Industry. Other awards include the Friend of the Children Award from Rheedlen Centers for Children and Families and the Business Leadership Community Builder Award from Phipps Houses. Chenault and his wife were also honored by the Citizens Committee of New York for their contributions to the city of New York.

Chenault's contributions extend to the educational arena, as well. He has volunteered significant time to his alma mater, serving on the Bowdoin College Board of Overseers and as a member of the Class of 1973 Reunion Committee, a Business Breakfast speaker, a member of the Presidential Search Committee, and a participant in Black Alumni Weekend activities.

Chenault's strong sense of values also earns him admiration. In his own words, "In the pursuit of opportunity and success, we all need a greater adherence to principles and values in guiding our behavior and actions." He acknowledges that a great deal of his success is due to his "simple, personal philosophy: I believe you can be the most determined competitor, totally focused on winning, which I am, but you can do it with integrity, grace, and always treating people with respect and dignity." His admonishment to a group of graduating college seniors sums up what he would expect from us all: "Act on your responsibility to contribute to the betterment of our society" (Chenault, 1996). Comments by American Express CEO Harvey Golub echo these attributes. He says, for example, that Chenault "holds himself and others to the highest standards of integrity and demonstrates respect for people at all levels of the organization" (American Express, 1997).

Even Chenault's sense of ambition and desire to lead seem tempered by these beliefs. He admits that as a child he knew he wanted to be a leader of something, although he was not sure of what. But this ambition was fueled by more than a need to succeed, materially and otherwise. Friends at college quote him as saying, "I've got to get into the system to help my people" (Shook, 1997). His personal goals reflect his deep sense of ethical and social responsibility: "What I want to do is to make a difference. Whether it's in the field of education or social services, what is most important is that I have a platform and an opportunity to bring about fundamental change" (Pierce, 1997).

He further reflects his deep sense of values and commitment when talking about his hopes for his two sons. He and his wife, Kathy, "want them to have a strong sense of themselves, to be confident, to have the capacity to be really happy and sad so that they have feelings and are sensitive to the needs of others, and that they want to make a difference in the lives of people." Like most parents, he wants them to be successful, but adds, "at the end of the day if you said to me, what do you want most out of your children, I would say I want them to be good people. That would be more important than saying this person is supersuccessful, but I don't really think this is a good person" (Pierce, 1997).

Importance of Learning

In 1987 after being promoted four times in five years, Chenault was listed in an article of "people to watch" in *Fortune* magazine. He states, "I basically believe I can learn anything" (Ballen, 1987). He apparently has continued to learn a great deal. As a child Ken was a late bloomer, and at one point his parents were concerned about what would become of him. While he was clearly bright, this did not always translate into high academic performance. He loved to read and made A's in his favorite subject, history, but his other grades were C's. However, Chenault points out, "I had a thirst for learning and that probably gave my parents hope. I'm sure it was frustrating for them that I was not applying myself."

Chenault attended the Waldorf School of Garden City on Long Island and had the good fortune to find teachers who recognized his abilities and encouraged him to apply himself. Ken remembers one teacher, Lee Lecraw, as "a unique and incredibly talented person." By the time he graduated, he was president of his class, an honor student, and captain of the basketball, soccer, and track teams.

Chenault continues to learn and grow in his position at AmEx. As one observer describes him, "He's very quick to turn a setback into a lesson, a lesson into an action plan, an action plan into an advantage" (Pierce, 1997). He seems driven, at least in part, by his perfectionism and need to constantly improve.

Despite his demanding schedule, Chenault manages to take time to reflect and to renew himself. He takes walks, enjoys occasional quiet moments, and reads, particularly biographies and the works of Howard Thurman, whose writings focus on "the brotherhood of man and reality of God." Chenault is known for his calm composure. As he explains, "I believe very strongly in keeping balanced. Don't get too up about the ups and too down about the downs" (Pierce, 1997).

A Leader Whom People Love to Follow

AmEx CEO Golub has called Chenault "the kind of leader whom people want to follow" (American Express, 1997). And he certainly seems to be leading the employees of American Express in the right direction. Known for his balanced judgment, high standards of integrity, respect for people at all levels of the company, and innovative repositioning of American Express in its markets, he remains a low-key, modest executive, not above making his own coffee and putting in long hours. These unique attributes and abilities will serve American Express well as it enters the twenty-first century.

CHAPTER TEN

Mary McAleese: Leading Ireland toward Peace and Prosperity

Unlike other leaders discussed in this book who are responsible for the management of hundreds, if not thousands of employees, Mary McAleese is a leader whose only power is that of her voice and her ideas. As the new president (a primarily ceremonial position) of the Irish Republic, she seeks to lead a country of 4 million people, a country that has endured hundreds of years of suffering and 70 years of violent division.

But both Ireland and McAleese are facing challenges and achieving successes at the end of the twentieth century that many other countries and leaders will be hoping to achieve during the twenty-first century. Ireland is emerging from wars and divisions to peace and unity, from poverty and hopelessness that caused its best to leave the country for the past 150 years to a country of richness and hope that is now calling and causing its children to return.

First President from Northern Ireland

Mary McAleese is the first president of the Irish Republic to come from Northern Ireland, the six counties of Ireland that remain contentiously under British jurisdiction. Born in 1951 into a Catholic Belfast family, McAleese grew up in a Protestant area, near Ardoyne. Her father ran a famous pub called the Long Bar in the Falls area of Belfast. The eldest of nine children, Mary attended high school in the Falls Road in Belfast. On the day she received the A-level results that guaranteed her place as a law student at Queen's University, she came home to find gangs of uniformed "B-Specials" terrorizing her neighborhood. Three years later her family home was machine-gunned while they were at Mass and the police advised them for their own safety not to return. In another sectarian attack, her deaf brother was badly beaten.

At the young age of just 24, she was appointed Reid Professor of Criminal Law, Criminology, and Penology, at Trinity College, Dublin. She conducted research into a range of issues, including the computerization of prison records and child custody.

Four years later, she joined Radio Telefís Éireann, the Irish State broadcasting service, as a current affairs journalist and television presenter. In 1981 she resumed her professorship at Trinity College, but continued her broadcasting career as the presenter of Europa, a TV program about the European Union.

In 1987, McAleese returned to Queen's University Belfast to become the Director of the Institute of Professional Legal Studies, a training center for members of the legal profession in Northern Ireland. She introduced a sign language module into solicitor's training in Northern Ireland, the first time such a course had been incorporated into legal training in Europe. She became associated with the development of affirmative-action programs that did much to alter the image of the university. Then in 1994, she was appointed pro-vice-chancellor of the University, the first woman and the first Catholic to reach such a position.

McAleese possesses obvious intellectual status and legal expertise. Combined with these professional talents are generous helpings of charisma, warmth, and down-to-earth humanity, which she displayed at the beginning of the presidential campaign when Marian Finucane introduced her to the nation on national television (Collins, 1998).

The New Ireland

A decade ago Ireland would have been dismissed as an economic basket case, with a high level of unemployment and a population smaller than before the potato famine of the 1840s. Now Ireland is being described glowingly as a Celtic tiger, combining low German inflation with high Southeast Asian growth rates.

In her inaugural address, McAleese spoke of how Ireland has become a nation transformed:

> This Ireland which stands so confidently on the brink of the twenty-first century and the third millennium is one our forbears dreamed of and yearned for: a prospering Ireland, accomplished, educated, dynamic, innovative, compassionate, proud of its people, its language and of its vast heritage: an Ireland

at the heart of the European Union, respected by nations and cultures across the world. (McAleese, 1997)

As Ireland commemorates the 150th anniversary of the Great Famine, which triggered a mass exodus of emigrants to the New World, it is enjoying the first signs of an inflow of overseas Irish, returning home to take jobs with the many foreign companies setting up factories. From a largely farm-based economy, Ireland has transformed itself into a key location for high-technology companies. It has fast become one of the most dynamic offshore financial service centers in Europe and has created a generation of indigenous companies that, in areas such as food processing, are taking on the world. Ireland has now become one of the favored foreign investment spots in the European Union. The government boasts of creating over 1,000 new jobs per week. One minister recently claimed that Ireland accounted for every other job created in the entire European Union. In short, Ireland has produced more jobs in the past 3 years than it had in the previous 30.

The education system, despite a lack of resources, now turns out proportionately more science graduates than any other Organization for Economic Cooperation and Development (OECD) member except Japan. Typically, the big U.S. companies already in Ireland, such as Intel and Hewlett-Packard, have special liaison officers who work directly with the universities to help shape the curriculum—and get first pickings of the brightest graduates.

Let's look at how McAleese's vision and leadership is helping to propel Ireland and Irish organizations into the twenty-first century, a century of peace and prosperity.

Building Bridges

In a recent interview with the *Irish News,* McAleese was clear as to her leadership role. It is "to reflect back to people a view that says we are capable of achieving." As president, she must instill a sense of pride in the nation by encouraging the Irish people to take a closer look at the enormous progress the country has made and celebrate its accomplishments (Collins, 1998). McAleese recognizes that the Irish people need a sense of achievement to provide the energy and momentum to keep on trying and achieving, and she is convinced that the Irish must first believe in themselves if they are all to share in the economic benefits of being a Celtic tiger.

Part of her responsibility as leader is to encourage a sense of unity and sharing. Recognizing that not everyone has benefited from recent economic growth, she envisions a nation in which all will share in this new prosperity. As she points out, it is not enough for those who have been successful to say, "I've arrived and I don't care about everybody else." Rather, she promotes a more collective effort, a synergy in which the Irish people, working together, will achieve far greater results than each working individually.

McAleese believes that her primary responsibility is to lead Ireland in its adaptation to changing political and economic realities. Because no one can predict with certainty what the next few years might bring, flexibility is a necessity. As history unfolds, she is prepared to constantly monitor its pulse and adapt and respond to the needs and priorities of the nation.

The cornerstone of the president's election campaign was her commitment to "building bridges." Her opponents claimed the slogan was a sham and that she cannot and will not deliver. McAleese insists, however, that her commitment to the concept is absolute. And she contends that she will demonstrate that commitment by more than words. In her eyes, bridges are not limited to north-south connections; they may be bridges between organizations, bridges in the north or in the south, linkages of many kinds. Noting that many people are already engaged in building bridges, she intends to celebrate their efforts and encourage others to buy into the concept.

Ultimately, her goal is to be able to demonstrate at the end of seven years that she and her party have done what they said they would do, with results that are definable, measurable, and identifiable. She recognizes that the nation must stay focused on its vision and not allow it to become dissipated or diluted. By celebrating and encouraging good practice throughout her presidency, she hopes to keep her message constantly in view.

Gone in the new President's speeches is the old nationalist language of victories, defeats, or historic conflicts. In its place, McAleese talks the new language of modern day nationalism—of inclusivity, of diversity, of consensus, of respect for all traditions.

She believes that the hothouse nature of the campaign has made her better able to cope with the demands of office. In fact, she sees the ability to endure difficulties or suffering as a legitimate way of proving oneself. "I think there is a crucible that you have to suffer; that there is a harsh, thorny path that you have to go through, and it's right that you should. That tests your mettle and, in a very public way, it shows to other people what you're made of." Asked if she learned anything about herself during her presidential campaign, she singles out two things in particular: the strength of her faith in God and the strength that comes from being surrounded by people committed to her. These forces sustained her through the worst parts of the campaign. Her profound faith that God was constantly with her gave her the courage to face each day, whatever might happen.

"We Have the Talent and Energy to Make Peace"

Before her election as president, Mary McAleese was heavily involved in the Clonard peace mission, which was working to reestablish the IRA ceasefire. The cause of peace in Ireland has dominated her life, and she knows where it lies in Ireland's scale of priorities—the peace process is "crucial."

She explains that the Irish people have achieved an enormous amount—economically, culturally, and in many other ways—over the last number of years, sometimes surprising themselves with their own capabilities. Thus, certainly, the achievement of consensus and peace is not beyond their abilities and talents. On the contrary, she believes that they have the energy, the imagination, and the flexibility necessary to achieve peace. The next step is to have the confidence to admit that they have these skills and tools and then to put them to use without fear.

A Vision for Ireland

Early in her presidential campaign McAleese spelled out, probably more clearly than any of the other three candidates, her vision for the Presidency. She saw three key elements in the job. First would be the president's role in ensuring that legislation is consistent with the wishes of the people as expressed in the Constitution. Second would be to continue her predecessor's (Mary Robinson) successful efforts to bring the "caring, reaching-out side" of the Presidency close to the people. And third would be the ambassadorial role—promoting an image of Ireland as "dynamic, very energetic, modern, fresh, a young country growing in confidence, in education, in self-understanding, and growing more comfortable in its complexity and diversity."

Echoing her campaign motif, McAleese stated in her inaugural address that the theme of her Presidency would be "Building Bridges." While requiring no engineering skills, these bridges demand patience, imagination, and courage to build in a rapidly changing and increasingly complex environment. She acknowledges that the tendency to dwell on the past has haunted the nation, slowing its progress. She advocates breaking with the past and moving on, instead of holding on to old wounds, real or perceived. She notes that in many arenas—dance, music, literature, sports, technology, and political leadership—the Irish have become giants on the world stage. These accomplishments can provide a sense of purpose and exhilaration for the nation to move forward.

McAleese recognizes the need for diversity, for a sort of creative tension, within Ireland. For example, she observes that some people exuberantly embrace innovation and change, while others are more cautious, even fearful. In her eyes, such tensions contribute to Ireland's dynamism and creative genius. One of her goals is to reconcile unproductive tensions and lead the nation to a more comfortable acceptance of the diversity flowering within its borders. In the words of Belfast poet Louis MacNeice, "a single purpose can be founded on a jumble of opposites."

McAleese emphasizes that the Irish are an energetic, dynamic, creative people in their own right, with a great capacity for achievement. But it is her vision that an achieving Ireland will not rest until all its people can benefit from the country's economic success. "We can only be happy when the rest of our big Irish family, those who still face unemployment, those who still face major problems in their lives, have been drawn into the charmed circle. Not until that happens can we rest" (Collins, 1998). This is truly an ambitious and exciting vision.

McAleese's vision for businesses was presented at the 1998 Conference of the International Federation of Training and Development Organizations (IFTDO) in Dublin, when she welcomed leaders from all over the world with these words:

> All successful organizations depend on people who are dedicated to the task of leadership and management, and who are able to react quickly and readily to the ever changing circumstances and fortunes of the marketplace—people who know that the person who uses yesterday's methods in today's work won't be in business tomorrow. To be such a person sometimes means being strong—being courageous—being the first to think the unthinkable, to suggest the thing that is hard to swallow—being prepared to persuade the crowd that yours is the right direction—the clearer vision. For us in Ireland—which has seen tremendous progress in the last decade— these are the people who transformed Ireland into a "can do" culture— who gave it energy and vision, and whose judgement was rewarded with success. That success has built up our self-confidence—our national self-esteem. (McAleese, 1998)

Innovation and Change for the Irish People

The ambitious vision that McAleese has depicted for Ireland requires a zeal for innovation. Recognizing that change is the key to success in all organizations and economies, she stresses that the Irish people are not afraid to adapt to change. In fact the rapid pace of change in Ireland evidences a drive for perfection. Advances in modern communications and the advent of the information superhighway have accelerated the rate of change and continue to profoundly affect the way businesses compete and also co-operate.

She notes how management theorist Igor Ansoff coined the phrase "environmental turbulence" in the 1960s to describe the change from a static to a dynamic view of business. That phrase has even more resonance today for enterprises facing the challenges of radically globalized, high-tech work. The science and art of management is all about meeting the challenge of change, generating competition, and yet ensuring that a stable economy is the backbone that allows us to control or harness that turbulence, and use it as a source of energy with which to drive forward.

Moving Ireland from Potatoes to Chips (Computer)

What Ireland produces has changed beyond what anyone would have believed a few years ago. The economy has moved from primarily state-owned enterprises to one of the preferred locations in the world of private investment.

McAleese has been a strong advocate of building Ireland into a technological powerhouse. The Industrial Development Agency is targeting the high growth areas of electronics, software, pharmaceuticals, and financial services. According to a study by KPMG, Ireland replaced the UK as the favorite site for U.S. electronics hardware investment, winning one third of the new projects located in the European Union, against 19% for the UK. Intel, Microsoft, IBM, and Hewlett-Packard all have major factories in Ireland. A sign of this high-tech focus is *Irish Expatriate*, an Internet-based newsletter produced by a retired software engineer among the dry stone walls of Galway. Its subscribers include leading universities in the United States, and its advertisements include numerous job vacancies in the electronics sector in Ireland.

Ireland has developed a strong information technology sector in recent years and has great potential in software, multimedia, and manufacturing. Realizing that sustainable economic development requires not simply rejecting international ties (pre-1958) or embracing them with little reservation (post-1958), Ireland must make choices about which international relationships are worthwhile and how their benefits can be distributed throughout society. The state has begun to play a critical role in mediating these relationships. However, time will tell whether the political will exists to extend the benefits to the whole society (Brown, 1997).

Service and Sharing

McAleese noted in her inaugural address that Irish people at their core are a sharing people. In her eyes, it is this commitment to the welfare of each other has animated generations of voluntary organizations and a network of every-day neighborliness that weaves together the caring fabric of the country. She points out that Ireland has sent missionaries, development workers, and peace-makers to the aid of distressed peoples in other parts of the world and is itself a country of refuge for the hurt and dispossessed of other troubled places. That sense of sharing is the driving force behind efforts to tackle the country's many social problems. She is firmly committed to bridging the gap between the comfortably well-off and those mired in poverty, unemployment, and despair, to spreading the benefits of prosperity throughout the country (McAleese, 1997).

This ethic of caring and service on a national level also lies at the heart of McAleese's own values and actions. The need to learn and innovate as the Irish people reach for the future is closely linked to the whole notion of service. As she puts it, "The quality of service that you give is directly related to your willingness to be open—to embrace change—to critique and amend—to try out new ideas and to learn" (McAleese, 1997).

Dialogue Rather than Hatred

McAleese is a strong advocate of peace through dialogue and consensus. She deplores the "cruelty and capriciousness" of the violent conflicts that have characterized Irish history and brought hardship to young and old alike. Many have paid with their lives, while those left behind cling to "shattered dreams and poignant memories." She is determined to replace violence with a renewed right to solve problems through dialogue and consensus, pursued without the language of hatred and animosity that has characterized past endeavors. Can peace be achieved? McAleese points to other nations in Europe who were once bitter enemies and who now "work conscientiously with each other and for each other as friends and partners." The greatest tribute to those who have died and those who have suffered these losses would be the achievement of agreement and peace (McAleese, 1997).

McAleese wants to create a presidency that "holds out a hand to victims." In an address to 2,500 disabled people in Dublin, she went to great lengths to show her empathy by recounting tales of her deaf brother and autistic cousin. McAleese's campaign managers squeezed a wheelchair into every photo call until foreign observers could be forgiven for thinking that half the Irish population was disabled (Walshe, 1997).

Continuous Learning

In her 1984 book, *Who's Who in Ireland: The Influential 1,000*, Maureen Cairnduff describes Prof. Mary McAleese as a "highly articulate, intelligent woman" and a "down to earth, approachable academic." During the 1997 elections, she was seen as having the training and experience to deal with the complex issues that face her as president.

In her speech to the IFTDO, she spoke of the importance of learning for global development. One of the key strategies of human resource development is to equip people to adapt to a changing, turbulent environment with confidence and self-assurance and to make use of the resources at their disposal. Meeting these developmental challenges requires an open, curious frame of mind and constant readiness to address new requirements. In her words, "Forging that curiosity into an energy, which drives effective change, calls for special people of rare insight and wisdom" (McAleese, 1998).

Leading Ireland into the Twenty-First Century

McAleese has a vision for Ireland and a burning desire to lead her nation toward that vision. In her words, "Ireland sits tantalizingly ready to embrace a golden age of affluence, self-assurance, tolerance, and peace. It will be my most profound privilege to be President of this beautiful, intriguing country. May I ask those of faith, whatever that faith may be, to pray for me and for our country that we will use these seven years well, to create a future where in the words of William Butler Yeats, 'Everything we look upon is blest.' "

Mary McAleese brings not only considerable intelligence and personal warmth to her role as president, but also a firm commitment to peace and reconciliation for all of Ireland. The President of Ireland has quickly become a model for public leadership in the twenty-first century.

CHAPTER ELEVEN

Cheong Choong Kong: Flying High with Singapore Airlines

In the late 1990s when most of Asia's airlines went into a financial tailspin, Singapore Airlines managed to not only survive but prosper. No wonder *Fortune* magazine chose Dr. Cheong Choong Kong, CEO of Singapore Airlines, as its 1998 Asian Businessman of the Year. While his excellent long-term financial performance certainly was a key factor in his selection, other less concrete capabilities, such as skillful management of people, willingness to take risks, appreciation for technology, and a clear global vision for the future were equally influential. Even though Cheong credits the entire SIA "team" for the company's impressive achievements over the years, he deserves the lion's share of the credit for his leadership of that team.

Professor, CEO, Actor—What Next?

Cheong, like many of today's leaders, has succeeded in more than one career. He served as an Associate Professor of Mathematics at the University of Malaya from 1968 until 1974, when he reportedly grew tired of his academic career and began looking for new challenges. His search led him to Singapore Airlines in 1974, two years after the company was formed from the original Malaysia-Singapore Airlines (*Singapore Airline Perspective*, 1999). As he progressed from his first position as an assistant manager of reservations, he got to know the company well, working in Personnel, Marketing, Planning, and Information Technology before becoming Managing Director in 1984 and Deputy Chairman and CEO in 1996.

Beyond his irrefutable abilities as a learned professor and shrewd businessman, he displays other unexpected skills and interests. His recreational interests include scuba diving, music (especially Italian opera), and good movies. He enjoyed acting in plays at the University of Malaya and has recently given movie acting a try. He appears in multiple roles—a priest, a stand-up comedian, a Chinese medicine shop owner, and a spiritual guru—in the film "Tiger's Whip," a comedy about an American porn star who comes to Singapore looking for a cure for his lost virility. Despite its seemingly risqué subject matter, it was tame enough to survive the formidable Singapore censors. Critics generally panned the film, and Cheong was not nominated for any Academy Awards for his performances. The film was one of the movie selections on SIA flights, however, and serves to remind us of the more human side of even the most serious business executive.

His sense of humor surfaces from time to time as well. In his acceptance speech for the *Fortune* magazine Asian Businessman of the Year award, he wryly noted, "So here I am, not a particularly pretty face like DiCaprio's but sufficient for the purpose." His comments about his acting "career" were equally light-hearted:

> So much has been said about my recent acting episode—even *Fortune* deemed it worthy of mention. How I wish, and how my producer must wish, that as many people had actually seen the movie as had talked about my acting in it! I cannot understand the commotion over a corporate figure being a part-time actor. After all, there are more natural actors in the corporate world, and far better ones, than in all of Tinseltown. (Cheong, 1999, January 21)

The High Flying Airline

Singapore Airlines has become synonymous with excellent customer service and financial success. In the words of Ian Wild, a regional airline analyst, "SIA stands head and shoulders above everyone else in the region" (Jayasankaran, 1999). Yet it is far more than a regional airline. Its route system covers 115 cities in 42 countries, including destinations served with alliance partners and cities served by SIA's regional airline, SilkAir. And its reputation is acknowledged throughout the world.

In a *Global Finance* survey (Best Hotels, 1998), business travelers picked Singapore Airlines (SIA) as the world's best airline, based on customer service, in-flight entertainment, and overall amenities. In the competition for best carrier in Asia, it also came in first, by a two-to-one margin over the number two choice, Cathay Pacific. The company was also ranked number one in the annual Review 200 survey in 1998, a spot it has occupied since 1993, when the rankings began. Companies in this survey are rated according to their focus, financial soundness, and service standards. In 1999 Singapore Airlines placed first in the annual Asia's Most Admired Companies survey, taking this coveted position for the fifth consecutive year.

And yet 1998 was a difficult year for the region and for SIA. In the midst of the Asian "meltdown," research analyst Lim Beng Eu predicted, "Singapore Airlines is going to find it's increasingly difficult and challenging to stay on top. No matter how well managed the airline, the impact of the regional turmoil will be felt." (Singapore Girl, 1998). Indeed, the company did experience declines along with the rest of the region. Net profits for the company lagged by 24% in the first half of the year, compared to the previous year, and revenues slipped 3.6% (Dolven, 1999). But its operating profit was $218.7 million on $2.2 billion in revenue for the period—a 10% profit margin and better than most U.S. airlines manage in good economic times (Nathan, 1999). It was the only Asian airline to post significant earnings during the Asian financial setback. Despite regional economic instability, SIA has expanded its holdings, built new alliances, and continued to invest. It is emerging from the Asian recession stronger than ever, in part because of its combination of strong cash reserves, focused business strategies, and the leadership of Cheong (Dolven, 1999).

How does SIA garner awards year after year? According to Jean-Louis Morisot, transport analyst for Goldman Sachs, SIA's frequency of flights, breadth of service, safety track record, quality of service, and profitability help explain its consistent performance. "They're innovative . . . they manage to stay one step ahead of everyone, constantly" (Hiebert, 1998).

Singapore Airlines, while a proud symbol of the economic success of this small island nation, is not a government-owned operation. Although state-owned Temasek Holdings owns a controlling 54% stake in SIA, the airline does not receive subsidies and is not protected against competition. Cheong and his management team are given free rein to run the airline.

Commitment to the Highest Quality of Service

Just as its CEO is a multifaceted individual, SIA has a unique corporate style, described by one writer as a "split personality." Despite flamboyant marketing campaigns and relatively open-handed spending for customer service, the company is otherwise conservative and hard-nosed (Kraar, 1999, p. 35). Perhaps it is this very dichotomy that explains the company's remarkable success in both good and difficult economic times.

Since its beginnings in 1972 as a small, insignificant carrier, SIA has soared to world-class stature in the airline industry. Cheong is widely credited with bringing about this transformation. By sticking with his long-term vision of SIA as a major international airline providing excellent service, he has succeeded in an industry where many others have failed.

Early on, Cheong described the keys to SIA's strategic plan to become a major, respected international airline: "service, growth, a commitment to free enterprise, and a willingness to make bold judicious investments" (*Singapore Airlines Perspectives*, 1999, p. 10) Cheong has promised that "Any airline that attempts to steal a march on us in the all-important area of customer service does so in the knowledge that his advantage can only be temporary" (Dolven, 1999).

Those bold investments have been particularly evident in marketing and customer service, which have helped secure SIA's reputation as a premium brand. Cheong explains, "In the early 70s we were starting as a very small carrier with only 10 planes. We built our reputation and our fortunes by doing things that were unheard of at the time, such as giving the passenger a cold towel as he boarded the aircraft, addressing the passenger in first class by his name, (and offering) free drinks and headsets in economy class. Thus a service culture evolved" (Sloan, 1998). Only 10 years after its emergence as an independent airline, SIA was ranked first in an Asian-Pacific survey in all categories: service and performance, esteem and preference, image, advertising recall, awareness, and familiarity.

The SIA fleet of aircraft exemplifies the company's focus on premium service and cost-effective operation. By 1977 it had built a fleet of seven 747s, three 727s, ten 707s and five 737s and ordered four DC10s. A year later it ordered ten more 747s and four 727s, at a cost of US$1 billion, the biggest single order ever made by an airline. Six Airbus A300s were ordered a year later. Such bold purchasing has continued over the years, giving SIA one of the youngest fleets in the world. What is the company's reason for such lavish spending on planes? As technology progresses, planes tend to consume less fuel and cost less to maintain, saving money in two of the most expensive categories of airline operating costs. More important, newer aircraft are more reliable, thus more punctual and more appealing to customers.

Cheong responded creatively to the Asian crisis, and his unconventional approach has paid off. During this period, the region saw significant drops in passenger volume and fare prices. But rather than retrench and cut back its flights and service, SIA took a totally different tack. It increased flights to America, Europe, India, and Australia and spent approximately $292 million upgrading service. As a result, it not only survived the recession but also won market share over other airlines operating in Asia (Jayasankaran, 1999). "Most passengers say they prefer Singapore Air even though it's expensive. They like its efficiency, punctuality and in-flight service," explains a senior ticketing officer at KenAir Travel Management Systems (Singapore Girl, 1998)

This refusal to cut back on service illustrates Cheong's ability to keep cool under pressure and remain focused on corporate priorities. "If you go back to the beginning, the early 1970's," he explains, "we made our reputation on our in-flight service. Even if we had known about the severity of the economic crisis, we would still have gone ahead with upgrading services. This is an investment in the product" (Bociurkiw, 1998). Cheong also urged other Asian airlines to continue to spend on the infrastructure necessary to the industry during the recession, noting that a decline in that area would be detrimental to growth in the region as a whole.

Innovation and Courage amid Crisis

The airline began a research and development effort at least a year prior to the Asian crisis, reviewing every aspect of travel experience in all three classes. First Class was remodeled to imitate the service traditions of luxury hotels. Employee escorts meet arriving customers at the curb and escort them to a comfortable reception lounge, where premium service staff members handle check-in formalities. Seats are covered in a supple leather supplied by the same company that outfits Rolls Royce and Ferrari. Seats can become beds, and an air mattress in the cushion inflates to provide maximum support and comfort when the seat is horizontal. Passengers receive a duvet and sleepwear, and on longer flights the crew adds a mattress and fresh bed linens to the seat. Meals are served at the customers' request and at their pace, as in a good restaurant. Dishes are served directly from the galley rather than on a trolley, along with fine vintage wines.

In Raffles (named after the world-famous hotel in Singapore) or business class, seats are wider and there is more room between rows than in any other airline with three classes. The seats offer electric footrests, leg rests, lumbar support, and adjustable headrests, so that passengers of various heights and dimensions can get comfortable. Seats are wider and higher, with privacy dividers between them, and power outlets are provided for laptop computers. Passengers arriving in Singapore also have seven days complimentary use of a cell phone. In economy, a personal video monitor is standard as well as a personal phone, improved neck supports in the headrests, and a choice of ethnic and international dishes—and Heidsieck champagne flows freely.

This approach is the opposite of what most other airlines have done when faced with financial problems. Delta, for example, went through an earnings slump in the early 1990s. The company cut 15,000 jobs and about 16% of its operating costs. The result was a return to record profit levels, but it lost its hard-earned reputation for excellent service and employee morale dropped precipitously. "We have a reputation for service that we believe is unrivaled, and we want to keep it that way, so we must be ready to invest," says Cheong (Nathan, 1999). Explains one analyst, "Singapore Airlines has always been a success story in branding. Its reputation as a well-managed airline company has been further boosted by its solid financial structure, which has enabled it to seek expansion through acquisition at a time when many other Asian airlines are retrenching" (Leung and Jordan, 1999).

While almost extravagant when spending on improvements to its service to customers, the company is fiscally conservative. The airline's expansion in Asia and on Western routes has been "organic, not debt-driven." Planes were purchased, for example, from cash flow, not through new debt. In fact, Cheong has always been a stickler for careful cost management. "Over the last eight years," he notes, "we've doubled the number of passenger kilometers we fly. But staff numbers have hardly moved. That's why retrenchment was never an option" (Jayasankaran, 1999). "We're emerging from this crisis better than the others because we have always been lean" (Nathan, 1999). "We don't swing into a cost-cutting mode only when times get tough" (Kraar, 1999).

Even in the midst of cutting expenses, the airline ordered five jets from Airbus to be delivered in 2002. This will make it the first regional airline to be able to fly Southeast Asia-North America routes nonstop. Despite immediate difficulties brought on by the recession, SIA could not afford to lose sight of its reputation and future needs. With a capitalization of $20 billion, zero debt, and cash reserves of S$1.6, it has "the best balance sheet in the industry," according to an aviation analyst with Goldman Sachs (Jayasankaran, 1999).

Beyond investments in the fleet and cabin amenities, Cheong understands that employees can make or break an airline's reputation for service. He relies on peer pressure among employees to keep quality high. The employees, not the bosses, are the first to criticize those who don't pull their own weight. The company monitors service closely—how long customers have to wait to check in, how often phones ring before being answered. Flight attendants are evaluated four times per year. Cheong describes his philosophy of customer service:

> We can be more efficient with computers and other forms of higher technology, but ultimately it is the human touch—that personal warmth—that wins friends and impresses people. This human touch must have, as its source, a genuine care for the welfare and comfort of the customer. We can show the customer that we care in many ways—a friendly nod of acknowledgement, a question, an expression of concern, an offer of assistance. Many of our customers will not need our assistance, but they will feel good knowing that someone in SIA cares. This is what outstanding service is all about. (*Singapore Airlines Perspectives,* 1999)

Small wonder that the airline won 23 awards for its service from international tourism groups in 1998 and continues to be singled out for its accomplishments.

Commitment to Learning and Training

When it comes to learning, Cheong leads by example. He holds a BSc with first class honors in Mathematics from the University of Adelaide (1963) and a PhD in Mathematics from the Australian National University in Canberra. As noted previously, he also spent six years in academia as a professor. In March 1999 he was granted a Distinguished Alumni Award from the University of Adelaide for his "sustained and distinguished service to management and communication, especially in Singapore," and he has been active in University of Adelaide alumni activities in Singapore and Adelaide.

To attain its high levels of customer service and safety, Cheong has not pinched pennies when it comes to investments in employee training and development. The company values all kinds of learning, from technical, job-specific training to management and executive development. Cheong sees training as important for everyone from the baggage handler to the managing director, whether the individual is based in Singapore or elsewhere, whether the individual is young or old. Its flight attendants, the well-known "Singapore Girls," are trained over four months, while most Western airlines settle for two months of training. Their skills range from handling emergencies in the air to explaining and correctly serving fine wines. Senior staff benefit from executive development programs from top institutions worldwide—Harvard, MIT, and others.

In fact, learning is central to SIA's corporate culture and beliefs. Cheong notes the fundamental importance of training at SIA: "Training is a necessity, not an option." SIA does not cut or postpone training when the going gets rough. In fact, during hard times, he believes that training is even more important. And he admonishes managers that deferring scheduled training of a subordinate because he needs to be working on a project is a sign of poor planning on the manager's part (*Singapore Airlines Perspectives*, 1999).

While not wasteful, SIA uses the best in training software and hardware that money can buy. Training is structured, yet flexible enough to adapt to changing market and economic conditions. And training is designed to produce not only competent workers but well-rounded people attuned to their environment. A central SIA Training Centre brings together people from many different parts of the airline's operations to learn from one another, better understand the diverse functions within the organization, and build stronger team bonds among employees.

Part of the company's success stems from its homegrown culture. Local flight schools and training programs make SIA an attractive career choice for many Singaporeans. The majority of SIA employees are Singaporean, including two thirds of its cabin crew and most of its senior management (Jayasankaran, 1999).

Global Mindset

Recognizing the need to remain adaptable in a global and ever-changing business environment, Cheong focuses on anticipating global changes rather than putting out day-to-day fires. This global viewpoint is crucial to SIA's continued success. As he explains, "We've recognized for quite a while our vulnerability if we remained a company based exclusively in Singapore. Because of the scarcity of resources on this small island, we will experience cost pressures" (Kraar, 1999). Over the years the company has diversified its markets to avoid reliance on any one area. During the economic downturn, other Asian competitors were hit much harder because of their regional focus. SIA was able to move resources from badly hit regions to the United States, Europe, and Australia.

Cheong emphasizes the need to remain flexible. In late October 1998, while the region was still in economic doldrums, he explained to his employees: "We don't know whether the worst is over. The experts themselves are divided. Our method is not to predict when the turnaround will occur, but to retain the flexibility to move quickly whenever the tide turns" (Kraar, 1999). One of the reasons SIA can react quickly to change is its ready store of cash.

Not only does SIA retain substantial cash reserves, its wholly-owned fleet provides another source of cash through sales or leases.

Global Alliances

Keenly aware of the latest trends in aviation worldwide, Cheong recognizes the integral role alliances play in any large airline's strategic development. A global alliance provides marketing advantages to its members. It can also provide passengers a seamless route network that enables them to complete a journey on several airlines using one ticket. Partners can enhance their competitiveness by combining buying power to reduce costs and can reduce excess capacity by combining routes. And yet SIA has been slow to enter the alliance game, a "wallflower" as others rushed to join hands. But the company is still looking around, and it has the funds to invest. Explains Cheong, "We do not enter an alliance, nor withdraw from one, lightly" (Singapore sees stars, 1998).

In its prudent, selective way, SIA has begun its move into the alliance arena. The company expanded capacity 40% on flights to Frankfurt after it formed an alliance with Germany's Lufthansa in 1998 (Nathan, 1999). It has formed alliances with Ansett Australia, Ansett International, and Air New Zealand and has signed Memoranda of Understanding with South African Airways and Air Canada. In June 1999 SIA and United Airlines formed a strategic bilateral alliance, allowing customers of both carriers to build up and redeem frequent flyer program miles and providing convenient one-stop check-in service for flights involving both airlines. SIA has also been negotiating an equity stake in China Airlines of Taiwan and most likely will be looking to the Taiwanese company to improve its safety record to keep SIA's image intact. SIA holds minority stakes in Delta and Swissair, which it acquired to bolster an earlier alliance that did not work out.

Cheong's ultimate plan is to use SIA's strong financial position to build the company into a group of global airlines and related companies. He would like to eventually generate 20%-30% of revenues from activities outside Singapore (the percentage is currently insignificant). SIA has begun acquiring or partnering with businesses with larger profit margins than its own. It owns aircraft maintenance operations in China, Hong Kong, and Taiwan and participates in a joint venture with Pratt and Whitney to overhaul jet engines for airlines worldwide. Its ground-handling subsidiary has invested in eleven other companies in Asian airports.

Servant Leader Who Encourages Teamwork

Often described in terms such as *humble* and *unassuming,* Cheong operates within an egalitarian framework. Unlike most executives, he occupies a small, unpretentious office at headquarters, itself a simple concrete building next to a maintenance hangar at the Singapore Airport. And it is not unusual to find him flying economy class on his own airline.

Cheong sets an example that his employees clearly respect and emulate. SIA's executives forego the standard corporate perks—stock options, free parking spaces, an executive dining room. At the lowest point of the Asian recession, Cheong and his managers voluntarily gave up their annual salary increase, leading most of SIA's 27,000 employees to follow suit (Kraar, 1999).

Cheong champions teamwork. He establishes clear goals and expects his subordinates to fulfill them with the least possible interference by management. Operations at SIA are transparent—everyone in the company is informed about the company's financial standing and progress (Kraar, 1999). Internal discussions and debate are encouraged. His humility and belief in team efforts are perhaps best illustrated by his acceptance speech when receiving the *Fortune* magazine 1998 Asian Businessman of the Year award: "I'll not make the customary statement on how humbling this experience is, but I will say that I'm terribly embarrassed. How do you accept personal credit for what is truly a collective effort? . . . In accepting this award, I'm under no illusion that I've earned it. . . . This award belongs rightly to my team, of whom I am immeasurably proud" (Kraar, 1999). He is quick to give credit to other executives on his management team, as well, for being the true leaders of the organization.

Technology to Serve the Customer

Cheong sees technological change, both in the air and on the ground, as one of the most significant forces in the industry today and in the future. He predicts that aircraft will continue to get faster and larger and fly longer distances, while costs per passenger or per ton of cargo decrease. Airlines, passengers, and the environment will benefit from the satellite-based Communications and Navigation System (CNS) which enables pilots to fly more direct routes at optimum altitudes. This equates to shorter travel time, less fuel consumption, and more accurate tracking of aircraft.

Technology makes flights more fun for the passengers as well. Advanced in-flight entertainment includes improvements such as individual video screens with numerous channels and video games, news updates, and even electronic blackjack and poker. Although currently reserved for first- and business-class, audio-and-video-on-demand provides even more choices for passengers, and live TV feeds and access to the Internet will be the norm in the future. Electronic ticketing, internet reservations, smart cards, and self-service check-in are all technology-based advances that make flying more pleasant for the customer and reduce the need for manpower, which is difficult to recruit in labor-scarce Singapore.

Perhaps the greatest barrier to technological change has been regulatory. According to Cheong, the regulatory climate worldwide has been slow to catch up to the dramatic structural and technological advances in the airline industry: "It's a bit like owning the latest Ferrari Testarossa and trying to drive it on roads, and under road rules, designed for Henry Ford's Model T" (*Singapore Airlines Perspectives*, 1999, p. 130).

Leader for the Second Century of Flying

From the Wright brothers' clumsy, two-winged plane to sophisticated jets, the growth of air travel during the twentieth century has been an amazing chapter in transportation history. No leader has had such an impact on the global airline industry as Cheong Choong Kong. We can be certain that leaders such as Dr. Cheong will continue to find new ways to make the twenty-first century even more exciting than the twentieth.

CHAPTER TWELVE

William Carris: Servant Leader of the Carris Community of Companies

William S. Brown

William H. (Bill) Carris, the dynamic owner and president of the Carris Financial Corporation of Rutland, Vermont, is a deeply self-effacing individual who is loath to talk about himself. He would much rather talk about his company's metamorphosis from an entrepreneurially owned and operated firm to an employee-owned company. In this sense, along with many others, he is not your typical entrepreneur-chief executive: "With his longish hair, flannel shirt and jeans, William Carris doesn't look like the typical President of an $83 million company. But little about Carris . . . is typical" (Daley, 1996b, p. A-1).

However reticent Carris may be to talk about himself, insights into the man can be gained by examining what he cares about. For years Carris (and his father before him) were known in the community for their discrete yet strong support of educational and social justice programs and of the arts. He is considered a dedicated volunteer and supporter of Dismas House, a recovery facility for former prisoners. He is also a member of the board of the College of Saint Joseph. And as a dyslexic, he is regarded as a role model for disabled students. Carris is widely known as a man who "walks the talk" concerning integrity, trust, and social concern. Given that, what follows in this chapter should not seem so surprising.

Carris Community of Companies

The company was founded in Rutland, Vermont, in 1951 as Carris Reels, Inc., by Henry Carris, father of the present owner, Bill Carris. The early company's principal business was the production of plywood reels of all sizes. Over the years the company grew from a two-employee operation to a viable and strong corporation. When Henry retired in 1980, his son Bill took over the leadership of the company. Bill Carris had spent many years working in all aspects of the company's operations preparing for this succession.

In the period of 1980–1996 Bill Carris began an aggressive growth strategy via the acquisition and start-up of a number of new divisions. These new divisions expanded the company to 775 employees and extended the product range beyond reels to include high-end furniture, shipping pallets, plastic tubes, and tin and bolts. During this time, company assets increased 664%, sales increased 415%, and the number of employees rose 372%. (Betit and Brown, 1998). The company, now called the Carris Financial Corporation (CFC), has operations in several Vermont locations, as well as Connecticut, North Carolina, California, Arizona, Indiana, Ohio, Michigan, and an international division headquartered in Seattle. Internally, the organization has adopted the name "The Carris Community of Companies" to reflect the strategic leadership initiative embarked upon by Carris and the employees of the company.

Tapping the Intelligence and Ideas of All Employees

"The answer with respect to the leadership issue is simple. Companies that take advantage of the intelligence and ideas of all their employees will be much more successful than those that rely on a few people to lead" (Carris, 1994, p. 5). This simple statement by Bill Carris describes the strategic thrust of the Carris Community of Companies. In doing this Carris hopes to build an organization that goes beyond being a business concern and moves into the realm of being a community. He hopes to accomplish this by building the values of trust, mutual respect, inclusion, employee participation, and lifelong learning in the corporate culture of this company.

Leadership Built on Sharing

Robert Reich, while Secretary of Labor, felt that old forms of leadership in the manufacturing sector of the U.S. economy created a situation where: "Workers don't feel a personal stake. Employees still regard the company as 'they'—perhaps benevolent, perhaps evil, but unambiguously on the other side of a psychological divide. The divide prevents them from investing very much of themselves in what they do every day" (Reich, 1997, p. 112). Carris is attempting to create a company where this is no longer the state of affairs. He is trying to build a company where trust, inclusivity, mutual respect, and participation are the active norms of behavior.

He is accomplishing his vision through an employee stock ownership plan (ESOP), which will transfer legal ownership of the companies to the employees, and through a structure that will support employee strategic governance. His rationale for this is a moral one:

> Legal owners are very willing to promote 'emotional' ownership because it clearly improves the performance of an organization and consequently, the value to the legal owner. As meaningful as emotional ownership is to the employee, however, legal ownership is what gives them their fair share of the fruits of their labors and control over the organization to which they devote so much "blood, sweat and tears." True devotion and loyalty to a company seem to be essential attributes of what ownership should be. Morally, such devotion should be complemented with legal ownership. (Carris, 1994, p. 6)

Carris's vision for employee ownership is laid out in his 1994 Long Term Plan (LTP). In addition to the moral arguments outlined above, Carris advances business reasons for the ESOP as well: "In a structure where all levels of employees have a voice in the distribution of wealth and the overall direction of the organization and see it as a vehicle to help them personally develop, they should be very interested in keeping the organization healthy" (Carris, 1994, p. 3).

The Mondragon Cooperatives of Basque, Spain, deeply influenced Carris's thinking in regard to employee ownership. These cooperatives, which are employee owned, produce most of the tools and appliances in Spain. They have consistently high productivity, and they are demonstrably more profitable than their competitors. In describing them, Robert L. Schwartz has said: "The Mondragon cooperatives are at once more effectively socialist than are doctrinaire socialists, and more militantly capitalist than a right-wing Republican. They take the best of both and create a wholly new economic reality" (Schwartz, 1984, p. 16). The collaborative environment of the cooperatives, with their strong emphasis on consensus, friendship, and profitability, resonated deeply with Bill Carris. (For more information on the Mondragon Cooperatives, see Mollner, 1991.)

The Carris Long Term Plan articulates a transition period of 10 to 15 years to full employee ownership, depending on the dynamics in the marketplace. There are several key differences between this plan and the usual ESOP. Perhaps most paramount, Carris is selling his company to the employees at a discounted price from the company's appraised value. Most ESOPs are designed by management and given to the employees as a *fait accompli* and usually are designated as a retirement plan. The Carris program differs markedly in this regard. Its intent is not as a retirement vehicle but rather to transfer ownership to the employees while they are still working at the company. Additionally, the plan was designed by a group employees called the Long Term Plan Steering Committee and will be managed by them. Furthermore, the annual allocation formula for the plan is nonhierarchical: 30% is divided among all eligible employees; 20% is allocated by seniority; and 50% is allocated by salary capped at a maximum of $30,000 adjusted annually for inflation. As of the end of 1995, employees owned 10% of the company, 20% as of the end of 1996, and 25.8% at the end of 1997. (For more information on the Carris ESOP, see Hahn, 1996; Skiffington, 1996; Daley, 1996a; Betit and Brown, 1998.)

Carris's stated objective is not just to sell the employees his company but to "teach the employees the business." Determined to have consensus-based, shared decision-making, Bill Carris brought together a group originally called the Long Term Plan Steering Committee. The LTP Steering Committee, now the Corporate Steering Committee (CSC), is made up of seven executives (including Carris) and one elected employee representative for every 50 employees (currently there are 34 representatives in the group). The CSC, via consensus decision making, administers the ESOP and sets the direction for the company toward its objective of 100% employee ownership. In explaining his approach to corporate governance, Carris says: "My feeling has long been that if employees own the company, they should be involved in the larger philosophical issues affecting it" (Daley, 1996a, p. A-10). Carris did insist on one feature in the design of the ESOP—that every employee-owner have one vote each in shareholder issues. The point behind this was to preclude the possibility that with time, decision making and the strategic direction of the company might become too conservative and risk-averse as more senior employees develop interests in the company.

Practicing Servant Leadership

In addition to the Mondragon Cooperatives mentioned earlier, the writings of Robert Greenleaf (1977, 1996) have been particularly influential on Carris's thinking. Of special significance is the concept of the leader as servant. Greenleaf attributes the origin of the leader as servant concept to his reading of Herman Hesse's *Journey to the East,* wherein the protagonist discovers a great and noble leader whom he first knew as a servant (see chapter 2). Max De Pree, chairman and CEO of the Herman Miller Furniture Company, Inc., expands on Greenleaf's concept of servant leadership. He calls it the art of liberating people to do what is required of them in the most humane and effective way available. In this manner the leader is the "servant" of the followership by removing obstacles that inhibit job performance and facilitating the realization of individual potential.

Carris has spoken quite clearly on his perspectives regarding leadership: "The most effective organizations are those that strive to find ways to generate and process . . . knowledge in practical, efficient ways. This will happen when employees are owners and we move from a 'monarch-type' leadership to where everyone participates in decision making" (Carris, 1994, p. 5). Besides this, he says, "One other benefit of moving away from being an organization led by a monarch is that a healthy organization does not owe its values and success to one individual. . . . Our leadership and governance approach must be one that encourages people to participate as owners and prevents any one individual from defining the goals and values of the organization" (Carris, 1994, p.5).

Creating a Visionary Organization

Collins and Porras (1991, 1996) distinguish between organizational vision and visionary organizations. They argue that visionary organizations are preferable to simple organizational vision in that visionary organizations have the capability to articulate, in vivid and descriptive language, the core values and beliefs that define not only a mission but also an organizational purpose. The role of top leadership in helping to focus attention on organizational purpose as a key strategic activity is also endorsed by Bartlett and Ghoshal (1994). They argue that this is accomplished through giving meaning to employees' work and by developing the potential of employees. By articulating the purpose of the company demonstrably and clearly, employees commit to the journey, thus moving the organization from a mere economic entity to a social institution.

Bill Carris is committed to building this type of organization. He writes, "For the longest time, I have had a faded, ragged piece of paper taped to the bookcase in my office. It reads: To improve the quality of life for our growing corporate community." Broadening this, Carris states,

> The employee-owned and governed company structure will enable individuals to solve their own problems by providing some powerful tools:
>
> — Security (profit)
>
> — Power (resources, money)

— Opportunity (education, services)

— Desire (new emphasis on improving their lives and the lives of others). (Carris, 1994, pp. 1–2)

Respect and Trust for All Partners

Kuhn and Shriver (1991) assert that the nature of relationships between business and its constituents has changed. They argue that the new constituencies of the corporate social responsibility movement (employees, suppliers, consumers, investors, etc.) open opportunities for partnerships that not only advance the economic well being of the business, but also enhance the quality of life for the constituents. These partnerships, they say, should be predicated on values of mutual respect, trust, caring, and cooperation. A key ingredient of trust and successful leadership is credibility, according to Kouzes and Posner (1993).

Among the many values that Carris has articulated to the CFC employees, trust and credibility rank high on his list. In his words, trust "has to be the major component of good communication and the ability to get things done. It is the result of honesty, openness and willingness. Trust is important enough to warrant working on it from both a formal, organizational level (i.e., classes, workshops, etc.) as well as on a personal basis" (Carris, 1994, p. 9).

Trust is one aspect of what Carris calls the spiritual realm of an organization. Other domains of the spiritual organization that Carris identifies include caring and enthusiasm, compassion and empathy, charity, the encouragement of goodness, and the exposure of evil. The guiding rubric in all of this is the golden rule: "Even though it is an impossible over-simplification, if there is one principle to live by, it is the golden rule. This rule applies to the individual and corporation alike" (Carris, 1994, p. 9).

The emotional organization is another domain that Carris discusses with the employees. Trust figures prominently here as well, but other values of importance include fairness, tolerance, personal growth, individuality, and motivation.

Organizational and Individual Learning

Senge (1990) defines a learning organization as one that continually expands its capacity to create its future. The Carris company is accomplishing this not only through the transition to employee ownership but also through a vigorous program of training and personal development. As Carris once noted, "The winners of the next decade will be those companies who have more people processing more information and making better decisions faster. These will be the companies that stay ahead of the market."

Thus, a standard feature of all company meetings is continuous learning. This is the follow-through on Carris's pledge to "teach employees the business. The company is training employees in the skills that will be needed in order for them to participate in the day-to-day running of the business. Classes are currently offered in listening, building trust, giving and receiving feedback, and coaching. Eventually classes will be offered in how to read and interpret financial statements and in the rights and responsibilities of stock ownership" (Hahn, 1996, p. 23). Additionally, "the Carris group has sponsored personal development programs ranging from literacy and math skills workshops, to stress management seminars and classes to introduce or improve on computer skills" (Skiffington, 1996, p. 24). Perhaps the most intriguing program of personal development is the Full Circle Program, described in the next section.

Part of the commitment to employee ownership at Carris is to teach the employees the business. Personal growth and individual learning are deeply ingrained in the culture at Carris: "This company is about personal growth. Whether it is growth in job responsibility, pay, education or psychological and spiritual growth, we need to encourage it all! Along with growth within the company, we need to make every effort to promote personal growth when we bring new people into the organization" (Carris, 1994, p. 12).

Global Service

When the Full Circle Travel Seminars, organized and hosted by the Center for Global Education at Augsburg College in Minnesota, came to Carris's attention, he recognized congruity with the espoused values of the Long Term Plan. Through Full Circle Travel Seminars, "participants leave home, reflect on themes central to home life (justice and security issues, what it takes to provide the minimum conditions of life, nurturance and survival), and return home to a place that is at once both familiar and newly strange" (Daley, 1996b, p. A-10).

Each month the names of two interested employees are drawn by lottery (with no consideration given to seniority or rank within the company), and those employees are sent on multiweek travel-learning sabbaticals. Employees have traveled to Guatemala, South Africa, Nicaragua, Namibia, Mexico, and Honduras. Upon return, employees share their experiences through interviews and articles in the corporate newspaper. Many employees have, upon return, described their experiences as life-changing.

Carris encourages employees to participate in the program because: "We believe a program like this not only empowers employees in their own life and their work, it also makes you a world citizen" (Daley, 1996b, p. A-10). His desire is that the program will "evolve into more volunteer kinds of projects, both in our local community and distant places" (Daley, 1996b). The cultural diversity awareness taught in the Full Circle Program is directly transferable to the workplace. As Carris has said: "Because the world is comprised of a diverse group of people, we should be able to understand and adapt to living and working in this diverse world. A rich mix of people in our organization brings with it a wide range of experience, ideas and cultures, which will, in turn, contribute to our greater mobility, flexibility and success" (Carris, 1994, p. 14).

Improving the Quality of Life for the Workplace and the Community

As articulated in the company mission statement, the goal of this strategic leadership initiative is "to improve the quality of life for our growing corporate community" and "to change a job, a workplace, a company, to a vocation, an extended family, a community" (Carris Corporate Community Mission Statement, 1997). It is a deeply ethical leadership style that is rooted in Carris's desire "to contribute toward effecting a change in the inequities and unfairness with which our society deals its cards." In the final analysis, he wants to create "a right to share wealth, to manage our daily work, to ultimately be in control of our lives" (Carris, 1994, p. 7).

CHAPTER THIRTEEN

Nobuyuki Idei: Bridging Electronics and Entertainment at Sony

Nobuyuki Idei, a multilingual, cosmopolitan marketing star, has created banner years for Sony since his surprise appointment as CEO in 1995. Sales of Sony televisions, Walkmans, and PlayStations are climbing; its once moribund movie division is on the move; and the company enjoyed a record $51.1 billion in sales and $1.6 billion in profits in 1998. It is poised for continued growth, and the market has taken notice. Since Idei became president, Sony's stock has doubled. Little wonder then that *Fortune* selected Idei as its first Asian Businessman of the Year in January 1998.

As *Fortune*'s editors noted, "It's painfully clear 1997 wasn't a year that produced a lot of business heroes in Asia. Many of the people who were riding high during the economic miracle took unprecedented blows, and some even went down for the count. That said, a handful of Asian executives demonstrated the courage to make big, smart bets. One name particularly stands out: Sony President Nobuyuki Idei" (Schlender, 1998).

The Surprise Choice to Lead Sony

In 1994, even as it was celebrating its 50th anniversary, Sony was facing an uncertain future. Sales had been weak for four years, and its strongest markets, televisions and stereos, were saturated. The company needed a new vision and a global manager who could take the lead in the increasingly complex digital marketplace.

Nobuyuki Idei, a lifelong Sony employee, took up the challenge. Idei started work in 1960, fresh out of Waseda University. His selection as President and COO in April 1995 came as a grand surprise, as he bypassed a dozen successful Sony executives with nicknames like "Mr. Walkman," "Mr. Semiconductor," and "Mr. Camcorder," proof of their pivotal roles in earlier Sony triumphs.

Idei is not what many experts would consider a typical Japanese executive. The son of an economics professor, he studied European history in college, and has held a number of marketing positions in Europe and Japan. In a land that values conformity, he personifies nonconformity. He drives a British-built Jaguar, speaks fluent English and French, and is said to be a movie enthusiast and a whiz at computer games, especially those played on Sony's PlayStation. Colleagues describe him as sophisticated, yet approachable, resourceful, and innovative.

Despite his marketing background, rather than a more traditional engineering base, Idei is a "corporate jack-of-all-trades." During his long stint at Sony, he has worked in key divisions at home and internationally. His goal now is to introduce his more cosmopolitan approach to Sony and make his personal mark. And he has proven that he is willing to break with tradition when necessary to openly scold fellow executives who have questioned his way of doing things (Palmer, 1996).

Sony Corporation—The Most Respected Brand Name in the World

According to a recent Lou Harris poll, Sony, not McDonald's or Coca-Cola or Marlboro, is the most respected and recognized brand name in the world. When it comes to electronic gear of all kinds, Sony sets the global standard for quality. Whether it is Trinitron televisions, Walkman stereo sets, or PlayStation game machines, Sony has a sterling reputation that allows the company to command a premium price—its products often sell at prices 15% higher than rival brands (Palmer, 1996). Sony also makes dozens of other products, including DVD players, batteries, cameras, computer monitors, flat screen televisions and telephones. Headquartered in Tokyo, the company has over 170,000 employees worldwide.

Sony's entertainment assets include Columbia TriStar Motion Picture Group and record labels Columbia and Epic. "Men in Black" is just one of a string of hits that has enabled its movie division to fly past $1 billion in U.S. box-office sales in record time. Its record division continues to churn out profits, even though the industry as a whole has been slow. Sony's PlayStation game player has blown away Nintendo, accounting for 10% of Sony's worldwide sales. And Sony sells over $25 billion a year of audio-video equipment. Results like these reflect the remarkable strategic and cultural overhaul of this $50+ billion company.

Sony's Need for a New Leader with a New Vision

Perhaps Idei's most immediate and daunting challenge is to equip the 50-year-old Sony for the next century. He has his eye on winning over a new generation of "digital dream kids," the new breed of young managers who expect a new corporate culture that is needed to flourish in the fast-paced, constantly changing world of electronics and entertainment. As Sony Chairman Ohga explains, "Right now, you don't need to be an engineer. You have to have a nose, and if you don't, you can't run a company like Sony" (Gibney, 1997).

Strategically, Sony is plunging into the digital market. It has little choice. Sony first made its name by building a series of innovative electronic devices—the transistor radio, the Walkman, Trinitrons—that took advantage of advances such as miniaturization. While it continues to make profits on items like Walkmans, its niche products are quickly moving to the digital language of computers.

Idei believes that the analog audio and visual electronics arena, in which Sony made its name, will rapidly be superseded by the digital world, a new arena with even faster cycles of change. "We have to react faster and make faster decisions," says Idei, "and without losing our creativity" (Palmer, 1996). Digital technology has propelled the electronics business to light speed. Sony must compete with computer giants like Compaq and IBM in the race to develop software, engage in complex battles over copyrights and industry standards in the entertainment business, and construct alliances and joint ventures before its rivals step in.

From Sony's vantage point, the home PC is at the center of a wide-scale convergence of the multimedia entertainment world. An electronic revolution is beginning to fuse televisions, DVD players, stereos, and computers, not to mention phone lines, cable, cellular, and satellite systems, plus Hollywood film libraries and the Internet. Japan's makers of television sets, compact-disc players, game machines, and other home entertainment equipment have long worried about America's personal-computer industry escaping from the office into the home. As Sony executive Stringer explains, "All of us are in a battle with Bill Gates for the living room" (Gibney, 1997). Idei is quick to point out that it is not so much a question of wanting to get into this game as not being able to afford to stay out (Young, 1997).

It is easy to understand why the Japanese are worried. PCs sit on half of all office desks and in one third of the homes in advanced countries, and hardware and software companies have begun targeting the 95% of households that watch television. Gateway 2000 and Compaq have already launched PCs with large screens that can double as television sets. Every year Microsoft's Windows software adds more entertainment functions, while the company expands its market into ever smaller, cheaper machines. Even giant chipmaking king Intel has become a big investor in Hollywood (Boot Up, 1997).

In its quest for new ventures, Sony's first step has been to turn as many as possible of its existing analog products into digital ones. This move has already begun to pay off, since digital models often can be sold for more, while costing less to make. Another solution has been for Sony to make personal computers with Intel, Netsurfing hardware for Microsoft's WebTV, and cell phones and pagers with San Diego–based Qualcomm. Sony factories are pouring out a wave of digital products, from high-resolution videodiscs and video-game machines to passport-size video and still cameras that plug into a PC.

Idei's quest is to combine Japan's technical magic with America's creative flair to reinvent Sony as the preeminent global multimedia entertainment company, "something," says Idei, "like a Disney or Time Warner with our manufacturing base in Japan." That means bridging the technology and enter-tainment worlds, not to mention the cultural chasm between Japan and America. Ultimately, Idei is striving to create a global wireless network, a world in which satellite communications would bring interactive entertainment to ev-ery living room and den. "Convergence is happening not only between audio and video but between computers and communication," he explains. "There is a fundamental change in society, and this is our opportunity" (Gibney, 1997).

Systems Thinking for Sony

During the 1970s and 1980s, Sony saw its market slip and stock prices fall. Since his appointment as president, Idei has moved aggressively to reverse this trend, in many cases countering decisions made by Sony cofounder Akio

Morita and his protege, Chairman Norio Ohga. Idei's ability to challenge worn-out strategies and direct the company in new directions has been paramount in one of Japan's most remarkable corporate turnarounds. "Sony is a classic turnaround situation," says Jim Coxon at Kemper. "Investors have missed the real story. This is a company that has gotten over its difficulties and is going to do much better in coming years" (Palmer, 1996).

One of Idei's first big changes after taking over was to split the unwieldy AV Company, one of its internal "companies within a company," and create an additional enterprise, IT Company. He arranged for all three U.S. operations to report directly to him and approved the reorganization of U.S. consumer operations.

He also engineered a radical reworking of the board. In May 1997 he trimmed the Sony board from 38 to 10, including three outside directors, with more outsiders to come. And he announced that executives' pay would be tied to the bottom line. According to Idei, "What we need now is a good operating system, a good application system and a good management team." He established an executive board, which he chairs, to oversee global corporate strategy.

He has also reworked the entire corporate structure, including taking charge of the board that supervises the 10 companies that make up Sony. He holds more concentrated executive power as a result. In his words, "We have to establish more modern management systems with greater central management controls to prevent the kind of things happening that led to our earnings downturn, and that's the reason I have more people reporting now directly to me" (Palmer, 1996).

While engineers rush to bring out new, innovative technology, Idei has been building new business alliances as well. Besides dealing with Intel, he is negotiating with Microsoft. In 1997, Microsoft paid $425 million for WebTV Networks Inc., an Internet software provider that uses Sony hardware. IBM's Lou Gerstner could be a key partner in shaping a future DVD format. Through Idei's personal connections with Rupert Murdoch, Sony announced it would cooperate with News Corp., Fuji Television Network, and Softbank (the Japanese company that owns Ziff-Davis and the COMDEX computer shows), in a venture to start JSkyB, a 150-channel satellite broadcasting service in Japan.

Sony's grand plans have been met with some skepticism in both the United States and Japan. "That doesn't mean there is a clear picture of where they are going," says Koichiro Chiwata, a Tokyo-based analyst for Salomon Brothers. "But Sony is the only company we can trust to do something about it. That may be a strong statement but people have faith in this company. They have shown they can change lifestyles before, and more important, they are not afraid to change themselves" (Hamilton, 1997).

Idei has developed a four-point strategy to systematically and synergistically take Sony into the twenty-first century:

1.　Offer state-of-the-art technology and service.

2.　Leverage the Sony brand name.

3.　Leverage strong retailer relationships.

4.　Build on Sony's broad strength in PC components and manufacturing.

One computer manufacturing executive said that Sony wisely understood that the key to winning the game-machine sweepstakes was winning over many software developers who write the games. Kids will buy the machines with the best games. Developers preferred Sony's CD-ROM format because it could hold more data. And Sony reduced the payments that game developers must make to hardware companies for each game sold.

Sony's VAIO is spearheading the company's long-term attempt to corner a piece of the multimedia home computer market. "The next growth market is digital imaging for PCs," says one Tokyo analyst. "And connecting digital cameras and computers is one of Sony's biggest strengths."

Since its inception, Sony has constantly created markets and proposed new lifestyles. The Sony mission is to "offer the opportunity to create and fulfill dreams to all kinds of people, including shareholders, customers, employees, and business partners. We pledge to continue to take on the challenge of preserving Sony's position as a unique and creative company" (Sony, 1998).

Becoming a Global Company

Despite its global presence, Idei admits that Sony remains a "purely Japan" company. Idei is resolved to bring younger, worldlier Japanese managers up through the ranks. Change will not come easily, however. As one observer notes, "Sony is steeped in tradition, which means seniority rules, and promotion still comes hard through the company's typically bloated management ranks" (Gibney, 1997).

Taken together, Idei's steps have restored Sony in many analysts' minds to its status as trailblazer for corporate Japan and the entire consumer electronics world. "I believe that Sony is the first truly global company to be able to offer hardware electronics, software content and distribution services" (Sugawara, 1997).

To better implement this mission, in June 1997, Idei drastically altered the composition of the Board of Directors and established the new position of corporate executive officer. This move was made to reinforce corporate governance by speeding up decision-making, making management more efficient, and clarifying the responsibilities of managers. The Board of Directors is now much smaller and includes more external directors. Additionally, the new management system separates individuals responsible for policy-making and oversight from those who are responsible for operational management. Through these steps, Sony is assembling a quality management system and infrastructure that is both efficient and capable of swiftly adapting to global change.

Creating a New Culture of Innovation and Risk-Taking

Japan's corporations, for all their technical expertise, tend to be slow-moving giants. Managers lean to the conservative side and are accustomed to consensus, not exactly the recipe for creativity in today's markets. In Japan, loyalty and longevity remain the paths to advancement. To compete in the fast-footed digital world, Sony needs to be more agile, more aggressive, and more American (Gibney, 1997). Many analysts credit record profits and sales in recent years to Idei's action-oriented style, a departure from the deliberate, rule-by-consensus approach of conventional Japanese management.

Idei expects Sony to be a world leader in innovation. As he explains, "It's a new world, and I'm the trigger man for change. We need new management styles to meet new challenges. We are out to rejuvenate the company's existing core businesses, get new growth from the mix of software and hardware, and create entire new operations" (Palmer, 1996).

As he was struggling to rebuild Sony America at one point, he realized that his reorganization efforts could not stop there. "The problems with Sony America were not just American," says Idei. "They were a mirror of the Japanese company." The advice of General Electric's Jack Welch and Eastman Kodak's George Fisher led Idei to realize that he had to set off a management revolution at Sony. For one thing, he adopted the American concept of "corporate governance"— the notion that the board of directors is supposed to represent the shareholders, not management. And changes continue. Declares Idei, with a hint of defiance: "Many Americans think the Japanese won't change, but we are. The government is changing; the companies are changing" (Gibney, 1997).

At the same time, Idei remains somewhat ambivalent about just how far he wants to take the lessons of American business culture. For example, he believes that corporate America, especially in the entertainment arena, still pays its executives too much for nothing. And he perceives that American companies often just do a deal, rather than staking an honest claim to new technology (Gibney, 1997). If Sony can combine politics and dealmaking with its legendary technological expertise, then instead of scrambling to react to digital convergence, Sony will be in a position to lead the move into every living room on the globe.

Some skeptics wonder whether Sony should be forging off into new highly competitive areas, such as satellite broadcasting. But Idei said he sees little risk in the satellite-broadcasting venture, noting that "from Sony's point of view, entering the field of digital satellite broadcasting will add the distribution element to our global strategy of supplying hardware electronics and software content."

Among its most recent developments, Sony has entered the telemedicine market with new videoconferencing systems. Building on its expertise in medical imaging and audio and video communications technology, Sony is marketing three new rollabout and desktop systems that will enable the "delivery of face-to-face, interactive medical care and education through the use of state-of-the-art communication and computer technology. Collaborative medical care has been elevated to unprecedented levels as a result of these new innovations" (Sony, 1998).

Regaining the Pioneering Spirit of Learning

During his first few months as CEO, Idei frequently urged Sony staff members to "find ways once again to capture the original pioneering spirit of our founders." He focused Sony's attention and resources on a digital future, an era in which traditional consumer electronic products would converge with computers and communications technology.

As a leader, Idei has always been willing and anxious to learn new things. He sought advice on the computer business from Intel's chief executive, Andrew Grove; on the movie business from media mogul Rupert Murdoch; and on the digital world from Masayoshi Son, head of Softbank Corp., a fast-growing Japanese Internet company. He has since done major deals with all three— getting Intel's help in entering the PC business and joining Murdoch and Son in a satellite broadcast service in Japan (Sugarawa, 1997).

Over the past half-century, Sony has had its Edsels—the electric seat warmer or the electric rice cooker, for example, the latter placed for all to see in the company's Tokyo museum. But there have been many more hits than flops, and that's likely to continue to be true, given the potential for the DVD, the PlayStation, HDTV, and the PC. Just as the company still has vocal fans in American consumers, it seems a fair bet Sony will soon restore its appeal to American investors, spurring new interest in the stock. "I don't talk the past,

I just talk the future," says Idei. "We have weak points but I am working on them. My staff and I are quick learners. We are going to make the restructuring and new products of Sony work."

Ethics and the Environment

When it comes to global corporate environmental standards, Sony stands above the crowd. Recognizing that environmental protection is one of the most pressing issues facing mankind today, Sony incorporates a sound respect for nature in all of its business activities. Its policies reflect this focus:

1. The Sony Group will form and maintain an organization that can promote a variety of environmental protection activities.

2. The Group will establish technically and economically viable environmental objectives and constantly seek to enhance the quality of its conservation activities.

3. Group companies will observe all applicable laws, regulations and agreements related to the environment. Moreover, the Group will create autonomous standards for even more effective environmental protection.

4. The Group will pursue improvements in all areas of operations, including resource and energy conservation, recycling, and the reduction of waste.

5. To the fullest extent possible, the Group will adopt alternative technologies and materials in place of environmentally-harmful processes and materials, such as ozone-depleting substances, greenhouse gases and other pollutants. The Group will also collect and recycle such substances and take other steps to minimize their use.

6. The Group will make products and develop technologies that minimize environmental impact.

7. Through environmental audits, the Group will continually endeavor to upgrade its environmental management capabilities.

8. The Group will contribute to society through community activities related to the environment.

9. Through education and internal communications, the company will strive to instill a better understanding of its environmental policy and raise awareness of environmental issues among all employees.

10. As required, Sony will publicly disclose information on its development of environmental technologies, materials and products as well as its environmental management activities.

Sony has established regional environmental centers in North America, Europe, and Asia. Through this infrastructure, the company engages in conservation activities on a global scale. The more than 170,000 people who make up the Sony Group worldwide represent a tremendous resource for achieving environmental goals, and Sony actively supports their efforts. The company works to keep awareness of these goals high among its people. In addition to educational programs, employees in administration are given specific targets for recycling and other activities, an environmental fund supports numerous initiatives, and grants are distributed. Equally important, group companies support employee contributions to worthy causes outside of work.

"Green" purchasing guidelines for overseas operations include:

1. Use of paper that is 70% bleached

2. Use of photocopying machines that can be recycled

3. Use of energy-saving computers

Sony offices are constantly on the lookout for new types of office equipment, stationery, and other goods that can be easily recycled—or discarded with little environmental impact. Sony has also been active in the movement to eliminate unnecessary idling of company vehicles.

A Leader in the Top Growth Industries of the Twenty-First Century

Entertainment and electronics will continue to be the top growth industries of the next century. Sony, through the leadership of Idei, has become recognized as a global leader in both these industries. Nobuyuki Idei has thus demonstrated the leadership attributes and competencies that will make him not only an Asian leader but also a global leader to be emulated in the twenty-first century.

Jorma Ollila: Taking Nokia from the Twilight to the Leading Light in Telecommunications

Stories abound worldwide about Nokia CEO Jorma Ollila's amazing success in powering the company to the top of the telecommunications market. *USA Today* describes how Ollila has enabled Nokia to set the standard in the wireless phone market. The *Malaysian Business Times* and the London *Financial Times* proclaim the unique leadership capabilities of Ollila in developing a global telecommunications giant. *BusinessWeek* is awed by his skills in keeping the cellular superstar flying high.

Jorma Ollila's successes have been recognized through numerous awards. The World Bank and IMF honored him with the CEO of the Year award based upon his accomplishment in taking over an ailing Nokia and turning it into the "number one corporate success story in the world" (Lim, 1998). Ollila's transformation of the Finnish electronics company from a largely unknown conglomerate concentrating on twilight industries such as paper and rubber to a leading light in telecommunications surely positions him as a model to emulate in becoming a global leader in the twenty-first century (Godier, 1997).

The Practical Philosopher

Close observers of Ollila's career are not surprised by the speed of Nokia's turnaround. Jorma joined Citicorp as an Account Manager in 1978 straight out of the London School of Economics. He rapidly advanced to Citibank's board of management in Finland. According to Kari Mannola, Ollila's boss when they both worked at Citicorp in the 1980s, "Jorma is intellectual in the sense that he grabs the theory and puts it into practice rather than philosophizing" (Baker, 1998).

Ollila joined Nokia in 1985 as Vice President of International Operations. The following year he was named Senior Vice President of Finance, moving up to President of Nokia Mobile Phones in 1990, and finally President and CEO of Nokia Group in 1992.

Ollila holds a Master of Science in political science degree from the University of Helsinki (1976), a Master of Science in Economics from the London School of Economics (1978), and a Master of Science in Engineering from the Helsinki University of Technology (1981). The University of Helsinki awarded him an honorary PhD in Political Science in 1995.

In addition to his extensive responsibilities at Nokia, Ollila serves as Deputy Chair of the Board of the Confederation of Finnish Industries and Employers, as well as Chair of the Council of the Finnish Foreign Trade Association. He is the Chairman of the Board of MTV Oy (Finnish Commercial Television) and the Council of the Finnish Foreign Trade Association and is also a member of the European Round Table of Industrialists and the Competitiveness Advisory Group of the European Commission. In the academic arena, he is Vice Chairman of the Advisory Committee of Helsinki University of Technology and a member of the Dean's Council of Harvard University, John F. Kennedy School of Government.

Nokia—The Corporate Leader in Digital Technologies

Headquartered in Finland, Nokia is a leader in digital technologies, including mobile phones, cellular and fixed telecommunications networks, wireless data solutions, and multimedia terminals. In 1986 telecommunications accounted for just 15% of Nokia's business, but today it derives over 90% of its revenues from telecommunications products. In fact, its only nontelecommunications activity is making computer monitors. It is the world's number one digital mobile phone handset supplier and the leading digital mobile phone network infrastructure supplier in Global Systems for Mobile Communications (GSM) 1800 networks. Nokia offers one of the hottest cell phones on the market— the 6100 series—whose battery and unique circuitry support a whole week of stand-by time and is the first company to develop a mobile phone that can surf the Web.

The company employs more than 45,000 people at locations in 45 countries, and its mobile phones are sold in over 130 countries. Sales have grown sevenfold in five years, from $2.1 billion to over $20 billion in 1999, and its shares are listed on the Helsinki, New York, London, Stockholm, Frankfurt, and Paris stock exchanges. In a remarkably short time, Nokia has succeeded in an industry dominated by giants with telecommunications pedigrees stretching back a hundred years or more.

How has the company accomplished such success? One answer is its ability to thrive, not just survive, in an era of fast-paced, continuous change that has caused the downfall of other well-known companies, including ITT in the United States, GEC in the UK, and CGCT in France. Perhaps the biggest factor in the company's success has been its leadership style—one that encourages everyone to work as one and head in the same direction, and yet still makes the most of individual creativity. Let's look at how Jorma Ollila has developed and practiced the eight attributes of twenty-first century leaders.

Visionary for a Digital Future

As head of the tiny cellular phone division, Ollila recognized that Europe was heading toward a digital standard for mobile phones that would provide European manufacturers with a vast unified home market. He realized that if Nokia could concentrate its resources on mobile communications, it could capture a leadership role. In 1992 he was abruptly named CEO, although he claims he was not seeking the job or even ready for it.

But he had a vision that inspired his colleagues, a vision that would transform the company's future. The reality of that vision is five factories around the globe turning out over 1 million phones per month. Cellular handset sales are increasing at 50% annually, compared to worldwide fixed line growth below 10% per year. Ollila's goal is for Nokia to be "number one in the world in the number of phones sold, in growth, and return on capital employed."

Having a vision is not enough. Ollila recognizes that a leader must be able to communicate the vision, and a clear strategy for reaching it, to the rest of the organization. Otherwise people will not be able to focus their energies on the things that are really important. The leader must strike a balance between innovation and implementation, between growth and profitability. Ollila's operating style is characterized by fast decision-making that, combined with a flat, nonhierarchical organization, enables Nokia to promptly apply new technologies.

Even when the company faces difficulties, Ollila steers with a steady hand. In mid-December of 1995 the company shocked Wall Street by warning that its earnings in its final reporting period would be below those of the same period the previous year. Wall Street responded by hammering the company's stock down more than 20% in one day. But that did not seem to faze the soft-spoken Finn: "I'm not losing my sleep over one bad period of earnings," Ollila has said. "I'm losing my sleep over meeting our future challenges." With his eye on the future, Ollila continues to lead Nokia toward his vision.

Innovative Risk-Taker

In looking for a new CEO, Nokia needed someone who would be willing to take risks and guide Nokia successfully into the twenty-first century. Ollila soon proved the wisdom of Nokia's choice. In 1993, as an untested CEO, he bet the future of the 135-year-old Nokia on cellular phones and, in the process, challenged and won against much larger rivals Motorola and Ericsson.

Survival in the highly competitive cellular phone market requires innovation. If Ollila is to survive in the highly competitive field of cellular phones, he must find a way to totally transform his $20 billion corporation. He faces a challenge many companies are grappling with these days: how to provide customers in a variety of markets worldwide with what management specialists call a "winning value proposition." That means constantly providing products and services with better features at increasingly lower prices—a customer's dream but a provider's nightmare (Lynch, 1997).

Ollila's answer is to turn one product into dozens of niche offerings, each one targeted to different moods, occasions, and age groups—a tiny phone encased in steel, much like a Zippo lighter, for executives; a phone with changeable color panels to match clothes or fingernail polish for teenage girls. Nokia pumps out new models and products every 35 days (Baker, 1998).

To keep ahead of Nokia's competition, Ollila has created a strategy panel comprising Ollila, the company's business-unit bosses, and its heads of R&D and of strategy. The panel recently gave the green light to a "smart car" project based in Germany. The project seeks to integrate the tiny computers in a car with digital cellular technology to transmit readings of mechanical problems back to the driver's dealership or even to provide navigational information.

In an increasingly competitive global environment, an industry leader cannot afford to depend on out-dated assumptions of proprietary solutions and protected markets. Instead it must concentrate its resources on building competencies, systems, and products that matter to the customer.

Systems Thinking Moves
Nokia to the Lead

When he took over the company in early 1992, Nokia was making everything from power-generation equipment to tires, but the one thing it wasn't making was money—in 1991 and 1992 it lost a total of $213 million. In August 1992 he came out of a brainstorming session and quickly scribbled "telecom-oriented, global focus," and "value-added" on a piece of paper. It isn't a literary masterpiece, but it has guided the company's strategy ever since. Ollila has been rapidly restructuring the unwieldy conglomerate he inherited to focus on telecommunications.

Today most of the 130-year-old company's profits stem from telecommunications, which includes sales of mobile-phone infrastructure equipment and handsets. Ollila constantly displays an unusual mix of the cerebral and the practical, whipping out a Swiss Army knife to open a bottle one moment before settling into an original discussion of corporate strategy. "In my opinion, the CEO has to understand the dynamics of each business the company is in," says Ollila, who speaks English with a slightly clipped British accent. "Otherwise you end up reading reports based on financial criteria rather than understanding where your future lies" (Baker, 1998).

Ollila is betting that he can make up what he loses on margin by boosting volume, but that requires making Nokia a powerhouse global brand. Although more than two thirds of its sales are currently in Europe and the United States, Nokia is rapidly expanding and pouring more resources into burgeoning markets like China—where the company is actively challenging Motorola and Ericsson.

Nokia also has held its advantage by keeping its worldwide research budget low. The company spends less on R&D than its competitors—6.4% of sales, which is less than half as much as Ericsson doles out—partly because a few years back it bet that one digital phone system, called GSM, would become the standard. By not developing infrastructure equipment, such as cellular-based stations, for other potential digital standards, Nokia saved millions. All of Europe and many Asian nations have now adopted GSM. In the U.S. market, though, many operators have chosen different standards.

Nokia also found ways to leverage its R&D dollars by creating high-tech partnerships. The company is able to keep its labs, which it operates in Japan,

Scandinavia, Hong Kong, Germany, Britain, the United States, and Australia, quite small. To gain the technical expertise it needs, its scientists work with outsiders. In the United States, for instance, Nokia taps into the diverse genius of software firms like Geoworks in California, with whom it is developing next-generation wireless products.

Taking Nokia Global

In an industry with worldwide sales and fierce competition, any CEO must understand the challenges of competing in a global market. After all, Helsinki is no further away from Tokyo, Bangkok, and New York than is London. Having spent his own formative years at a British boarding school, the London School of Economics, and Citibank, Ollila became convinced of the value of international experience at a young age.

Ollila fully comprehends that globalization is a force that cannot be stopped or reversed. To meet the challenges of worldwide competition, Nokia must recruit the best people possible and bring seasoned international managers on board. Ollila also realizes the need to plan for global adaptability: "As all the key functions—manufacturing, marketing, and research and development—become global, we have to introduce more complicated management structures." He faces the challenge of globalizing a company whose European revenues still account for about 70% of total sales, building the Nokia brand worldwide, and sustaining innovation in a cutthroat pricing environment.

To speed Nokia's international growth, Ollila is engaging his managers from around the world in strategy development, while teaching them to act locally in foreign markets and to develop an acute understanding of local cultures. For instance, a five-month project that ended in May 1998 brought together a wide cross section of hundreds of Nokia employees at airport hotels in London and Frankfurt. In three-day sessions, they brainstormed about technological and lifestyle trends the company might ride.

Humility and Teamwork

At the young age of 34, Ollila moved to Nokia to work in finance but was determined to learn about industry as well. A co-worker recalled the tall, thin financier making his way through the mostly deserted headquarters on a Saturday, introducing himself to the few people there, in his low-key way, as "the cashier" (Baker, 1998). He has maintained a rather humble, gentlemanly approach, with concern for customers and employees. Speaking of the company's future challenges, he encourages employee participation: "It is a challenge we must humbly accept; one that requires that each and every employee be open, cooperative, receptive to new ideas and have the boldness to shoulder responsibility with others." A key element of his leadership style "is to empower people in a way which gives them direction on possibilities."

Ollila understands that to remain an industry leader, Nokia must be successful in recruiting, keeping, and motivating the best talent. More important than financial incentives, this requires an open, nonhierarchical corporate culture based on fundamental principles of respect for the individual, the possibility to achieve and excel, accountability while accepting that mistakes will happen, and foremost, a culture based on continuous learning, hard work, and fun (Carnegy, 1997).

He promotes the need for teamwork throughout the organization: "We must entrust others with responsibility and offer opportunity. Mutual dependencies among Nokia business groups and the development of common core technologies create a greater need for cooperation. . . . Cooperation and teamwork are the best ways of dismantling hierarchies and rigid structures, and preventing their establishment where they have thus far been avoided" (Baker, 1998).

Finnish Culture and Collegiality

When Nokia experienced a drop in earnings and stock value in 1995, Ollila resisted pressure to fire his executives. (He estimates that a typical U.S. company would have fired 12 execs.) Instead, he views the crisis as a valuable lesson, and the company's swift recovery as vindication for his vision of gentle Finnish management.

Despite the global nature of Nokia, Ollila has preserved a predominantly Finnish corporate culture. He believes that part of Nokia's strength comes from its "understated collegiality" which he associates with Finnish culture. Unprejudiced attitudes and humility toward learning are also examples of the Finnish heritage. He adds that "there is also a flexibility that has allowed the nation of Finland to survive." Also, "The way we work here is very representative of our non-hierarchical management style, where people are always to be seen to be available" (Nokia, 1998). All of these characteristics are well suited to success in today's changing world.

Ethics at the Core of Nokia Culture

Ethical practices and social responsibility are at the core of Nokia's operations. As Ollila explains, what drives the telecommunications expansion is the "pragmatic realization that in a networked economy, telecommunications brings together widely dispersed functions at all levels to create greater economic efficiency, to better utilize scarce natural resources, to safeguard the environment, and to provide greater choice, more freedom and democracy."

The four Nokia values—customer satisfaction, respect for the individual, achievement, and continuous learning—are incorporated globally, with local emphasis on different aspects depending on national culture. Additionally, Nokia recognizes three fundamental principles in its operations: (a) always operating according to strict, ethical principles, (b) always serving the society in which you work, and (c) always protecting the environment in which you work and live.

These shared values and principles permeate the Nokia culture, forming a strong foundation of corporate responsibility. The company management concentrates on implementing its values, developing a way to further integrate these values into the performance management system, and encouraging employees to focus on internal cooperation at all levels. Senior management plays a critical role in this value implementation process. As Ollila points out, "Nokia employees are aiming for excellence in performance. Achieving this presupposes personal involvement on the part of all of us in our work and in sharing our common goals. That involvement is manifested in the level of innovativeness, flexibility, team spirit and efficiency of our people—and the satisfaction it brings" (Nokia, 1998).

Protecting the Environment

Nokia also emphasizes its commitment to protecting the environment as part of its core values and strives to make environmental issues a part of the everyday life of all employees. Through training efforts, employees at all levels develop a deeper understanding of environmental concerns and learn ways to integrate this knowledge into work practices. Employees make eco-efficiency and life-cycle thinking a primary consideration during the development, production, and marketing of new products. Nokia's environmental program includes optimizing energy and material use, reducing pollution and waste, enhancing product durability, and facilitating end-of-life product treatment. Through an open and ethically sound approach, Nokia is committed to the goal of sustainable development and seeks ways to meet the needs of the present without jeopardizing the rights and resources of future generations.

Technology Leader

As a leader in high-tech telecommunications products, Nokia constantly researches new technologies, looking for new features to offer, products to sell, and snappy improvements to update its current line. Ollila embraces technology and its many benefits, recognizing the powerful role Nokia will continue to play in the technology marketplace. "Technology gives us a new flexibility to arrange work and leisure according to need. The benefits our businesses will realize are not measured only in terms of processes, organization, and operational efficiency, but in terms of creating new forms of cooperation with our vendors and customers in networked ventures and partnership."

In the telecommunications industry, having the right technology at just the right time can provide the edge needed to dominate. When the digital phone standard, GSM, took off in Europe, Nokia was ready with user-friendly cell phones that could be adapted to varying frequencies and standards around the world. When mobile phone growth accelerated, Nokia was positioned to expand into new markets. Nokia takes a long-term perspective in order to be in the right place at the right time as new services or technologies come to the commercial stage. Under Ollila's leadership, Nokia has actively developed third generation technologies to be standardized in Europe, Japan, and the U.S.

Technology driven by a continued focus on R&D will, according to Ollila, remain a key force in the industry. Ollila envisions a world in which tax forms will be filled out and submitted electronically, bills will be paid from a mobile phone, and companies will create networked teams with people in different countries and different time zones working on the same project (Ollila, 1998). Convergence of a variety of gadgets—telephones, computers, televisions and appliances—in one digital device is the dream of many high-tech companies, including Nokia.

At a recent European Telecommunications Standards Institute meeting that established a future Universal Telecommunications Service (UMTS) technology based on Wideband Code Division Multiple Access (WCDMA) radio access technology, Ollila cited the solution as one beneficial to equipment manufacturers, operators, and end-users globally, noting that "harmonizing standards is a cost efficient solution that will be advantageous for the entire wireless industry" and represents "a major step toward the wireless information society." The new UMTS technology will

> provide wideband wireless multimedia capabilities over mobile telephone networks, allowing for the introduction of personalized, innovative video, Internet/intranet and high-speed data services . . . as well as accelerate capacity improvements, make high speed mass communications fully possible and enable the introduction of extensive range of new services, leading to even higher global volumes, economies of scale, and rapid further development towards a wireless world. (Ollila, 1998)

Continuous Learning at All Levels

Ollila's strategy also calls for continuous learning at all levels. He urges everyone to pursue continuous learning "so that we are fully prepared to meet those expectations anticipated of us." "As the level of uncertainty in our environment grows," he noted in a recent annual report, "knowledge empowers us to act with purpose and confidence. And investment in continuous learning is reflected in a company's personnel and product developed. Nokia will substantially invest in continuous learning" (Annual Report, 1998).

Ollila recognizes that competence development will be a critical factor in Nokia's success in a rapidly changing business environment. Thus, the company encourages continuous learning by providing a wide range of training, from induction, skills, and technology training to management and leadership development. Training programs are local or global. Because company leaders believe that most learning occurs outside the monitored learning environment, Nokia encourages action learning in many of its programs and provides new assignments and opportunities for growth and job rotation. Employees participate in training 11 working days per year on average; this increases to 20 days per year for new employees.

Ollila is improvising a brand-new style of high-tech management, replacing the usual "slip and you die" thinking with a "slip and you grow" philosophy. In his viewpoint, disasters are learning opportunities. He shuns comfort and complacency, looking instead for challenges and plunges into the unknown and unconquered. For example, just at the point when Nokia seemed to be performing in high gear, Ollila switched the jobs of all his top managers, removing them from their comfort zones. Such an upheaval is designed to sharpen their skills and inject a sense of urgency into a successful operation. According to *BusinessWeek*, he "lives by the plunge." He believes that "it takes a dive into the unknown, or a push, to tap into employees' strongest instincts— those that guide survival" (Baker, 1998).

Learning must be an inherent part of the organization, not an event but an ongoing process. "You can't issue instructions every day or run a company like a conductor runs an orchestra. Whatever it is, has to be deep within the organization—almost in its genes—it is all about the ability to scan ideas, the willingness to take new ideas on board—it's about not having any of the 'not-invented-here' syndrome." Nokia's corporate culture is receptive to change and new ideas aimed at a continuous learning process. Part of the learning process is not just sitting in an office but getting information from colleagues and expecting to be able to challenge the truths or the obvious feelings that other colleagues have. Another technique for re-creating job enthusiasm is by rotation.

Ollila involves top managers and employees in strategic reviews because he sees these reviews as strategic learning opportunities. By engaging more people, the ability to implement strategy becomes more visible. Such reviews force managers to look for the convergence of different technologies and how these might affect the company. The most tangible benefit and learning to date is the recent creation of a new "smart-car" unit in Germany to develop products for the auto industry. Nokia hopes to use its expertise in cellular networks to create such products as integrated navigation and road guidance systems.

"The smart-car project needed a multitude of disciplines to master the solution that will win in the future," said Ollila. "The think-tank approach addressed this challenge effectively." The company's top executive team now meets monthly with a strategy agenda. And the line managers, who spend a quarter of their own time over six months on the exercise, now have the training and perspective to make strategy a regular part of their jobs (Byrne, 1996).

Nokia's ability to maintain its leadership position in the fastest growing telecommunications segments is based on the learning of its employees, the cornerstone of its success. In Ollila's words, the key is "Getting the right people, mobilizing them, and putting in place a concept of continuous learning. You have to have something in your organization to attract people who are willing to achieve something different. And then you will have to reward people who get things done—people who learn from their mistakes."

Leading Nokia into the Twenty-First Century

Several years ago, many business gurus were predicting that Finnish Nokia was too small to succeed in the big business of telecommunications. Now they are saying that Nokia is like the bumblebee that theoretically should not be able to fly because it doesn't have enough wing surface to support the body. The bumblebee (Nokia) doesn't know, however, so it just goes ahead and flies anyway.

Ollila recognizes, though, that there will always be new challenges. As he noted recently, "My major fear for the future is that we will not be able to avoid the dangers that come with growth from a medium-sized company. We must resist becoming bureaucratic. My hope is that we can continue to focus on the right things, We have great ideas. We must continue to be able to make them work" (Nokia, 1998). Most futurists are betting that Ollila will continue to do the right things and keep Nokia as a leading light in the telecommunications world as the company enters the twenty-first century.

CHAPTER FIFTEEN

Problems, Pathways, and Prospects for Twenty-First Century Global Leaders

As we enter the twenty-first century, we will set foot into an era more challenging and chaotic, but also more exciting, than any before. Leaders will face ever more complex problems and perplexing opportunities, yet have less time to prepare and develop themselves to manage these challenges.

What will be the most difficult problems of the twenty-first century? How can we prepare future leaders to handle these challenges? Is there a leadership development approach or tool that works best for twenty-first century leaders? How can we build leaders who will be able to cross the chasm into the next millennium with the attributes and perspectives possessed by the 12 leaders described in this book? What will high-performance and high-people twenty-first century organizations and communities look like? In this chapter we will seek the answers to the problems, pathways, and prospects awaiting those who seek to lead in the twenty-first century.

Twenty-First Century Problems

As we noted in chapter 1, the twenty-first century workplace will involve rapidly changing socioeconomic trends and markets, overnight innovation from competitors, mergers across disparate corporate cultures and industries, new distribution channels, and globalization of business. In confronting such challenges, leaders will not be able to look for ready-made solutions. Problems will become ever more confusing and difficult to identify, much less solve. And solving problems will no longer be the domain of any one person or leader—

we will need to incorporate the information, imagination, perspectives, and talents of many people to find answers to tomorrow's dilemmas. No one person, however prescient, will have all the answers.

Heifetz and Laurie (1998) distinguish the problems that are more common to the twentieth century from those that will be most critical in the twenty-first century by contrasting what they term as *technical* versus *adaptive* problems.

Technical problems (twentieth century) are those in which the necessary knowledge to solve the problem already exists in a legitimized form or set of procedures. The challenge in solving these problems is to obtain and apply the knowledge in an efficient and rational way. Technical problems have a linear, logical way of being solved, with precedents within or outside the organization. (As we note below, these types of problems are termed *puzzles* in action learning programs.)

Adaptive problems (twenty-first century) are problems for which no satisfactory response has yet been developed and no technical expertise is fully adequate. The challenge is to mobilize the people with the problem to make painful adjustments in their attitudes, work habits, and other aspects of their lives, while at the same time learning their way into the creation of something that does not yet exist. Adaptive problems have no ready solutions. They require people collectively "to apply their intelligence and skills to the work only they can do. The responsibility requires unlearning the habits of a managerial lifetime, new learning to meet challenges where current skills are insufficient, and capacity to explore and understand competing values at stake."

Because of the significant differences in these two types of problems, leaders and organizations will be need to respond in different ways, as seen in Table 14.1.

Perhaps the reason that many efforts to transform organizations (through reengineering, downsizing, restructuring, mergers, or acquisitions) are less than successful is because leaders do not recognize this change from technical to adaptive work. Treating adaptive challenges like technical problems leads to unsatisfactory solutions. And the failure of technical strategies is blamed when, indeed, the true nature of the problem was not understood. Because of the technical orientation that most managers have come to accept as reality, other perspectives go unrecognized from the beginning, when the problem is defined. Leaders often fail to identify and tackle the adaptive dimensions of the challenge and to ask themselves: Who needs to learn what to develop, what to understand, what to commit to, and how to implement the strategy? (Heifetz and Laurie, 1998).

Table 15.1

Comparison of Appropriate Responses to Technical and Adaptive Problems

Responsibilities	Twentieth Century: Technical Problems	Twenty-First Century: Adaptive Problems
Leadership	Take charge, provide decisive leadership.	Allow leadership to emerge close to the action, become a facilitator.
Organization	Create an effective hierarchy of roles and responsibilities.	Build a community of trusting relationships.
Roles and tasks	Clarify roles and define responsibilities.	Continually challenge the pressure to define new roles.
Stress	Shield the organization from external pressure.	Let the organization feel the external pressure within a range it can tolerate.
Communication	Define problems and clearly tell people what is expected.	Frame the key issues and continually ask questions.
Learning	Learn from successes, share best practices.	Learn from failure as well as success.
Human resources	Find competent people and put them into the right roles.	Create richly connected networks of mutually involved people.
Direction	Define problems and provide solutions.	Identify the adaptive challenge and frame key questions and issues.
Orientation	Clarify roles and responsibilities.	Challenge current roles and resist pressure to define new roles quickly.
Managing conflict	Restore order.	Expose conflict or let it emerge.
Shaping norms	Maintain norms.	Challenge unproductive norms.

Adaptive challenges are more difficult to define and resolve, precisely because they require efforts of people throughout the organization. In an adaptive environment, leaders will need to encourage everyone within the organization to take responsibility for the problematic situations that face them.

This is not to say that technical problems are unimportant or easy to solve. But they are called technical because the information and knowledge needed to resolve them already exist, and those in authority have a concrete set of procedures or guidelines to follow as they work through the issues at hand. As the workplace continues to become more complex, however, strategic and operational problems will require more than a technical response. Leaders will be faced with learning more adaptive approaches in order to solve problems for which no plan of action has yet been developed and current technical expertise is not fully adequate.

Adaptive work will mean leading people to make difficult changes in their attitudes, work habits, and lives. While clearly articulated objectives, detailed work plans, flow charts, and carefully scheduled target dates may help them achieve technical solutions, adaptive processes will be more helpful when they are forced to take on the design and implementation of new processes and other challenges of the future.

As the number and frequency of adaptive problems increase, the leader's role also begins to change. The concept of leadership in which the leader has a vision and aligns people with that vision, which may have been effective in an era of mostly technical problems becomes less possible or even desirable in the new era of the twenty-first century.

Leadership and Continuous Learning

One cannot lead adaptive change without a strategy for continuous learning throughout the organization. We will need to constantly ask ourselves, "Who needs to learn what and how?" Taking an adaptive approach means that all those having a stake in a particular problem will need to think together and learn together to find new solutions. The leader's role will be to ask good questions, remain flexible as groups work through their issues, and accept uncertainty as a necessary part of the process.

Leadership, when seen in this light, requires a learning strategy as well as a teaching strategy. A leader, from above or below, with or without authority, has to engage people in confronting the challenge, adjusting their values, changing perspectives, and learning new habits. To authoritative persons who pride themselves on their ability to tackle hard problems, this shift may come as a rude awakening. "The adaptive problems and demands of our time require leaders who take responsibility without waiting for revelation or request. One can lead with no more than a question in hand" (Heifetz and Laurie, 1997).

Building Leaders for the Twenty-First Century—The Leadership Engine

Tichey and Cohen (1997) spent a decade researching the world's most successful organizations (e.g., General Electric, Hewlett-Packard, Intel, Service Master, and others that consistently outperformed market averages). They discovered that these organizations were successful mainly because "developing leaders at all levels was a critical priority, pursued with the same zeal as new products, new customers, and competitive edge. Leaders felt it was their job to develop others, and they did it personally instead of delegating the task to consultants or professors" (p. 60). The authors found that the best way to get more leaders was to encourage leaders to develop new leaders. Leaders passed on their experience to others who were expected to use it and develop their own leadership style. Leaders, in short, must be able to develop future leaders if they wish their company to "win in tomorrow's world."

Preparing Twenty-First Century Leaders at GE

Many people have called Jack Welch, who retired in the year 2000, the last great leader of the twentieth century. And what does he consider his most important role? Developing GE's future leaders. Let's look at how Jack Welch prepares GE's leaders for the twenty-first century.

> Whisked by chopper from New York City, Jack Welch arrives early at the General Electric training center at Croton-on-Hudson. He scoots down to the [training center], peels off his blue suit jacket, and drapes it over one of the swivel seats. This is face-to-face with Jack, not so much as the celebrated chairman and chief executive of GE, the company he has made the most valuable in the world, but rather as Professor Welch, coach and teacher to 71 high-potential managers attending a three-week development course.
>
> The class sits transfixed as Welch's laser-blue eyes scan the auditorium. . . . For nearly four hours, he listens, lectures, cajoles, and questions. In this classroom, where Welch has appeared more than 250 times in the past 17 years to engage some 15,000 GE managers and executives, something extraordinary happens. The legendary chairman of GE, the take-no-prisoners tough guy who gets results at any cost, becomes human. . . . The students see all of Jack here: the management theorist, strategic thinker, business teacher, and corporate icon who made it to the top despite his working class background. No one leaves the room untouched. (Byrne, 1998)

Preparing Leaders in Organizations

In their classic book, *The Leadership Engine,* Tichey and Cohen (1997) describe how three of the top leaders of the twentieth century are preparing company leaders for the twenty-first century:

— *Andrew Grove,* CEO of Intel, goes into the classroom several times a year to teach Intel managers how to lead an industry in which the products (microprocessors) double in capacity every 18 months. A key challenge: Helping leaders detect and navigate the turbulent industry shifts. Grove does this because he believes having leaders at all levels of Intel who can spot the trends and who have the courage to act will enable Intel to prosper while competitors falter.

— *Roger Enrico,* CEO of PepsiCo, runs his own personal "war college" to develop a new generation of leaders for PepsiCo. At remote sites in Montana and the Cayman Islands, "far away from the daily demands of making potato chips, selling sodas, and resolving assorted day-to-day problems," Enrico prepares PepsiCo to survive and thrive into the twenty-first century.

— *Rear Admiral Ray Smith,* a Navy SEAL since the Vietnam War, regularly visits SEALs about to graduate from Basic Underwater Demolition SEAL training. Only 20% of the candidates who enter this elite six-month program survive its great physical and mental demands to graduate. Throughout the day, Smith, in his 50s, participates in the same physical training as the SEAL candidates who are in their 20s. At the end of the day, he meets alone with the graduates. Speaking as a successful leader who has been exactly where they are, he lays out for them personally his teachable point of view of the leadership duties of becoming a SEAL, the conduct, honor, and teamwork required, and the need for them to develop other leaders.

As we have seen thus far in this chapter, twenty-first century problems requiring the most attention and skill of leaders will be adaptive in nature and will obligate the organization's leaders to be at the forefront in developing people who can handle these problems. The question that naturally arises is: What is the best tool or approach to prepare twenty-first century leaders to handle such problems? For more and more organizations, the answer is "action learning."

Action Learning as a Tool for Building Twenty-First Century Leaders

Organizations and leaders that change too slowly will not survive for long in the twenty-first century. They will quickly become dinosaurs unless they continuously learn about and quickly respond to their changing environment (customers, technology, political upheavals, etc.) But where does a company or leader find time to learn and develop long-range capabilities for change when the day-to-day problems must be solved and critical crises must be met? Simply put, today's organizations and leaders are often too busy fighting alligators to find time to drain the swamp.

They must find a way to fight (act) and drain (learn) simultaneously. Learning and acting must become concurrent since too many demands and too little time prohibit focusing exclusively on one or the other. The days when workers, especially leaders, could be absent from the action to concentrate solely on learning, or to be absent from learning to focus on action, are over.

And learning in the more traditional ways of corporate training or executive development at institutions of higher learning, according to Dilworth (1996, p. 49) "produce individuals who are technologically literate and able to deal with intricate problem-solving models, but are essentially distanced from the human dimensions that must be taken into account." Leaders may be good at downsizing and corporate restructuring but cannot deal with a demoralized workforce and the resulting longer-term challenges. These so-called development programs provide excellent technical skills, but the "social and interpersonal aspects of the organizations that largely create the dynamics of corporate culture are left unattended."

Action learning has the power to provide both the best content (what) and the best methodology (how) for building the vital attributes of leadership for the twenty-first century. Leadership is built on the premise and expectation of getting things done. To take effective action is an essential task. Action learning programs introduce real-life, real-time practice of those skills. And they focus on the learner/leader, not just the tasks to be undertaken by the learner/leader.

What exactly is action learning? Simply described, action learning is both a dynamic process and a powerful program. It involves a small group of people solving real problems, while at the same time focusing on what they are learning and how their learning can benefit each group member, the group itself, and the organization as a whole.

Action learning contains a well-tested framework that enables people to effectively and efficiently learn and to simultaneously handle difficult, real-life situations. It is built on the application of new questions to existing knowledge as well as a reflection on actions taken during and after the problem-solving sessions.

Perhaps action learning's most valuable capacity is its amazing, multiplying impact to equip individuals, especially leaders, to more effectively respond to change. Learning is what makes action learning strategic rather than tactical. Fresh thinking and new learning are needed if we are to avoid responding to today's problems with yesterday's solutions while tomorrow's challenges engulf us (Dilworth, 1998).

Reg Revans (1982), the father of action learning, writes:

> When in an epoch of change, when tomorrow is necessarily different than yesterday, new ways of thinking must emerge. New questions need to be asked before solutions are sought. Action learning's primary objective is to learn how to ask appropriate questions under conditions of risk rather than find answers to questions that have already been identified by others. We have to act ourselves into a new way of thinking rather than think ourselves into a new way of acting.

Components of an Action Learning Program

Action learning programs derive their power and benefits from six interactive and interdependent components (Marquardt, 1999). The strength and success of action learning is built upon how well these elements are employed and reinforced.

1. A problem (project, challenge, opportunity, issue, or task)

Action learning is built around a problem (be it a project, a challenge, an issue, or a task), the resolution of which is of high importance to an individual, team, or organization. The problem should be significant, be within the responsibility of the team, and provide opportunity for learning. Why is the selection of the problem so important? Because it is one of the fundamental beliefs of action learning that we learn best when undertaking some action, which we then reflect upon and learn from. The main reason for having a problem or project is that it gives the group something to focus on that is real and important, that is relevant and means something to them. It creates a "hook" on which to test stored-up knowledge.

2. An action learning group or team

The core entity in action learning is the action learning group (also called a *set* or *team*). The group is composed of 4–8 individuals who examine an organizational problem that has no easily identifiable solution. Ideally, the make-up of the group is diverse so as to maximize various perspectives and to obtain fresh viewpoints. Depending upon the type of action learning problem, groups can be composed of individuals from across functions or departments. In some situations, groups include individuals from other organizations or professions; for example, the company's suppliers or customers.

3. A process that emphasizes insightful questioning and reflective listening

By focusing on the right questions rather than the right answers, action learning focuses on what one does not know as well as on what one does know. Action learning tackles problems through a process of first asking questions to clarify the exact nature of the problem, reflecting and identifying possible solutions, and only then taking action.

Action learning employs the formula: $L = P + Q + R$; i.e., Learning = *Programmed* knowledge (in other words, knowledge in current use, in books, one's mind, the organization's memory, lectures, case studies, etc.) + *Questioning* (fresh insights into what is not yet known) + *Reflection* (recalling, thinking about, pulling apart, making sense, trying to understand).

4. A resolution of taking action

For action learning advocates, there is no real learning unless action is taken, for one is never sure the idea or plan will be effective until it has been implemented. Therefore, members of the action learning group must have the power to take action themselves or be assured that their recommendations will be implemented (barring any significant change in the environment or the group's obvious lack of essential information). Action enhances learning because it provides a basis and anchor for the critical dimension of reflection described earlier.

5. A commitment to learning

Solving an organizational problem provides immediate, short-term benefits to the company. The greater, longer-term, multiplier benefit, however, is the learning gained by each group member and how the group's learning can be applied on a system-wide basis throughout the organization. The learning that occurs in action learning has greater value strategically for the organization than the immediate tactical advantage of early problem correction. In action learning, the learning is as important as the action. Action learning places equal emphasis on accomplishing the task and on the learning and development of individuals and organizations.

6. A group facilitator / learning coach

Facilitation is important to help the group slow down their process in order to allow sufficient time to reflect on learning. A facilitator may be a working group member (possessing familiarity with the problem being discussed) or an external participant (not necessarily understanding the problem content or organizational context, but possessing action learning facilitation skills).

The facilitator is important in helping participants reflect both on what they are learning and how they are solving problems. The facilitator helps group members reflect on how they listen, how they may have reframed the problem, how they give each other feedback, how they are planning and working, and what assumptions may be shaping their beliefs and actions. The group advisor also helps participants focus on what they are achieving, what they are finding difficult, what processes they are employing, and the implications of these processes.

Developing Twenty-First Century Leader Capabilities via Action Learning

The process, principles, and practice of action learning can be effective in developing each of the eight attributes necessary for a successful twenty-first century leader. Let's examine how action learning accomplishes these capabilities.

1) Action learning and visionary leaders

Often, action learning groups are challenged with a problem for which, initially, no one knows which direction to steer. Yet, through the process of sharing ignorance, the group begins developing a vision of where they need to go to solve the problem. Ann Brooks (1998, p. 53) notes how action learning builds leaders who "metaphorically speaking, (have) the capacity to find a new and better path through the jungle, rather than be the first one down a path that already exists."

Learning how to conceptualize complex issues is a skill gained through action learning. Creating vision, particularly shared vision, occurs frequently in action learning groups as the members develop system-oriented, holistic resolutions to complex problems.

Trying to get people to comprehend a vision of an alternative future is also a communications challenge of a completely different magnitude from organizing them to fulfill a short-term plan. It is much like the difference between a football quarterback attempting to describe to his team the next two or three plays versus his trying to explain to them a totally new approach to the game to be used in the second half of the season. Action learning gives people the skills of understanding and preparing such a vision of the future.

Through action learning, leaders recognize the importance of "carving new paths," of living in a state of constant inquiry. We recognize the importance of continually asking questions, gathering information, and analyzing the situation. Dealing with all these uncertainties is fraught with risks and requires a willingness to admit the things we do not know, something no one likes to do. Yet it is when we are overwhelmed with possibilities and things go wrong that we achieve our greatest accomplishments. Revans cites how the great successes at the Cavendish Laboratory occurred when the scientists admitted and shared their "bloody ignorance." Handling problems and confusions is what leadership is all about and is what action learning develops.

2) Action learning, risk-takers, and innovators

Action learning enhances the ability to think in new and fresh ways—critical reflection, reframing, context shifting—about existing reality and problems. The synergy of diverse groups asking fresh questions generates creativity. Risk-taking is encouraged in action learning so as to generate numerous solutions and to inspire action.

Marsick (1988) states, "the capacity to dig below the surface layer of perception and examine taken-for-granted assumptions and values" is necessary in order to determine whether or not one is addressing the right problem. Members take risks in being frank and honest in helping each other learn about themselves. And adapting and applying the learning to one's organization and to one's professional lives requires flexibility and creativity.

3) Action learning and systems thinkers

Action learning is built around a diverse group of people (whole systems) asking new and fresh questions so as to gain a full picture of the problem and its context before attempting to solve it. Questions that focus on examining underlying causes and long-range solutions, that seek to provide the greatest leverage, that recognize that importance of relationships and one's own role in problems and solutions, these are the core of the questions asked in action learning. Making connections, analyzing seemingly contradictory data, and seeking new possibilities rather than old answers are inherent parts of the action learning process.

During action learning, participants learn how to handle many problems, often in the same meeting. They learn how the problems interconnect. The group advisor must note the numerous dynamics occurring simultaneously between and among several members.

4) Action learning and multicultural or global perspectives

Although action learning does not directly help in creating a global mindset, it forces people to see problems and issues from a variety of perspectives. When organizations use action learning with multicultural leaders, the global mindset is better built through employing action learning processes. Action learning programs create and manage global projects in culturally diverse settings. Cultural dimensions that are often hidden or buried in normal group settings are brought out in the open and lead to synergetic successes through action learning.

5) Action learning and servant-leadership

The group facilitator, in many ways, is a model of the servant-leader. The tasks that the facilitator carries out mirror in a remarkable way the roles identified in chapter 2 for the servant-leader, namely:

— Design opportunities for participants to find their own answers to problems.

— Design opportunities for participants to learn from each others' perspectives, successes, and mistakes.

— Encourage a climate in which participants will both support and challenge each other.

— Refrain from displaying one's own knowledge and understanding.

— Challenge individual and group assumptions.

— Provide difficult feedback to members.

— Ask questions that assist participants in exploring the reasoning behind their assumptions.

— Acknowledge mistakes publicly, framing them as learning experiences.

6) Action learning and ethics

The success of action learning programs depends upon the establishment and fulfillment of high ethical standards. Members cannot really help each other in solving problems unless there is a genuine caring for and strong support for each other. Group norms are set relative to confidentiality, openness, sincerity, and commitment. Unethical behavior is clearly seen and discussed. Decisions need to take into account people and not just profits or convenience.

McNulty and Canty (1995, p. 57) remark how action learning "develops the ability to create change" and to have the courage "to do so." Iyer (1989) adds that "the action learning process is founded on the concept that one cannot change the system to the better unless one is changed to the better as well."

7) Action learning and technology

In action learning groups, the leaders become much more aware of the systematic impact of technology as well as its potential and limitations. Members recognize that technology, like any large-scale factor, demands the "recreation and redefinition of leadership" as we now see it.

8) Action learning and coaching or facilitating

The primary focus of action learning is to learn, and to learn how to learn. All members of the set, not only the group facilitator, are encouraged to assist fellow members in the learning process. Thus, learning occurs naturally in action sets, as individuals and teams reflect on their thinking, their actions, and their learning. Coaching and enabling skills are enhanced and developed in action learning. Members help the problem-presenter identify the true problem and assist him or her in developing possible actions to take in resolving it. They seek to empower the client to take "appropriate levels of responsibility in discovering how to develop themselves" (McGill and Beaty, 1995). Mentoring is also developed in action learning through the process in which the members enable the presenter or client to work through the issues. As a presenter, the person also gains an understanding of what it is like on the receiving end of mentoring.

Prospects and Perspectives for the Twenty-First Century Leader

Since the seventeenth century, the world and the workplace have been built upon Newtonian physics—the physics of cause and effect, of predictability and certainty, of distinct wholes and parts, of reality being what is seen, of quantifiable determinism, of linear thinking and controllable futures. This mindset, as Wheatley (1992) notes, will be "unempowering and disabling for all of us" as we enter the twenty-first century. Twenty-first century leaders will be required to understand and apply the science of quantum physics, which deals with the world at the subatomic level, examining the intricate patterns out of which seemingly discrete events arise, where relationships between objects and between observers and objects are what determine reality, where surprises are more common than predictions. It will force us to change the way we think, the way we attempt to solve problems, the way we deal with order and change, autonomy and control, structure and flexibility, planning and flowing. Holistic ways of seeing things will emerge in importance. Leaders will need to educate (draw out), inspire, nurture, and be co-creative insiders.

Table 15.2

Twentieth Century Managers versus Twenty-First Century Leaders

WORLD OF TWENTIETH CENTURY MANAGER	WORLD OF TWENTY-FIRST CENTURY LEADER
Newtonian physics	Quantum physics; chaos and complexity theory
Atomism	Holism
Stress on separate working parts	Stress on relationships
Fragmentation	Integration
Determinism	Indeterminism and unpredictability
Specifics, logical and linear thinking	Systems thinking
Instructor (put in)	Educator (draw out) and mentor
Detached outsider	Co-creative insider
Hands-on control, resulting in alienation	Service and support, resulting in self-organization and freedom
Constrains	Enables and nurtures
Finite opportunities	Infinite opportunities
Fear, present and past	Courage and self-confidence, future

Ideal Workplace of the Twenty-First Century

What would be the ideal workplace of the twenty-first century? According to a recent Development Dimensions International (DDI) survey, people want the following:

— Employees control resources, systems, methods, working conditions, and work schedules.

— Leaders build an environment of trust by listening to and communicating with employees.

— Understood vision and values help guide decision-making.

— Decision-making occurs at the lowest level.

— Individuals have the ability and data to measure their own performance and progress.

— Leaders and associates work together to establish clear goals, expectations, and accountabilities.

— Leaders champion continuous improvement, facilitate learning, and reinforce effective performance.

— Risk-taking is encouraged, mistakes are treated as learning opportunities.

— Performance feedback comes from peers, customers, and direct reports.

— Systems—selection and promotion, rewards and recognition, compensation, information management, and so forth—are aligned to reinforce and drive desired behaviors.

— Effective training is provided to build skills at the teachable moment (just-in-time).

— Jobs are designed to provide employee ownership and responsibility.

The 12 global leaders described in this book have already produced such workplaces and will continue to create even better communities of work in the twenty-first century. Their competencies and commitment, their visions and victories, their energies and ethics have set the standards for all twenty-first century global leaders.

References

Preface

Cleveland, H. (1997). *Leadership and the information revolution*. Minneapolis: World Academy of Art and Science.

Tichey, N. and E. Cohen (1997). *The leadership engine: How winning companies build leaders at every level*. New York: Harper Business.

Chapter 1: A New Century

Bassi, L., S. Chenny, and M. van Buren (1997). Training industry trends. *Training and Development,* 51, (11), 46-59.

Bates, A. W. (1995). *Technology, open learning, and distance education*. London: Routledge.

Carey, J. (1998, August 24–31). We are now starting the century of biology. *BusinessWeek,* 86–87.

Drucker, P. (1992). The new society of organizations. *Harvard Business Review,* 5, 95–104.

Goleman, D. (1997). *Emotional intelligence*. New York: Bantam Books.

Goleman, D. (1998). *Working with emotional intelligence*. New York: Bantam Books.

Gross, N. (1997, June 23). Future of technology. *BusinessWeek,* 72–84.

Marquardt, M. (1999). *The global advantage: How world-class organizations improve performance through globalization*. Houston: Gulf Publishing.

Morton, M. (1991). *The corporation of the 1990's*. New York: Oxford University Press.

Stewart, T. (1997). *Intellectual capital: The new wealth of organizations*. New York: Doubleday.

Toffler, A. (1990). *Powershift*. New York: Bantam.

Wheatley, M. (1992). *Leadership and the new science.* San Francisco: Berrett-Koehler.

Zuboff, S. (1988). *In the age of the smart machine: The future of work and power.* New York: Basic Books.

Chapter 2: Attributes and Competencies

Block, P. (1996). *Stewardship.* San Francisco: Berrett-Koehler.

Byrne, J. (1998, June 8). Jack—A close-up look at how America's #1 manager runs GE. *BusinessWeek,* 92–111.

Cleveland, H. (1997). *Leadership and the information revolution.* Minneapolis: World Academy of Art and Science.

Cohen, E., and N. Tichey. (1998). The teaching organization. *Training and Development,* 52, (7), 27–33.

Curtin, L. (1996). February, The Caux Round Table for business. *Nursing Management,* 27(2), 54–58.

Dechant, K. (1990). Knowing how to learn: The "neglected" management ability. *Journal of Management Development,* 9 (4), 40–49.

Galen, M., and K. West. (1995, June 5). Companies hit the road less traveled: Can spirituality enlighten the bottom line? *BusinessWeek,* 82–86.

Goleman, D. (1997). *Emotional intelligence.* New York: Bantam Books.

Goleman, D. (1998). *Working with emotional intelligence.* New York: Bantam Books.

Greenleaf, R. (1997). *Servant leadership.* New York: Paulist Press.

Hamel, G. and C. Prahalad (1994). *Competing for the future.* Cambridge: Harvard Business School Press.

Hamilton, M. (1998, August 2). Shell's new worldview. *Washington Post,* pp. H1, H5.

Jacques, E. (1989). *Requisite organization.* Arlington: Cason Hall.

Kiechel, W. (1990, March 12). The organization that learns. *Fortune,* 133–136.

Kotter, J. (1996). *Leading Change.* Boston: Harvard Business School Press.

Marsick, J. (1987). *Learning in the workplace.* New York: Croom Helm.

Maruca, R. (1994, March–April). The right way to go global. *Harvard Business Review,* no. 2, 134–135.

Rhinesmith, S. (1993). *A manager's guide to globalization.* New York: McGraw-Hill.

Senge, P. (1990). *The fifth discipline.* New York: Doubleday.

Spears, L. (Ed.). (1995). *Reflections on leadership*. New York: Wiley.

Tichey, N., and E. Cohen. (1997). *The leadership engine: How winning companies build leaders at every level*. New York: HarperBusiness.

Wheatley, M. (1992). *Leadership and the new science*. San Francisco: Berrett-Koehler.

Chapter 3: John Chambers

Baum, G. (1998, February 23). John Chambers. *Forbes*, pp. 52–53.

Brandt, R. (1998, October). *Upside,* 10 (10), 122–130.

Chambers, J. (1998, August 31). The InternetWeek interview. *InternetWeek*, 730, 13–14.

Annual Report. (1994, 1995, 1996, 1997, 1998, 1999). *Cisco Systems.*

Corcoran, E. (1998, August 9). The Cisco connection—Network giant has seen the future—And is poised to piece it together. *Washington Post*, p. H1.

Kupfer, A. (1998). The real king of the Internet. *Fortune*, 138 (5), 84–93.

Marshall, J. (1998, November 11). Cisco stepping out. *San Francisco Chronicle,* p. Cl.

LaPlante, A. (1997, December). The man behind Cisco. *Electronic Business,* 23 (12), 48–53.

Mr. Internet. (1998, March 28). *The Economist*, 346 (8061), 64.

Nee, E. (1996) John Chambers. *Upside,* 8 (7), 54–63.

Schmit, J. (1998, September 23). Cisco embraces "Internet economy." *USA Today*, p. 3B.

Schlender, B. (1997). Computing's next superpower. *Fortune*, 137 (9), 88–101.

Scouras, I. (1998). John Chambers, president, CEO. *Electronic Buyers News Online.* Available: http://www.techweb.cmp.com/ebn.hot25/chambers.html.

Chapter 4: Ricardo Semler

Fierman, J. (1995, February 6). Winning ideas from maverick managers. *Fortune*, 131 (2), 66–80.

Lloyd, B. (1994). Maverick! An alternative approach to leadership, company organization, and management. *Leadership & Organization Development Journal,* 15 (2), 8–12.

Man who drives Brazil nuts. (1993, September). *Director,* 47 (2), pp. 82–83.

McNerney, D. (1995). Maverick: The success story behind the world's most unusual workplace. *Organization Dynamics*, 24 (2) 92.

Muehrcke, J. (1998, January–February). Let tribal customs thrive. *Nonprofit World*, 16 (1), 2–3.

Pottinger, J. (1994, September). Brazilian maverick reveals his radical recipe for success. *Personnel Management,* 26 (9), 71–72.

Semler, R. (1993). *The maverick.* New York: Warner Books.

Semler, R. (1989, September–October). Managing without managers. *Harvard Business Review,* 67 (5), 76–84.

Semler, R. (1994a, January–February). Why my former employees still work for me. *Harvard Business Review* 72 (1), 64–71.

Semler, R. (1994b, February). Who needs bosses? *Across the Board,* 31 (2), 23.

The new mavericks. (1993). *Incentive,* 167 (10), 18–20.

Wheatley, J., and J. Blount. (1997, May). The maverick. *Latin Trade,* 59–64.

Chapter 5: Kofi Annan

Berg, S. (1998, February 21). College friends say Annan's the man for the job. *Star Tribune,* p. 18A.

ITAR-TASS. (1997, May 17). *Domestic News Digest* [On-line]. Available: http://www.elibrary.com.

Keen, J. (1998, February 24). 'Moral force' speaks for Annan: Secretary-General takes on challenges with quiet persistence. *USA Today,* p. 7A.

Ratnesar, R. (1998, March 9). World: A star turn for the peace broker. *Time,* 61.

Reform at the UN? (1997, October 1). *The World & I, 12,* 40.

Shawcross, W. (1996, December 15). Good man from Africa. *Independent on Sunday,* p. 17.

UN Department of Public Information. (1997, June 13). Kofi Annan United Nations Secretary-General [On-line]. Available: http://www.un.org/overview/sg/sg7bio.html.

UN Press Release. (1996, December 17). Secretary-General-Designate outlines goals for term. Press Release GA/9211 [On-line]. Available: http://www.un.org/ Docs/ SG/quotable/ga9211.htm.

UN Press Release. (1997, January 9). Secretary-General urges staff to strive for excellence, stressing UN performance will turn detractors into supporters. Press Release SG/SM/6140 [On-line]. Available: http://www.un.org/ Docs/SG/quotable/6140.htm.

UN Press Release. (1997, January 24). Secretary-General stresses need for partnership, building consensus for UN reform to succeed, in address to National Press Club. Press Release SG/SM/6149 [On-line]. Available: http://www.un.org/ Docs/SG/ quotable/6149.htm.

UN Press Release. (1997, April 23). World needs instrument of global action "as never before in history," says Secretary-General in address to Council on Foreign Relations. Press Release SG/SM/6218 [On-line]. Available: http://www.un.org/ Docs/ SG/quotable/6218.htm.

UN Press Release. (1997, May 27). Secretary-General calls on International Women's Forum, friends and supporters of United Nations, to spread knowledge and understanding of organization. Press Release SG/SM/6242, WOM/972 [On-line]. Available: http://www.un.org/Docs/SG/quotable/6242.htm.

UN Press Release. (1997, June 5). International organization helped tilt balance towards domain where power of human reason prevails, Kofi Annan says. Press Release SG/ SM/6247 [On-line]. Available: http://www.un.org/ Docs/SG/quotable/6247.htm.

UN Press Release. (1997, July 16). Secretary-General pledges "quiet revolution" in United Nations, presents reform proposals to General Assembly. Press Release SG/ SM/6284/Rev.2, GA/9282/Rev.2 [On-line]. Available: http://www.un.org/ Docs/ SG/quotable/6284rv.htm.

UN Press Release. (1997, October 24). Secretary-General, in UN Day message, calls for renewal of faith "in our one and only" universal instrument of progress. Press Release SG/SM/6367, OBV/17 [On-line]. Available: http://www.un.org/ Docs/ SG/quotable/6367.htm.

UN Press Release. (1997, November 19). Power of television should be "partner" in pursuit of better future, says Secretary-General to World Television Forum. Press Release SG/ SM/6401 [On-line]. Available: http://www.un.org/ Docs/SG/quotable/6401.htm.

UN Press Release. (1997, December 3). Talented, courageous people must believe their public service can make difference, Secretary-General says. Press Release SG/SM/ 6412 [On-line]. Available: http://www.un.org/Docs/SG/quotable/6412.htm.

UN Department of Public Information (1998) Dynamics of UN reform felt system wide [On-line] Available: http://www.un.org.

UN Press Release (1998, April 27) Press Release #SG/SM/6359GA 9404 [On-line] Available: http://www.un.org.

Chapter 6: John Browne

Arnst, C. (1997, November 10). When green begets green. *Business Week,* 3552 [On-line]. Available: http://www.elibrary.com.

British Petroleum. (1998, January 30). BP opens new solar plant in California. Press release [On-line]. Available: http://www.bpamoco.com.

Browne, J. (1997, June 6). Creating the sustainable company. Presentation to the Andersen Consulting World Forum on Change [On-line]. Available: http://www.bpamoco.com.

Browne, J. (1997, September 30). Global climate change: The policy options. Presentation to the Berlin Parliament, Berlin, Germany [On-line]. Available: http://www.bpamoco.com.

Browne, J. (1997, October 28). Science, technology and responsibility. Presentation to the Royal Society, London [On-line]. Available: http://www.bpamoco.com.

Browne, J. (1997, November 13). Corporate responsibility in an international context. Presentation to the Council on Foreign Relations, New York [On-line]. Available: http://www.bpamoco.com.

Browne, J. (1998, January 27). *Financial Times* survey names BP one of Europe's' most respected companies. Presentation at an award dinner marking the annual *Financial Times* list of Europe's most respected companies. [On-line] Available: http://www.bpamoco.com.

Browne, J. (1998, February 2). Public pressure and strategic choice. Presentation at the World Economic Forum, Davos, Switzerland [On-line]. Available: http://www.bpamoco.com.

Browne, J. (1998, February 6). Climate after Kyoto: The business response. Presentation at the Royal Institute of International Affairs Conference, "Climate After Kyoto: Implications for Energy," London [On-line]. Available: http://www.bpamoco.com.

Browne, J. (1998, February 27). Learning to be distinctive. Speech at Goldman Sachs, London [On-line]. Available: http://www.bpamoco.com.

Browne, J. (1998, September 18). Leading a global company: The case of BP. Presentation at Yale University [On-line]. Available: http://www.bpamoco.com.

Energy Intelligence Group. (1997, November 18). BP's John Browne receives Energy Intelligence Group's Petroleum Executive of the Year Award. News release from the 18th Annual Oil and Money Conference, London, England [On-line]. Available: http://www.energyintel.com.

Fagan, M. (1998, January 11). BP raises the bar. *Sunday Telegraph* [On-line]. Available: http://www.elibrary.com.

Fisher, A. (1997, October 27). The world's most admired companies. *Fortune* [On-line]. Available: http://www.elibrary.com.

Garten, G. E. (1998, February 9). Globalism doesn't have to be cruel. *Business Week*, 26.

Guyon, J. (1999, July 5). When John Browne talks, big oil listens. *Fortune,* 140 (1), 116–122.

Hamilton, M. M. (1998, September 18). British Petroleum sets goal of 10% cut in "greenhouse" gases. *Washington Post,* p. A6.

Hoover's. (1998, April) Hoover's company capsule: The British Petroleum Company. [On-line] Available: http://www.hoovers.com.

Intel (1997, January 27). Intel elects John Browne to its board of directors. Press release [On-line]. Available: http://www.intel.com/pressroom.

Kemezis, A. (1997, May 20). Browne predicts $1 billion sales goal for 2007. *Stanford Daily* [On-line]. Available: http://daily.stanford.online

Landberg, R. (1997, December 21). BP's heretic hailed. *Independent on Sunday.* [On-line]. Available: http://www.elibrary.com.

Lean, G. (1997, August 24). Stormy ride for two unlikely friends. *Independent on Sunday* [On-line]. Available: http://www.elibrary.com.

Price Waterhouse. (1997, September 24). ABB nominated Europe's most respected company for fourth successive year [On-line]. Available: http://www.pw.com/uk/most_respected_ companies.htm.

Prokesch, S. (1997, September–October). Unleashing the power of learning: An interview with British Petroleum's John Browne. *Fortune* 6, 147–168

Reed, S. (1997, May 5). Britain: BP: A well-oiled machine. *BusinessWeek International, 3528* [On-line]. Available:http://www.elibrary.com.

Stewart, T. A. (1999, June 7). Telling tales at BP Amoco. *Fortune,* 139 (11), 220–224.

Chapter 7: Carol Bartz

Autodesk. (1998a, February 1). Career opportunities [On-line]. Available: http://www.autodesk.com/compinfo/career/culture/htm.

Autodesk. (1998b, March 26). Company information [On-line]. Available: http://www.autodesk.com.

Autodesk. (1998c, March 26). Welcome to the Autodesk woman: Carol Bartz [On-line]. Available: http://www.autodesk.com.

Bartz, C. (1996, November 18). Piracy on the PCS. Transcript of speech given at the Commonwealth Club of California [On-line]. Available: http://www.autodesk.com/compinfo/todaynew/piracy.htm.

Bartz, C. (1997a, June 30). Women in technology: Look how far we haven't come. Keynote speech to the National Coalition of Girls' Schools Girls and Technology Conference [On-line]. Available: www.autodesk.com/compinfo/welcome/girls.htm.

Bartz, C. (1997b, December 1). No time to change others. *Forbes ASAP* [On-line]. Available: http: www.forbes.com/asap/97/1201/140.htm.

Bartz, C. (1997c, December 9). Women of the world chat with Carol Bartz. An on-line forum [On-line]. Available: http://quest.arc.nasa.gov/women/todtwd/cb.12-09-97.html.

CNBC. (1997, August 28). Interview with Autodesk CEO Carol Bartz. CNBC Power Lunch [On-line]. Available: http://www.autodesk.com.

Computer captain. (1997, June). *Architecture: The AIA Journal,* 86 (6), 71–73.

Hamm, S. (1997, August 25). Silicon Valley: The culture: Why women are so invisible. *BusinessWeek,* 3541, 136.

Leadership experts explain the secrets. (1996, April 8). *Forbes,* 102.

Levin, C. (1997, August). CEOs go to Washington: The software industry's lobbying effort intensifies. PC Magazine [On-line]. Available: http://www.zdnet.pcmag/issues/1614/ pcmag0067.htm.

McKee, B. (1997, June). Autodesk's upgrade. *Architecture: The AIA Journal,* 86 (6), 112–115.

Verespej, M. A. (1996, January 8). Growth by design. *Industry Week,* 245 (1), 391.

WITI. (1997, May 5). Hall of fame press release [On-line]. Available: http://www.witi.org/center/museum/hall/97/cbartz.html.

Wolfson, J., and M. Talitenu. (1997). An interview with Carol Bartz. *San Jose Mercury News* [On-line]. Available: http://www.thetech.org/exhibits_events/online/revolution/bartz/ sound/gender_gap.ram.

Wylie, M. (1997, August 11). Software's grand dame [On-line]. Available: www. news. com/newsmakers/bartz/bartz.html.

Chapter 8: Felipe Alfonso

Alfonso, F. (1997a, September 25). Asian managers facing the challenges of the global economy in the new millenium. Speech to the 29th Management Congress of the Philippine Council of Management, Manila.

Alfonso, F. (1997b, August 9). Developing Asian managers for the new millenium. Speech at the 24th ARTDO International Human Resource Development Conference, Kuching, Sarawak, Malaysia.

Alfonso, F. (1997c). Strategic issues in technology management. Speech at Strategies Issues in Technology, PICMET Conference, Portland, Oregon.

Alfonso, F. (1997d). The manager of tomorrow. Speech at the opening of the Management Association of the Philippines Annual Conference, Manila.

Alfonso, F. (1998a). Global innovations in learning. Keynote Speech at the 1998 Australian Institute for Training and Development Conference, Sydney.

Alfonso, F. (1998b, August 22). Interview with Rowena Figueroa, Manila, Philippines.

Alfonso, F. (1998c). Speech at the signing of the memorandum of agreement between the Department of Foreign Affairs and the Asian Institute of Management for the establishment of the Asia-Europe Management Program at AIM (AEMP-AIM), Manila.

Asian Institute of Management. (1997, 1998) Annual Report.

Manila Electric Company (Meralco). (1996, 1997, 1998). Annual Report.

Mendoza, I. (1995, August 31). The Asian Institute of Management: Breeding ground of future Asian managers. *Manila Bulletin.*

Syrett, M. (1995, September). View from the top: What Asia's business leaders want from MBAs. *Asian Business,* 31 (9).

Tripathi, S. (1996, September). Who needs Stanford? Asia's business schools can't match the best MBA programs, but the product is improving and some prefer the 'Asianized' curriculum. *Asia, Inc.,* 5 (9).

Tripathi, S. (1997, September). The best MBA schools: Asia's top 25 business programs. *Asia Inc.,* 6(9).

Chapter 9: Ken Chenault

American Express Company. (1997, February 27). Kenneth I. Chenault appointed President and Chief Operating Officer of American Express Company [On-line]. Available: http://www.americanexpress.com.

American Express names Chenault COO. (1997, February 27). *Reuters Business Report* [On-line]. Available: http://www.elibrary.com.

American Express names president, COO; Executives: Kenneth Chenault will be first black to control one of the country's largest firms. (1997, February 28). *Los Angeles Times* [On-line]. Available: http://www.elibrary.com.

American Express snapshot: Rethinking inside the box—a blue box. (1996, September). *ABA Banking Journal,* 88 (9), 50.

Authers, J. (1997, February 27). American Express president breaches white stronghold [On-line]. Available: http://www.worldafricannet.com/news/newsinformation/news5.html.

Ballen, K. (1987, March 2). People to watch. *Fortune* [On-line]. Available: http://www.elibrary.com.

Bianco, A. (1998, December 21). The rise of a star. *BusinessWeek*, 60–68.

Bowdoin College. (1996, June 3). Kenneth I. Chenault Doctor of Laws [On-line]. Available: http://www.bowdoin.edu/cwis/events/news/chenault.html.

Charkalis, D. M. (1997, February 28). Chenault moves up at American Express. *USA Today* [On-line]. Available: http://www.elibrary.com.

Chenault appointed president and COO of American Express Company. (1997, March 17). *Jet,* 91 (17), 8–9.

Chenault, K. (1996, May 25). Remarks delivered at Bowdoin College's 1996 commencement [On-line]. Available: http://www.bowdoin.edu/cwis/events/miss/chenault.html.

Clarke, C. V. (1995, August 31). Meeting the challenge of corporate leadership. *Black Enterprise* [On-line]. Available: http://www.elibrary.com.

Curtis, E. (1994, February 16). Black history month special: National black achievers profiled. *Sun Reporter* [On-line]. Available: http://www.elibrary.com.

Day-Foley, J. (1994, February 22). Kenneth Chenault. *Michigan Chronicle* [On-line]. Available: http://www.elibrary.com.

Dugas, C. (1997, May 19). Making changes inside and out, Chenault combines profit and good will. *USA Today* [On-line]. Available: http://www.elibrary.com.

Executive Leadership Council. (1997, December 9). James Daniel, Jr. named Executive Director of the Executive Leadership Council [On-line]. Available: http://www.elcinfo.com/ press1.htm.

Grant, L. (1995, October 30). Why Warren Buffett's betting big on American Express. *Fortune* [On-line]. Available: http://pathfinder.com./@5prakgyaeufjyg2j/fortune/magazine/ 1995/951030/cover.html.

Greenwald, J. (1998, January 12). Charge! *Time,* 151 (1), 60–62.

Hubbard, C. (1995, November 23). CDFC 20-year gala stresses need for minority businesses. *Bay State Banner* [On-line]. Available: http://www.elibrary.com.

ISWire. (1997, April 16). Do you know me? I'm Jackie Robinson in a suit [On-line]. Available: http://www.urbansportsnetwork.com/main/square/iswire/do041697.htm.

Lloyd, F. (1995, April 30) American Express promotes Chenault. *Black Enterprise,* p. PE (On-line) http://www.elibrary.com.

Pierce, P. (1997, July). Blazing new paths in corporate America. *Ebony,* 52 (9), 58–62.

Reingold, J., and J. Byrne, (1997, August 11). The top 20 heads to hunt. *Business Week*, 35–39 [On-line]. Available: www.elibrary.com.

Sherrid, P. (1997, June 23). A new class act at AMEX. *U.S. News & World Report*, 122 (24), 39–40.

Shook, C. (1997, December 1). Leader, not boss. *Forbes*, 160 (12), 52–54.

Smith, E. L. (1997, May). Someone's knocking at the door. *Black Enterprise*, 27 (10), 97–99.

Stone, S. (1995, December 26). Leadership Council honors American Express official. *Philadelphia Tribune* [On-line]. Available: http://www.elibrary.com.

The 25 top managers of the year. (1998, January 1). *Business Week* [On-line]. Available: http://www.businessweek.com/1998/02/b3560004.htm.

Chapter 10: Mary McAleese

Brown, J. M. (1997, July). Irish highs. *Accountancy*, 12 (1247), 34–36.

Collins, T. (1998, July 12). Help me to build bridges. [On-line]. Available: http://www. Irishnews.com/mary.html.

McAleese, M. (1997, November 11). Inauguration speech.

McAleese, M. (1998, July 20). Keynote speech, presented at the International Federation of Training and Development Organizations (IFTDO) Conference, Dublin, Ireland.

Walshe, J. (1997, November 14). A law professor and political outsider is elected president of Ireland. *Chronicle of Higher Education*, 44 (12), A52.

Chapter 11: Cheong Choong Kong

Best hotels and airlines. (1999, February). *Global Finance*, 13 (2), 52–54.

Bickers, C. (1998, October 1). Sharing the pain. *Far Eastern Economic Review*, 161 (40), 79–80.

Bociurkiw, M. (1998, December 14). Time for champagne. *Forbes*, 162 (13), 68–69.

Cheong, C. (1999, January 21). Acceptance Speech at Asian businessman of year award.

Dolven, B. (1999, January 7). Easy riders: Transport firms glide into top spots. *Far Eastern Economic Review News: Review*, 162 (1), 24.

Hiebert, M. (1998, January 1). A perennial winner. *Far Eastern Economic Review*, 161 (1) 82–84.

Jayasankaran, S. (1999, July 1). Gaining speed. *Far Eastern Economic Review,* 162 (26), 48.

Kraar, L. (1999, February 1). Asia's businessman of the year. *Fortune (Asian Ed.).* 138 (2), 32–37.

Leung, J., and T. Jordan. (1999, May). Asia's most admired companies. *Asian Business,* 35 (5), 24–32.

Nathan, S. (1999, March 16). Singapore Air soars through Asian financial crisis. *USA Today* [On-line]. Available: www.usatoday.com.

Pascoe, M. (1998, September 27). Dr. Cheong Choong Kong, CEO Singapore Airlines. Interview transcript [On-line]. Available: www.businesssunday.ninemsn.com.au.

Singapore Airlines Perspectives. (1999). Singapore: SIA Press.

Singapore girl has little to smile about. (1998, July 2*). South China Morning Post.*

Singapore sees stars. (1998, January). *Air Transport World,* 35 (1), 9.

Sloan, G. (1998, October 2). Culture defines Singapore Airlines: Executive Cheong Choong Kong takes a hard look at the industry. *USA Today,* p. 8D.

Chapter 12: William Carris

Bartlett, C. A., and S. Ghoshal. (1994, November-December). Changing the role of top management: Beyond strategy to purpose. *Harvard Business Review,* 79–88.

Betit, C. G., and W. S. Brown. (1998, July). Building trust, inclusivity and community in a learning organization. Paper presented at the Professor's Forum of the 27th International Federation of Training and Development Organizations World Conference, Trinity College, Dublin, Ireland.

Bigley, G. A., and J. L. Pearce. (1998). Straining for shared meaning in organizational science: Problems of trust and distrust. *Academy of Management Review,* 23 (3), 405–421.

Carris, B. (1994). Long term plan for the Carris Community of Companies. Rutland, VT: Carris Financial Corporation.

Carris corporate community mission statement. (1997). Rutland, VT: Carris Financial Corporation.

Carris Reels Website: http://www.carris.com.

Collins, J. C., and J. J. Porras. (1991, Fall). Organizational vision and visionary organizations. *California Management Review,* 30–66.

Collins, J. C., and J. J. Porras. (1996, September-October). Building your company's vision. *Harvard Business Review,* 65–77.

Daley, Y. (1996a, December 31). Not your typical company president. *Boston Globe,* p. A10.

Daley. Y. (1996b, December 31). Worldly workers: Vermont firm sends its employees abroad. *Boston Globe*, pp. A1, A10.

Greenleaf, R. K. (1977). *Servant leadership: A journey into the nature of legitimate power and greatness.* New York: Paulist Press.

Greenleaf, R. K. (1996). *On becoming a servant leader.* San Francisco, CA: Jossey-Bass.

Hahn, W. (1996, February–March). Carris Reels Company has begun a gradual transition to employee stock ownership plan. *Rutland Business Journal*, 23.

Kouzes, J. M., and B. Z. Posner. (1993). *Credibility: How leaders gain and lose it, why people demand it.* San Francisco, CA: Jossey-Bass.

Kuhn, J. W., and D. W. Shriver, Jr. (1991). *Beyond success: Corporations and their critics in the 1990's.* New York: Oxford University Press.

Mollner, T. (1991). *The profits of the Pyrenees: The search for the relationship age.* Northampton, MA: Trustee Institute.

Reich, R. B. (1997). *Locked in the cabinet.* New York: Vintage Books.

Renesch, J. (Ed.). (1992). *New traditions in business: Spirit and leadership in the 21st century.* San Francisco, CA: Berrett-Koehler.

Schwartz, R. L. (1984, August). The Mondragon Cooperatives: In Spain a new economic model combines capitalism and kinship. *The Tarrytown Letter*, 16–17.

Senge, P. M. (1990). *The fifth discipline: The art and practice of the learning organization.* New York: Doubleday.

Skiffington, K. K. (1996, February–March). Vermont Tubbs, furniture manufacturer plans expansion and internal restructuring. *Rutland Business Journal*, 24.

Strong, K. C., and J. Weber. (1998). The myth of the trusting culture: A global, empirical assessment. *Business & Society*, 37 (2), 157–183.

Chapter 13: Nobuyuki Idei

Boot up the television set. (1997, June 28). *The Economist*, 343 (8023), 63–65.

Gibney, F. (1997, November 17). A new world at Sony. *Time*, 150 (21), 56–60.

Hamilton, D., and J. Lippman. (1997, May 14). Sony's Idei finds winning path: Reject tired thinking. *Wall Street Journal*.

Palmer, J. (1996, April 15). Back in the game. *Barron's*, 76 (16), 31–37.

Schlender, B. (1998, January 12). Asia's Man of the Year. *Fortune*, 137 (1), 32.

Sony. (1998, September 2) Sony enters telemedicine market [On-line] http//
www.sony.com.

Sugawara, S. (1997, May 29). Nobuyuki Idei's shrewd restructuring has lifted the giant
back on top. *Washington Post*, p. E1.

Young, L. (1997, January). The conversion of Sony. *Electronic Business Today,* 23 (1), 30–34.

Chapter 14: Jorma Ollila

Baker, S. (1998, August 10). Nokia. *Business Week,* 54–60.

Byrne, J. (1996, August 26). Strategic planning. *Business Week*, 46–52.

Carnegy, H. (1997, March 3). Revolution leader regains his poise. *Financial Times.*

Godier, K. (1997, September 22). Jorma Ollila—CEO of the year. *Emerging Markets
IMF/World Bank Daily.*

Lim, W. (1998, July 16). From an ailing group to a success story the Nokia way. *Malaysia
Business Times.*

Lynch, D. (1997, April 4). Nokia sets standard in wireless phone market. *USA Today,*
pp. B1, B9.

Nokia Annual Report. (1993, 1994, 1995, 1996, 1997, 1998, 1999).

Nokia—The creation of an industry leader. (1998). *FT Telecoms World,* 36–38.

Ollila, J. (1998, June 4). Speech at World Federation of Investors, Helsinki, Finland.

Chapter 15: Problems, Pathways, and Prospects

Brooks, A. (1998). Educating human resource development leaders at the University of
Texas. *Performance Improvement Quarterly,* 11 (2), 48–58.

Byrne, J. (1998, June 8). *Business Week,* pp. 92–93.

Cohen, E., and N. Tichey. (1997, May). How leaders develop leaders. *Training and
Development,* 51 (5), 58–73.

Dilworth, R.L (1996). Action learning: Bridging academic and workplace domains.
Employee Counseling Today, 8 (6), 48–56.

Dilworth, R. L. (1998). Action learning in a nutshell. *Performance Improvement Quarterly,*
11 (1), 28–43.

Heifetz, R., and D. Laurie. (1997). The work of leadership. *Harvard Business Review,* 75 (1), 124–134

Heifetz, R., and D. Laurie.(1998). Leadership: Mobilizing adaptive work. (unpublished).

Iyer, C. (1989). Action learning through quality circles. *Sri Lanka Journal of Development Administration.*

Marquardt, M. (1999) *Action learning in action.* Palo Alto: Davies-Black.

Marsick, V. (1988). Learning in the workplace: The case for critical reflectivity. *Adult Education Quarterly,* 38 (4), 187–198.

McNulty, N., and G. R. Canty. (1995). Proof of the pudding. *Journal of Management Development,* 14 (1), 53–66.

McGill, I. and L. Beatty (1992). *Action learning.* London: Kogan Page.

Revans, R. (1982). *The origins and growth of action learning.* Bromley: Chartwell-Bratt.

Tichey, N., and E. Cohen. (1997). *The leadership engine.* New York: HarperBusiness.

Wheatley, M. (1992) *Leadership and the new science.* San Francisco: Berrett-Koehler.

Index